22.95

Who's Your Mama,
Are You Catholic,
and
Can You Make A Roux ?

Who's Your Mama,
Are You Catholic,
and
Can You Make A Roux?

Marcelle Bienvenu

Acadian House
PUBLISHING
Lafayette, Louisiana

ON THE COVER: *The birthday party for my grandfather, Lazaire "Pop" Bienvenu, was well attended, in January 1953. Among those at the party were 11 of his 12 children, plus a granddaughter, all shown here. Left to right are: Bobbie Lee Stewmon (granddaughter), Marcel M. "Blackie" Bienvenu (my father), Corinne Cecile "Coco" McCoy, Ralph Roch Bienvenu, Rita Rose Patout, Annabelle Valentine "Billy" Bienvenu, Marie Therese "Taye" Chataignier, Margaret Vida "Git" Laborde, "Pop" (the birthday boy), Msgr. Clay Anthony Bienvenu, Genevieve Gertrude "Jenny" Durand, and Louis Lawrence "Shorty" Bienvenu. Pop's other child, the one not in the photo, was Claudia Helen "Taudie" Brosius.*

ISBN-13: 978-0-925417-55-8
ISBN-10: 0-925417-55-6

♦ Published by Acadian House Publishing, Lafayette, Louisiana. (Edited by Trent Angers; designed and illustrated by Don Fields; produced by Jon Russo.)

♦ Printed by Walsworth Printing, Marceline, Missouri

To my father, who showed me how

to see the brighter side of life,

and to my mother, who taught me

the pleasure of cooking

Growing up in south Louisiana

I was born and reared in St. Martinville, Louisiana, in the heart of Acadiana, sometimes known as Cajun country.

When I was growing up, I believed I lived in a romantic Eden. The town was one of the settings for Longfellow's poem, "Evangeline," which tells of the deportation of the French-Acadian people from their beloved *Acadie* (Nova Scotia) and of their search for a new home. Among the exiles were the famous betrothed couple, Evangeline and Gabriel. As a child I played at the feet of the statue of Evangeline at the rear of the St. Martin de Tours Catholic Church in the center of town.

St. Martinville, once known as *Poste des Attakapas* because it was a French and Indian trading post, later became known as *Le Petit Paris*, for it was here that many French aristocrats came to settle after the French Revolution. There were visitors from New Orleans who came every year for fashionable balls and operas and long hours of formal dining and dancing. The little town developed a unique culture, with food an integral part.

So it was in this atmosphere that I grew up. My father's father, Lazaire Bienvenu, was a pioneer in the newspaper business, establishing St. Martin Parish's oldest newspaper with his brother, Albert. It was then called *The Weekly Messenger*. Now in its third generation and called *The Teche News*, it continues as the official journal of the parish. Pop Lazaire and his wife Leoncia Tertrou (whose family had been in the hotel business) had 12 children. Their home was a mecca for much cooking and eating. The old stove never got cold.

My mother's father, Alphonse Broussard, was an overseer for several large sugarcane plantations. Their family of six children and the workers on the plantations required hearty food and lots of it.

I can't remember a day that tables were not filled with tureens of gumbo or stew, platters of baked chicken or variously prepared seafood, bowls of garden

How this cookbook got its name...

I have been asked countless times about how I came up with the name for this cookbook, so here goes...

It's important in the South for people to make a connection when being introduced to strangers or newcomers. It's long been a tradition, especially in south Louisiana, to find out, "Who are your people?" This is not only to make conversation, but also to find out about a new person's background.

Through this line of questioning, one will often find long-lost cousins or some kind of family connection.

It should be noted also that when the Acadians were deported from Nova Scotia in the 1750s, families were separated, and when many made their way to French-Catholic south Louisiana, they sought to find relatives (close or distant) in their new homeland.

Although it may seem rude to visitors and those unacquainted with the local customs, we Acadians are innately curious. So, you may very well be asked about your mother's maiden name, what vegetables, and baskets of French bread and biscuits. There were pitchers of milk heavy with cream, jars of fig preserves, and crocks of pickled meats.

Many noon meals were taken at Pop Lazaire's house. Back then, time allowed businessmen to go home for lunch. Weekends found us in the country participating in *boucheries* or carrying pails of food to the workers in the fields.

I walked through my childhood believing everyone enjoyed the pleasure of preparing and consuming jambalaya, crawfish *bisque*, and stewed okra. Children and adults all participated in the tasks of cooking. Aunt Grace, with her kitchen helpers, Yola and *La Vielle* ("the Old One"), showed me how to bake biscuits and corn bread that were so light they could have floated on air. Papa, who with his 11 siblings assisted in Leoncia's kitchen, patiently showed me how to make a roux. Mama, who grew up on a plantation, was the source for information on canning and preserving fresh produce.

We were not aware that we were assimilating any special kind of cuisine. We only knew that our food was good. Food and its preparation were at the center of our lives.

Not only was I surrounded by good cooks and good food, but I was also enchanted by the family newspaper. When I was six years old, I hand-folded the newspaper on press day. Later I learned to proofread "hot type" coming off the Linotype machine. I was my father's shadow around the plant, watching him and Pop Lazaire as they sat on old rockers at their desks discussing what news was to be included in the paper. After I became an adult, I had careers in both the newspaper business and the food business. I operated my own restaurant, worked for the Brennan family of New Orleans, and wrote for *The Times-Picayune*.

I offer this collection of recipes – some traditional and some new – because I want to share with others the dear memories and delicious food that are the natural result of a lifetime of good times spent with family and friends.

– Marcelle Bienvenu

LOUISIANA

Cajun Country (Acadiana)

schools you attended, and what your father does for a living.

With all of this in mind, you'll understand why, in 1989, I was inspired by the dialogue in a play called *The Band Inside Your Head*. It was written by Raleigh Marcell Jr. of New Iberia and produced by the University of Southwestern Louisiana's Opera Theater.

The story line in the play is that a young Acadian fellow left the area to find fame and fortune, and when he returned he did so with his bride-to-be. Naturally, the members of his family were anxious to know more about this young lady.

Thus, there was a dialogue between the local women and the newcomer. They couldn't help but ask about her family connections, her religion, and what she knew about cooking. So, of course, they needed to know:

Who's your mama?
Are you Catholic?
Can you make a roux?

These words kept going round and round in my head for days, and I finally settled on them as the title for my book.

And now you know.

– M.B.

Preface to the New Edition

It is with great pleasure that I re-introduce this, the fourth edition of *Who's Your Mama, Are You Catholic and Can You Make A Roux?*

Though the book was out of print for a number of years, demand for it has continued. It seems that the reading and cooking public can't get enough of Cajun and Creole recipes – which is music to my ears!

The first edition was published in 1991, and it has been re-designed three times since. I hope you enjoy this spruced-up new hardcover edition. It includes the original narrative and recipes, all of which have been reviewed, some of which have been tweaked and polished to make them more accurate and easy to follow.

– M.B.

TABLE OF CONTENTS

ACKNOWLEDGEMENTS

I must, first of all, thank my many aunts and uncles, my countless cousins, and, of course, my brothers Henri Clay and Bruce, my sister Edna and their families for giving me all the memories that are at the heart of this collection of recipes and stories.

I will be forever indebted to my many friends who constantly urged me to do this book, and a special thanks to Ella Brennan, who gave me the courage to put it all together.

I am also indebted to Trent Angers, editor and publisher of Acadian House Publishing, for offering to republish my book; to Don Fields, who designed this new edition; and to Jon Russo for his patience and dedication in reconstructing the old manuscript and producing the book.

Last, but not least, I thank my husband Rock Lasserre for his encouragement and suggestions.

Who's Your Mama,
Are You Catholic,
and
Can You Make A Roux?

SPRING

Spring arrives quickly in south Louisiana. One day the landscape along the highways and country roads is desolate. Strands of Spanish moss hang on barren tree limbs. Then suddenly, in early March, the purple, pink and lavender of Japanese magnolias and redbud trees burst into the leafless countryside.

With the last cold front behind them, men and women don straw hats and *garde-soleils* (sunbonnets) and begin to work the soil for spring gardens. Soon it will be time to put in Creole tomato plants, eggplant, bell pepper, corn and squash. The glory of nature and the renewal of life are celebrated with a unique combination of reverence and gaiety during springtime in Louisiana.

Growing up in St. Martinville, Louisiana, one of the things I loved about Spring was dressing up for Mass on Easter Sunday, in this case in 1951.

Easter Bonnets, Painted Eggs and a Feast

I love Easter time!

The countryside is alive with color – the lavish hues of azaleas mingling with bright white bridal wreath – and yards and pastures alike are lush dark green carpets.

Everyone is frantically getting Easter outfits together. Girls decorate straw bonnets with ribbons and flowers, while boys dig out their white linens. Our family goes through its own special rites of spring.

For years now, the weekends leading up to Easter find us all at the camp, cleaning and sprucing, planting and planning for the long Easter weekend. Our large Bienvenu family gathers annually at the camp on Good Friday. Early in the day we pile into a pickup truck or van and go for a ride on the levee between Catahoula and Henderson. It seems that everyone has taken a holiday. Hundreds of families gather along the waterways to picnic, fish or put out crawfish nets. Children sit in patches of clover and amuse themselves by making flower necklaces.

We pick up a few sacks of live crawfish and go to three o'clock church services. Then we head back to the camp for a crawfish boil. As we are just about finishing up the crawfish, the ladies of Catahoula come by to drop off SWEET DOUGH PIES.

There is a wonderful custom in Catahoula. For many days prior to Good Friday the ladies of the town make sweet dough pies, or *tarte a la bouillie*, and then on Good Friday all the families gather to eat the pies. Miss Tootie Guirard, a local historian and storyteller, says the ladies know they're supposed to have just one meal on Good Friday, so they make it a good long one. They eat practically all day long!

Tarte a la Bouillie (Sweet Dough Pies)

Makes four 9-inch pies

¾ cup of vegetable shortening
1 cup of sugar
½ cup of milk
2 eggs
1 teaspoon of vanilla extract
4 cups of all-purpose flour
4 teaspoons of baking powder
Filling (Recipes follow)

Preheat the oven to 350 degrees.

Cream the shortening and sugar in a large mixing bowl. Combine the milk, eggs and vanilla in another mixing bowl and stir to blend. Add this mixture to the shortening and sugar and blend well.

Combine the flour and baking powder in a mixing bowl. In another bowl, alternate blending the liquid mixture with the dry ingredients. Continue to alternate adding the mixtures until the dough comes away from the sides of the bowl.

Divide the dough into four equal parts and roll out on a lightly floured board. Place the dough in four 9-inch pans, crimp the edges, and add the filling.

Bake until the crust is golden brown, about 30 minutes. Cool and add the filling of your choice.

BLACKBERRY FILLING

Wash the berries and drain well. Pick them over and remove any stems.

For every quart of berries, use 1½ to 2 cups of sugar (depends on how sweet you like it) and ¼ cup of water.

Combine the sugar and water in a large pot and bring to a boil. Add the berries and cook, stirring often, until the mixture thickens, 20 to 30 minutes.

CUSTARD FILLING

1 (12-ounce) can of evaporated milk
12 ounces of water in which ½ cup of
    cornstarch has been dissolved
1 cup of sugar
2 eggs
1 teaspoon of vanilla extract

Combine all the ingredients in a large saucepan. Slowly bring the mixture to a gentle boil and stir until the custard thickens.

Cool and spoon into the sweet dough crusts.

To make coconut filling, add one cup of shredded coconut to the custard while it is cooling.

Note: The Catahoula ladies usually do not put tops on the large pies, but any extra dough can be used to make a lattice top for each pie. If you're making pies on a hot and humid day, it is wise to refrigerate the dough for an hour or two so that it will be easier to work with.

You can also use the dough to make small turnovers. Simply roll the dough into smaller circles than described above, add filling, fold over, and bake.

The dough can also be used to make sugar cookies. Roll out the dough a bit thicker and cut with a cookie cutter. Place on cookie sheets and bake at 350 degrees until golden brown.

Friends and relatives join us every year for our Easter celebration. Sometimes we have a baked ham and barbecued chicken, and other times it might be lamb with all the trimmings. Whatever the fare, the important thing is that we are all together sharing a big meal.

The following recipe is not a traditional family dish, but rather a new twist on one. A friend of mine who would rather be a chef than the attorney he is shared this with me. His hobby is cooking, and he is always improving on a dish. Personally, I don't think he needs to do anything to this one.

Hallman's Leg of Lamb with Spinach and Feta Cheese

Makes 8 to 10 servings

3 pounds of fresh spinach
¼ cup plus 3 tablespoons of virgin olive oil
1 teaspoon of garlic powder
1 teaspoon of salt
1 teaspoon of sugar
1 cup of French bread crumbs
2 teaspoons plus 3 tablespoons of Dijon mustard
Freshly ground black pepper, to taste
1 boneless leg of lamb, about 5 to 6 pounds
1 (5-ounce) package of feta cheese
2 tablespoons of chopped fresh rosemary leaves mixed with ½ cup of fine dried bread crumbs

Clean the spinach and chop coarsely in a food processor or by hand. Transfer to a mixing bowl and add one-fourth cup of the olive oil, the garlic powder, salt, sugar, bread crumbs, black pepper, and two teaspoons of the Dijon mustard. Mix well and set aside.

Either debone the leg of lamb or have your butcher do it for you. Be sure the outer membrane is removed. Butterfly the leg by slitting it open so that it lies flat on a cutting board, skin side down. Make horizontal cuts the length of the leg, about two inches apart, being careful not to cut all the way through. Brush the inner surface of the meat with two tablespoons of the olive oil and two tablespoons of the Dijon mustard. Sprinkle with freshly ground black pepper. Crumble the feta cheese and press evenly over the entire inner surface and into the slits in the lamb.

Then pat and press the spinach stuffing mixture evenly onto the lamb. Roll the lamb back into shape and tie it up with kitchen twine about every two inches.

When completely secured, pat the roll with the remaining olive oil and Dijon mustard. Rub the rosemary-bread crumb mixture over the meat and insert a meat thermometer into the thickest part of the roast.

Cook in a smoker or covered grill, or in a 350-degree oven, until the thermometer reaches 125 to 130 degrees for medium-rare.

Remove from the smoker or oven, and let rest for 30 minutes before slicing to serve. This can be refrigerated overnight and served cold on a buffet.

When I was 4 I wore a white organdy dress for our town's May Festival.

I don't know about anybody else, but I associate food memories with people. For instance, every time I make a sandwich I think of my friend, Judy. Meat pies bring my old Aunt Belle to mind. Caviar and *Dom Perignon* conjure up great memories of a couple who used to invite me over for this treat on cold Sunday afternoons after the football games. And whenever Mama fixes STUFFED ONIONS, I think of her old friend from Boston who thought these were a mouthful of heaven.

Every once in a while the stuffed onions show up on a holiday table, and are great when served with the Easter lamb. They take a little time to prepare, but they're worth it.

Stuffed Onions

Makes 6 to 8 servings

6 to 8 medium-size yellow onions
4 tablespoons of butter
1 large tomato, peeled, seeded and chopped
½ cup of finely chopped fresh mushrooms
2 garlic cloves, minced
1 pound of lean ground beef, or sausage of any
   kind, removed from the casing, or chopped
   raw shrimp
¼ to ½ cup of unseasoned bread crumbs
1 egg, beaten
2 tablespoons of chopped parsley
¼ teaspoon of dried basil leaves
¼ teaspoon of dried marjoram
Salt and cayenne pepper, to taste
Freshly grated Parmesan cheese
1 cup of chicken broth

Peel the onions. Cut off a slice from the top and bottom of each onion. With a spoon, scoop out the center of each onion, leaving a thick shell. Reserve the extra onion pieces.

Place the onion shells in a large, deep pot and cover with water. Bring to a gentle boil and cook until they are slightly tender, about 10 minutes. Carefully remove them from the water and drain on paper towels.

Chop the reserved onion pieces. Heat two tablespoons of the butter in a large skillet over medium heat. Add the onion pieces and cook, stirring, until slightly soft, about three minutes. Add the tomato, mushrooms and garlic, and cook, stirring, for five minutes. Add the ground beef, sausage, or shrimp and cook for another 10 minutes, stirring gently.

Remove from heat and stir in the bread crumbs and beaten egg. The mixture should thicken. Add the parsley, basil and marjoram, and season with salt and cayenne.

Preheat the oven to 350 degrees.

Melt the remaining two tablespoons of butter and pour into a baking dish large enough to accommodate the onions.

Stuff each onion with equal amounts of the filling and arrange in the baking dish. Sprinkle with the Parmesan cheese and pour in the chicken broth.

Bake for 30 minutes, then increase the oven temperature to 400 degrees and bake until the tops of the onions are lightly browned, about 10 minutes.

Serve warm and baste with the pan juices.

My Aunt Lois makes a vegetable casserole that's pretty good and ideal for serving a large Easter Sunday crowd.

Lois' Vegetable Casserole

Makes about 12 servings

2 (1-pound) cans of green beans
2 (15-ounce) cans of green or white asparagus
2 (14-ounce) cans of artichoke hearts (packed in water)
1 (2-ounce) jar of sliced pimiento
1 (4-ounce) can of sliced mushrooms
½ cup of fried crumbled bacon
½ cup of melted butter
¼ cup of fresh lemon juice
Garlic juice, to taste (optional)
Salt and black pepper, to taste
2 (8-ounce) cans of sliced water chestnuts

Preheat the oven to 350 degrees.

Drain all the vegetables. Gently toss all ingredients, except the water chestnuts, with seasonings in a large baking dish.

Sprinkle the top with the water chestnuts and bake for 30 minutes.

Note: If there are some picky children around for the meal, consider serving scalloped potatoes or *petit pois* simmered with lots of butter.

Forego the green salad and make a festive fruit salad. Use your imagination. Any and all fresh fruit combined with freshly grated coconut makes a delicious and refreshing salad. Add a little powdered sugar and whipped cream to make it really luscious. Top with fresh mint from the garden.

Once Lent is over and we are into Eastertide, it's like being released from unyielding bindings. With winter behind me, I look forward to outdoor activity and all the food treats that go with it. Spring is crawfish season! There will be crawfishing trips, followed by crawfish boils and crawfish cooked a hundred different ways. Ah, what good times we have.

There is a fable that Acadians tell about how the crawfish came to live in south Louisiana. Before the Acadians were exiled from their beloved *Acadie* (now known as Nova Scotia) in the 1750s, they were accustomed to eating lobster, which they caught in the cold waters of the North Atlantic. When the Acadians began the journey in search of a safe haven, their travels took many of them along the Eastern Seaboard, and eventually they arrived in Louisiana, where they made a new home for themselves.

The lobsters followed them (so the story goes), but the long and arduous journey caused the crustacean to become smaller and smaller until it became the size it is today. The crawfish, like the hearty Acadians, adapted to its new home and soon there were thousands and thousands of these delicious crustaceans for all to enjoy.

For ever so long, the tasty crawfish were known only to the natives along the Louisiana and Texas Gulf Coast. In 1959, the small town of Breaux Bridge, in St. Martin Parish, decided to honor the crawfish, and since then there has been a festival held every spring. There's dancing in the streets (called a *fais do do*), parades, crawfish-eating and -cooking contests and, yes, even crawfish races. The people of Breaux Bridge are a tireless and innovative group, and because of their loyalty and faith in the crawfish the whole world now knows about the little lobster-like delicacy.

Through the years, cooks and chefs have discovered just how versatile the crawfish can be. You can boil them, stew them, stuff them, fry them, bake them, and combine them with other seafood to create innovative new dishes.

Back before crawfish was king, local fishermen brought the crawfish from the swampy waters primarily for consumption by their own families. If there was more than enough for even the largest Acadian family, the fishermen peddled the crawfish to friends and neighbors.

Once crawfish were recognized for their sweet tasty meat, the world clamored for them. To meet the demand, crawfish farming has developed into a science. Crawfish-peeling and -processing plants have sprung up all over the region. There are now crawfish ponds dotting the land from Lake Charles to Grand Isle. Before all of the technical innovations came about, crawfish were caught in the swamps from April through June; now they are harvested at crawfish farms from January to July.

One of my favorite ways to enjoy crawfish is in "stew-fay." It's a cross between a stew and an *etouffée*. The crawfish meat is so delicate and sweet I don't want to dress it up too much. My rule is to keep it simple and, above all, to not overcook the crawfish.

Crawfish Stew-fay

Makes 8 servings

2 pounds of peeled crawfish tails
1 stick (8 tablespoons) of butter
2 cups of chopped onions
1 cup of chopped green bell peppers
1/2 cup of chopped celery
1 tablespoon of cornstarch
1 cup of water
Salt and cayenne pepper, to taste
1/3 cup of chopped green onions
1/4 cup of chopped fresh parsley

Melt the butter in a large saucepan over medium heat. Add the onions, bell peppers and celery and cook, stirring, until the vegetables are soft and golden, eight to ten minutes. Add the crawfish tails and cook, stirring occasionally, until they throw off some of their liquid, six to eight minutes.

Dissolve the cornstarch in a cup of water and add to the crawfish mixture. Simmer, stirring occasionally, until the mixture thickens, four to five minutes. Season with salt and cayenne.

Serve immediately over steamed rice. Garnish with a sprinkling of green onions and parsley.

In my First Communion dress, inside St. Martin de Tours Catholic Church in St. Martinville in 1952...

Once I have my first taste of the season's crawfish, it is difficult to resist eating more. I do try to pace myself so I won't have too much all at one time.

I watch the advertising signs at roadside stands and at the seafood market, and just when I think the price is getting right I take the plunge and have a crawfish boil.

It must be understood that each person in south Louisiana has his very own way of boiling, so there are no hard and fast rules about how it should be done. Some cooks add tons of salt, cayenne pepper and other spices. Others are not so heavy-handed with seasonings. It's perfectly acceptable to throw whole onions, new potatoes, corn on the cob, smoked sausage and even whole fresh artichokes into the boiling pot. These are wonderful accoutrements to eat along with the crawfish.

I also recommend that the boiling be done outdoors in large boiling pots over butane burners. If you do it indoors you run the risk of having live crawfish escaping from sacks and running around the kitchen. Plus, there'll be a mess to clean up if the pot boils over. Anyway, it's practically a sacred ritual to spread old newspapers on a large picnic table in the yard and let everyone gather around to peel and eat at their own pace. Here is one way to boil crawfish.

Boiled Crawfish

Makes 4 servings

20 pounds of live crawfish (allow 5 pounds per person)
5 gallons of water
1 (26-ounce) box of salt
6 heaping tablespoons of cayenne pepper
4 lemons, halved
10 bay leaves
6 medium-size whole onions
12 new potatoes
6 ears of shucked corn
¼ cup of olive oil (optional, but it makes peeling easier)

If the crawfish appear to be a little muddy, rinse them well with cool water in a large tub, changing the water several times until it runs clear.

Put the five gallons of water in a 10-gallon boiling pot. Add all the ingredients except the crawfish. Bring the water to a rolling boil.

Add the crawfish, cover and allow the water to return to a boil. Cook for eight to ten minutes.

Drain and serve on trays or on that big newspaper-covered outdoor table.

Note: The corn and potatoes will absorb the seasonings, and they are delicious.

When crawfish are plentiful, you can bet there's a pot of something made with them on just about every stove in south Louisiana. Crawfish pies, bisques, stews and jambalaya are traditional favorites, but innovative cooks and chefs have created many different recipes. I was once served a martini with, what else, a marinated crawfish tail instead of an olive.

When time is short, a quick way to make a delicious crawfish jambalaya is in an electric rice cooker. A tossed green salad, hot French bread, and something cold to drink make a great meal.

Crawfish Jambalaya

Makes 6 to 8 servings

1 (10½-ounce) can of beef consomme
1 cup of chopped onions
1 cup of chopped green bell peppers
1 jalapeño pepper, seeded and minced
1 (4-ounce) can of sliced mushrooms, drained
1 stick (8 tablespoons) of melted butter
1 pound of peeled crawfish tails
2½ cups of uncooked long-grain rice
½ teaspoon of salt
¼ teaspoon of cayenne pepper

Place all the ingredients in an 8- to 10-cup rice cooker. Do not add water. Turn on the cook cycle. When the cycle is completed, keep on the warm cycle for at least 30 minutes. Do not attempt to cook in a smaller rice cooker or to double the recipe when using an 8- to 10-cup rice cooker.

There are times when friends shove me out of the kitchen and cook for me. Now, that's what I call a real treat. There are also times when friends challenge me with a recipe they claim is better than mine. I always allow them to cook their recipe for me because that gives me the opportunity to sit back and learn something new.

Such was the case when my husband Rock came home one evening with a bag of groceries under his arm and offered to cook supper. His only clue as to what was in store was that it was going to be something with crawfish. He ordered me out of the kitchen saying this was a secret recipe passed on to him by his father. His challenge to me was to determine the secret ingredient.

I could hear him chopping and stirring as I contented myself with swinging in my hammock, watching the late afternoon clouds brewing into one of those Louisiana thunderstorms. I was a bit mystified when I noticed Rock wrapping up the garbage and depositing it in the outdoor garbage bin. When I asked him what all that was about, he explained that he was getting rid of the evidence.

While the crawfish bubbled on the stove, I was allowed to come in for a whiff. It smelled like an *etouffée* and it had a rich golden color. In fact, it had a gravy that looked better than Mama's. I couldn't wait to taste it.

Finally, I was invited to the table, which had been grandly set with my best china and crystal. Rock stood over me, rubbing his hands as I took my first bite. Ah, it was delicious!

"Well," Rock asked anxiously, "what do you think?"

I admitted it was quite good and although it didn't taste exactly like a traditional *etouffée*, which is usually made with extra fat, it certainly had a rich, full taste. He was pleased with himself when I admitted that I couldn't detect the secret ingredient.

The next day when my garbage was being picked up, I ran out to investigate what Rock had deposited in the garbage. *Aha!* I found the evidence.

Lasserre's Magic Crawfish

Makes 6 to 8 servings

1 pound of peeled crawfish tails
6 tablespoons of butter
2 cups of chopped onions
2 garlic cloves, minced
½ cup of chopped green bell peppers
½ cup of chopped celery
1 (10¾-ounce) can of cream of shrimp soup
   (the secret ingredient)
½ cup of water
¼ cup of dry white wine or dry sherry
Salt, cayenne pepper and hot sauce, to taste
Minced green onions, for garnish

Heat the butter in a large, heavy pot over medium heat. Add the onions, garlic, bell peppers and celery. Cook, stirring, until the vegetables are soft and golden, eight to ten minutes.

Add the crawfish tails and cook for five minutes. Add the soup, water and wine or sherry. Reduce the heat to medium-low and simmer for about 20 minutes.

Season with salt, cayenne and hot sauce. Simmer for five minutes longer.

Serve over steamed rice or your favorite pasta, and garnish with the green onions.

Note: If there is any leftover crawfish mixture, combine it with cooked rice or bread crumbs to make a stiff dressing and stuff into green bell peppers. Bake at 350 for 20 minutes.

The kitchens of Acadiana are the heartbeat of its unique cuisine. The parlors or living rooms of Acadian homes are seldom used. I often wonder why we have them. They are probably used only for special occasions, and even rarely for those. The only way Mama is able to shoo family or guests out of the kitchen is to turn off the lights and close the door. And even then, sooner or later, we find ourselves back at the kitchen table or hanging around the stove.

An old friend of mine says much the same about her mother's kitchen. I have spent many hours in Marie Angelle's kitchen. I do not remember a single time I went there to visit that a pot was not simmering on the stove. Mrs. Angelle, if not busy stirring a pot or chopping up vegetables, sat in a rocking chair near her stove and shared endless cups of coffee with us, listening to the news and gossip of our lives. Bustling around us, checking the pots or refilling our cups was *'Tite Fille*, Mrs. Angelle's faithful kitchen helper and companion.

When I called my friend Tina, Mrs. Angelle's daughter, to come for a visit one April, she declined emphatically.

"Impossible, Marcelle. We're just getting started on making a batch of Mama's famous CRAWFISH *BISQUE*. The crawfish are beautiful and the whole family says it's time for their first share of the season."

My mouth was watering and I was hoping they would either invite me to come help or at least tell me they would keep some for me. In my heart, though, I knew the family came first, and before the season was over I, too, would have a couple of quarts of bisque of my very own.

Having been around several times when the making of crawfish *bisque* took the better part of the day, I allowed my spirit to be with the Angelles as they worked diligently at their task.

For instance, I knew they had gone and hand-selected the crawfish from their supplier, for you must have just the right size to make bisque. Then the heads and tails have to be perfectly cleaned and readied. The vegetables have to be chopped just so, and then begins the arduous task of stuffing, stirring and cooking. Although I wouldn't have the *bisque* made by the

Sister Mary Elaine, who taught at Our Lady of Mercy School in St. Martinville, looks over her brood of first-graders who were going to receive First Communion on Mother's Day 1952. That's me with the cape in the center of the picture.

After receiving my First Communion, my siblings and I got together for a picture in front of the altar of St. Martin de Tours Catholic Church. That's Edna Marie on the left and Henri Clay in the middle.

magical hands of Mrs. Angelle, Tina did give me the recipe and I can vouch you will never have better – maybe different, since each cook has his or her own version – but definitely not more delicious, in my opinion.

Crawfish *Bisque*

Makes 10 to 12 servings

STUFFING

1 cup of vegetable oil or butter
3 medium-size onions, minced
4 celery ribs, chopped
4 medium-size green bell peppers, seeded and minced
5 garlic cloves, minced
1½ pounds of peeled crawfish tails
8 to 10 slices of day-old bread, soaked in water and squeezed dry
2 tablespoons of salt
1 tablespoon of black pepper
1 tablespoon of cayenne pepper
1 cup of unseasoned bread crumbs
1 cup of seasoned bread crumbs
150 crawfish "heads," cleaned

Heat one-half cup of the oil (or butter) in a large, heavy pot over medium heat. Add the onions, celery, bell peppers and garlic, and cook, stirring, until they are soft and golden, eight to ten minutes. Remove from heat and set aside.

Grind one pound of the crawfish tails and the bread together in a meat grinder or food processor.

Heat the remaining one-half cup of oil (or butter) in a large, heavy pot or Dutch oven over medium heat. Add the crawfish/bread mixture, the cooked vegetables, the salt, black pepper, cayenne and the remaining one-half pound of crawfish tails. Cook, stirring, for five to eight minutes. Remove from the heat and cool to room temperature, stirring several times as it cools.

Combine the bread crumbs in a small bowl and set aside.

Preheat the oven to 375 degrees.

Stuff each of the crawfish "heads" with about one tablespoon of the Stuffing and place on a large baking sheet. Cover the Stuffing in the crawfish "heads" with a generous amount of the bread crumbs, patting it gently to adhere to the Stuffing.

Bake until the bread crumbs are lightly golden brown, 15 to 20 minutes.

Remove from the oven and set aside.

BISQUE

1 cup of vegetable oil
2½ pounds of peeled crawfish tails
2 tablespoons of salt
1 tablespoon of cayenne pepper
2 tablespoons of paprika
1½ cups of hot water
4 tablespoons of dark brown roux
4 medium-size onions, chopped
4 medium-size green bell peppers, seeded and chopped
4 celery ribs, chopped
6 to 8 cups of tepid water
2 tablespoons of chopped green onions
2 tablespoons of chopped fresh parsley

Heat one-half cup of the oil in a large, heavy pot or Dutch oven over medium heat. Add the crawfish tails, salt, cayenne and paprika, and cook, stirring, for three minutes.

Combine the water and the roux in a small pot over medium heat and stir to blend. Add to the crawfish mixture and cook, stirring, for two minutes.

Meanwhile, in another large pot, heat the remaining one-half cup of oil over medium heat. Add the onions, bell peppers and celery. Cook, stirring, until soft and golden, about eight minutes. Remove from the heat and add to the crawfish mixture.

Add three to four cups of water, stirring to blend. Cook, stirring, until the mixture thickens, about two minutes. Reduce the heat to medium-low and add the remaining water and cook until the bisque is slightly thick, about 15 minutes. It should be the consistency of a thick soup.

Add the stuffed crawfish "heads," the green onions and the parsley. Cook for about five minutes, stirring gently.

Serve over steamed rice.

Note: After cooling, the *bisque* can be frozen in airtight containers.

Members of my family gather at my grandfather's farm, Banker Plantation, near our hometown in 1944. Bottom row, left to right: Aunt Lois Broussard, my brother Henri Clay sitting on Uncle A.P. Broussard's knee, and my father Blackie Bienvenu. Standing, left to right: My great-aunts May Judice Haines and Belle Judice, my maternal grandfather Alphonse Preval Broussard, my mother Rhena Judice Bienvenu, and my great-aunt Grace Broussard.

From the Basin to the Bay

When the snow begins to melt up north the waters of the Mississippi River and its tributaries often rise to dangerously high levels. Held in check by intricate levee systems, it's not uncommon to see huge vessels prowling along the river above sea level. Some of south Louisiana is below sea level, so no one pays much attention to the situation.

The gradual influx of fresh water into the rivers, streams and bayous creates ideal fishing conditions. Many early mornings find fishermen armed with simple bamboo poles trying their luck along the banks of the nearest bayou.

Bass anglers with more sophisticated equipment head out to numerous lakes. Deep sea sportsmen make their way into the bays and the Gulf of Mexico seeking the big ones. Shrimpers and crabbers begin hauling in their catches, and the waterways are alive with vessels heading in and out of ports. It is time for fish fries, shrimp boils and outdoor suppers featuring seafood taken from the rich waters of the Atchafalaya Basin and Vermilion Bay.

When I was a child, late afternoon was my favorite time to bicycle around the neighborhood checking out who was having what for supper. Mama's only instruction was to be back by sundown because that was when our supper was served. If I was lucky, I would be invited by neighbors to sample whatever was coming off the grill, simmering in their pots, or being spread out on backyard tables. I sometimes ate three suppers before I arrived home for Mama's evening meal. The fresh evening air kept my gastric juices flowing!

Even after growing up and moving to New Orleans, I continued the habit of scouting the neighborhood, checking out what other people were eating for supper. I made friends with local seafood shop owners, asking them to call me when fresh seafood arrived.

One spring afternoon, walking home from the streetcar stop, I spotted a family in their back yard frying up a batch of catfish. I quickened my pace and dashed into the nearest seafood market. I must have appeared to have had a pack of wild dogs on my heels as I rushed in the door and ran to the counter. The shopkeeper looked at me anxiously.

"What do you need today?"

"Catfish!" I responded.

After we checked out several big cats, he happily skinned and filleted my pick. I tucked the package under my arm and headed home. I had enough for a small feast. I hoped my neighbors hadn't eaten supper yet.

I found a few willing friends who generously offered to bring the trimmings – potato salad and hush puppies. I agreed to make a batch of tartar sauce and homemade mayonnaise for the salad.

The first task at hand was to prepare the fish for frying. I had a large, deep, black iron pot – perfect! Let's see now. Does Mama fry her catfish in cornmeal or cracker meal? Do I dredge the fillets in an egg wash before dredging them in meal? It appeared that I would have to reach out and touch someone. No answer at Mama's. I dialed Aunt Lois. She gave me directions.

Fried Catfish

Makes about 4 servings

2 pounds of catfish fillets, cut into 2-inch
  square pieces
2 teaspoons of salt
1 tablespoon of yellow mustard
1 tablespoon of Creole mustard
¼ teaspoon of hot sauce
2 tablespoons of fresh lemon juice
4 cups of yellow cornmeal
3 tablespoons of all-purpose flour
Vegetable oil for frying

Season the fish with the salt, rubbing it in well. Blend the mustards, hot sauce and lemon juice, and spread the mixture all over the fish. Let it sit a while to soak up the marinade.

Pour four fingers of vegetable oil into a deep, heavy frying pot. Mama always said the fish must have enough oil in which to float. Heat the oil to 350 degrees.

Put the yellow cornmeal and flour into a large paper bag. Add the fish fillets and shake the bag to coat the catfish evenly.

Put two or three pieces of fish into the hot oil at one time. Fry until the fish floats to the top.

Drain on paper towels.

My friend Matt says the best thing about fried catfish is the TARTAR SAUCE he makes to go with it.

Matt's Tartar Sauce

1 cup of homemade mayonnaise
  (Recipe follows)
1 large garlic clove, mashed
1 large sweet pickle, minced
5 dashes of Tabasco
3 good shots of Worcestershire sauce
1 teaspoon of grated onion

Mix all the ingredients together in a bowl, cover and chill before serving.

HOMEMADE MAYONNAISE

1 hard-boiled egg yolk
1 raw egg yolk
2/3 cup of vegetable oil
1/2 teaspoon of sugar
1/2 teaspoon of salt
1 teaspoon of vinegar
1/4 teaspoon of black pepper

Combine the egg yolks in a small mixing bowl, stirring and mashing until the mixture is smooth. Slowly add the oil, about a tablespoon at a time, and whip with a wire whisk each time you add the oil. When you have one-fourth cup of oil left, add the sugar, salt and vinegar; whip well. Add the remaining oil and whip again.

Note: While you're at it, you might as well make a double batch – some for the tartar sauce and the rest for potato salad.

When I was living at Oak Alley Plantation, upriver from New Orleans, I always opted to cross the Mississippi by ferryboat. One Saturday evening, I had a few minutes to kill before the next ferry, so I decided to cruise around the riverside village near the ferry landing. I spied a seafood market and went in to browse. There was a wonderful aroma of boiled crawfish, and my mouth began to water. A glass-fronted cooler displayed beautiful fresh shrimp and containers of lump crabmeat. I also spotted bags of "gumbo crabs," so called because they are perfect for simmering in a stew or gumbo.

I hesitated to buy anything because I wasn't expecting company and it seemed a waste to cook such delicacies just for me.

But my time was running short. I heard the ferry blowing, announcing departure from the other side of the river. Oh, what the heck! I grabbed a bag of six gumbo crabs and a pound of large shrimp. I made it just in time to board the ferry.

As I floated to the other side, I gave some thought to what I was going to do with my purchases. Nothing else would do but to make a CRAB AND SHRIMP STEW – the kind that's thick and full of flavor.

On the way to my cottage, I stopped and invited a neighbor and his girlfriend to join me the next afternoon for an early Sunday dinner.

I was just beginning to make the roux when my neighbor called and informed me that a few friends had dropped by unexpectedly and wondered if it was okay to bring them along. No problem. I could stretch my stew. Imagine my chagrin when they arrived and I realized there would be a total of seven at my dinner table!

I would just have to do what Mama does when assorted hungry nieces and nephews drop by with friends. I would have to add a little more stock, cook more rice, and make a bigger salad. Luckily I had a two-loaf bag of French bread.

As everyone gathered in my tiny kitchen, my mind was racing. I didn't even have seven matching dinner plates. I did have eight small soup bowls shaped like fish. As I dug around the cabinet looking for them, I managed to break one. That left seven. Perfect.

Just when I was about to begin serving, everyone decided to crowd around the stove to have a taste test. I hated to tell them that if everyone had a spoonful, servings would be small. Oh, what the heck! Everyone oohed and aahed during dinner, and that helped to relieve my anxieties.

Crab & Shrimp Stew

Makes 6 servings

6 medium-sized crabs
1 pound of large shrimp, peeled and deveined (reserve heads and shells)
1 pound of lump crabmeat, picked over for shells and cartilage
4 tablespoons of vegetable oil
4 tablespoons of all-purpose flour
1 onion, chopped
2 celery ribs, chopped
1 medium-size green bell pepper, seeded and chopped
5 cups of seafood stock (Recipe follows)
2 pinches of ground thyme
2 bay leaves
Salt and cayenne pepper, to taste
½ cup of chopped green onions
2 tablespoons of finely chopped parsley

If you're using live crabs, you'll have to scald them. Bring eight cups of water to a boil in a large pot. Add the crabs and scald for three minutes. Remove the crabs from the water and cool.

Pry off the top shells of the crabs and remove the legs. With a small spoon, remove the rich yellow fat and reserve it. Remove the gills and inedible parts.

To make seafood stock, return the crab shells and legs to the pot of boiling water along with the shrimp heads and shells. Reduce the heat and simmer while you make the roux.

Combine the oil and flour in a heavy pot over medium heat. Stirring slowly and constantly, make a roux the color of peanut butter. Add the onion, celery and bell pepper. Cook, stirring, until the vegetables are soft and golden, eight to ten minutes.

Meanwhile, strain the seafood stock and measure five cups. Slowly add the stock to the roux, stirring and blending. Simmer for 45 minutes.

Add the crabs, lump crabmeat and shrimp along with the seasonings and reserved fat. Cook for 15 minutes.

Add the green onions and serve immediately over rice in soup bowls. Garnish with chopped parsley.

Toting his camera and briefcase, my father Blackie Bienvenu heads for work circa 1949. He was editor and publisher of The Teche News at the time.

From the time I was a toddler until I was well into my teens, I learned all there was to know about the blue hard-shell crabs caught in both freshwater lakes and saltwater bays of south Louisiana.

But it wasn't until Papa deemed me old enough to accompany him on a business trip to New Orleans that I was introduced to the true delicacy known as soft-shell crab. The term "soft-shell" refers not to a kind of crab, but to a specific point in a crab's life.

Crabs periodically outgrow their shells and live for a few hours in a soft-shell state before the new shell begins to harden. It is at this point that they must be removed from their water environment for immediate consumption.

It's a time-consuming and arduous task for the workers who must check the submerged boxes holding the crabs several times a day, waiting for just the moment the crabs begin to molt.

Soft-shell crabs are an epicure's delight and have always been a popular item in the famous and not-so-famous restaurants of the Crescent City.

Papa chose a waterfront restaurant on Lake Pontchartrain to christen my taste buds with what he said was a secret passion of his. Without even perusing the menu, he gave the waitress the order.

"Fried soft-shell crabs for the young lady and myself," he boomed. "And make sure they're done just right!"

Sailboats glided past our seaside perch while Papa and I waited for our order. He explained that I would be able to eat the entire crab. No peeling or messing with hard shells. I was a bit apprehensive, but having trusted Papa all my life, I figured this was no time to have misgivings.

Our platters arrived, piled high with two golden fried soft-shell crabs, French fries and hot, buttered French bread. I watched Papa snap off a huge claw encrusted in a crunchy batter and pop it into his mouth. A look of ecstasy appeared on his face. That was all the encouragement I needed. I dug in. Oh, what fun it was not to have to do battle with the hard crab shell. No pieces of shell to spit out. And the flavor! I savored the legs then tore into the body where the lump crabmeat and rich fat were held together by the light batter. I dared not dip the chunks into my little cup of tartar sauce lest I lose the taste of the sweet lake crab.

I had a new and dear respect for Papa.

Throughout the rest of his life, whenever he and I shared a meal of soft-shell crabs we exchanged secret winks and remembered that wonderful meal on the lakefront.

When I had my own restaurant near Lafayette, one of my chefs, Bryan Richard, created a dish using SOFT-SHELL CRABS that became a fast favorite of our clientele.

Stuffed Soft-Shell Crabs & Shrimp Jambalaya

Makes 6 servings

6 jumbo soft-shell crabs
1 cup of chopped green onions
1 garlic clove, minced
1 pound of lump crabmeat, picked over for shells and cartilage
1 pound of small shrimp, peeled and finely chopped
½ cup of dry white wine
2 teaspoons of salt
1½ teaspoons of cayenne pepper
½ teaspoon of white pepper
3 cups of stale bread crumbs
½ pound of mushrooms, finely chopped
3 egg yolks
1 (3-ounce) jar of diced pimientos
All-purpose flour for dredging
2 cups of buttermilk
4 eggs, beaten
3 cups of cracker meal
Peanut oil for deep frying
Creollaise Sauce (Recipe follows)

Begin to clean the soft-shell crabs by cutting crabs across the face with a pair of kitchen shears. Remove the eye sockets and the lower mouth. Carefully lift up the apron and remove the gills. Rinse gently with cool water and pat dry.

Cook the green onions, garlic, crabmeat and shrimp in the wine for several minutes over medium heat. Add one teaspoon of the salt, one-half teaspoon of the cayenne, one-fourth teaspoon of white pepper and the bread crumbs. Stir to mix. Add the mushrooms, egg yolks and pimientos. Mix gently. Remove from heat and cool to room temperature. Chill the stuffing for at least one hour or until firm.

Carefully lift the "shoulders" on each crab and gently press about one tablespoon of the stuffing into this area. Press the "shoulders" down to hold the stuffing. Be careful not to break off any of the legs of the crabs. Lay the crabs on a baking sheet and sprinkle with one-half teaspoon of salt and one-half teaspoon of cayenne.

Combine the flour with the remaining one-half teaspoon of salt, one-half teaspoon of cayenne and one-fourth teaspoon of white pepper in a shallow bowl. In a mixing bowl combine the buttermilk and the eggs. Whisk to blend. Put the cracker meal in another shallow bowl.

Heat the oil to 360 degrees in a deep pot.

Dredge the crabs in the seasoned flour, then dip them in the buttermilk mixture. Then dredge them in the cracker meal, making sure that the legs are well-breaded.

Hold each crab by the body, allowing the legs to dip into the hot oil for a few seconds before dropping the whole crab into the hot oil. Fry the crabs until they float to the surface of the oil and are golden brown. Drain on paper towels.

SHRIMP JAMBALAYA

3 tablespoons of vegetable shortening
2 tablespoons of all-purpose flour
1½ cups of chopped onions
½ cup of chopped green bell peppers
1 cup of chopped celery
1 garlic clove, minced
1 (1-pound) can of whole tomatoes
¾ cup of tomato sauce
2 cups of uncooked short-grain white rice
1 teaspoon of salt
1¼ teaspoons of cayenne pepper
2½ cups of water
1 pound of medium-size shrimp, peeled and deveined

Heat the shortening in a large saucepan over medium heat. Add the flour and stir over medium heat to make a golden brown roux. Add the onions, bell pepper, celery and garlic. Cook slowly in the roux until the vegetables are soft, three to four minutes.

Add the whole tomatoes and the tomato sauce and cook until an oil film rises to the surface.

Stir in the rice, salt, cayenne, water and shrimp. Cover and cook over a low heat until the rice is tender, 20 to 30 minutes. Add more water if the mixture becomes dry.

Serve the crabs, legs up, over a bed of the jambalaya. Ladle a tablespoon of Creollaise Sauce over the crabs. Garnish with a wedge of lemon and fried parsley.

CREOLLAISE SAUCE

2 cups of béarnaise sauce
2 tablesoons of Creole mustard

Combine the sauce and mustard and keep warm.

Oh, if Papa could see me now!

Before the spring shrimp season gets into full swing, I like to test the waters, so to speak. I call a friend who has a small fishing camp near the mouth of the Mississippi River and suggest an excursion. Just the two of us go down late in the afternoon and prepare for an early morning adventure.

All we need to pack is a small ice chest, the fixings for a cold breakfast, a throw net and bathing suits. The kitchen at the camp is equipped with a small butane stove and a collection of iron pots. If we're lucky we'll catch our supper. On our way down, we pick up some vegetables from roadside stands. We're on an adventure!

The plan is to rise with the sun and be on the wharf for our first cup of coffee. Who's going to cast the net first? We flip a coin. He wins. I stand aside as he spins the net gracefully into the water that at this time of morning is the same color as the sky. The spinning net looks like a giant spider web as it sinks into the gray-blue water. He adroitly pulls the rope in his hand and quickly drags in the net.

What treasures will it hold? I stand at the edge of the pier, my toes curled around the rough, weathered cypress boards. The net is hauled up onto the wharf. In its folds we count six, seven, eight shrimp, a small crab and a couple of large minnows. I pick out the shrimp, still kicking, and carefully put them into our small pail containing a bit of crushed ice. Everything else goes back to the sea.

My turn now with the net. I'm not as adept as my companion, but I manage to set the net spinning into the cool blue depths. I yank the cord and pull in the net. *Aha!* Another eight or ten large, sweet shrimp. A few more castings bring in enough for our late afternoon meal.

Now we can while away the day. We set out a small crab trap in hopes of catching a few to go with our meal later in the day. With ham sandwiches and soft drinks packed in the small ice chest, we tie a small dinghy on a tether rope, jump in and spend the day on the water.

With a large umbrella to protect us from the sun and armed with a small radio, we are perfectly content. We discuss how we plan to prepare the catch. We doze off and

on, pointing out now and then the egrets and seagulls soaring above us. No one comes our way throughout the day, and we feel secluded from the outside world of hot afternoon traffic and ringing telephones. Is this the little bit of heaven we all dream about?

Before we know it, the sun is moving into the western sky. It's time to check the crab trap, take a quick shower under the watering hose that hangs from a post on the pier, change into shorts and T-shirts, and prepare supper before heading back to the city.

Let's see, we have a couple dozen shrimp, six medium-sized crabs, a couple of red-ripe tomatoes, one Vidalia onion, and a loaf of French bread we brought from the city. On the pantry shelf in the camp I find a can of small potatoes, a can of sliced beets, and a surprise – a can of hearts of palm.

We pull out the collection of iron pots and choose our weapons. He's to take care of the shrimp and crabs. I will try to be innovative with the potatoes, beets and hearts of palm.

Pot Crabs & Shrimp

Makes 6 servings

2 dozen shrimp
6 medium-sized crabs
2 cups of water
1 teaspoon of salt
1 teaspoon of cayenne pepper
2 tablespoons of butter
1 small onion, chopped
2 ripe tomatoes, peeled, seeded and chopped
1 cup of seafood stock

Peel the shrimp, reserving shells and heads. Scald the crabs, cool them and then pick out the crabmeat. Reserve the shells.

To make seafood stock, place the shrimp and crab shells in a small saucepan with two cups of water seasoned with the salt and cayenne. Simmer for about 30 minutes. Strain the stock.

In a large skillet, melt the butter over medium heat. Add the onion and tomatoes, and cook, stirring for two to three minutes. Add the shrimp and crabmeat, stir for a few minutes and then add the seafood stock. Simmer for 10 minutes. Serve immediately.

While my friend cooked the seafood, I drained the canned potatoes and dredged them in some flour seasoned with a little salt and black pepper and a pinch of nutmeg. I deep-fried them to a golden brown.

The beets and hearts of palm were sliced, chilled, drizzled with vinegar, and garnished with sprigs of fresh parsley I found near the back door steps.

We loaded all of the food onto a large cutting board and set it out on the wharf, where we dined *alfresco*. We sopped up every drop with chunks of French bread.

Oh, dear, do we really have to go home?

There comes a point in late spring when I feel it in my bones – the need to head out toward the open waters of Vermilion Bay. I want to smell the salty sea air and see the horizon, uninterrupted by land or trees.

I believe that feeling comes from listening to Mama and Papa talk as summer neared and they too yearned to get away to the camp at Cypremort Point. Situated on the northeastern edge of Vermilion Bay, practically dead center on the Louisiana Gulf Coast, The Point is often referred to as the "Cajun Riviera."

At the Cypremort Point of my childhood, camps were strung out along the water, each with its own covered pier and many with names such as "Camp Sip-More." The camps were simple, with screened porches wrapped around the fronts and painted bright red and yellow with green roofs and trim.

Mama loaded up all of us kids, along with boxes of towels and sheets, a portable washing machine and bags of food. We stopped in New Iberia to pick up Aunt Eva and her daughter Candy, and headed south.

Louisa was the last stop before we got on the only road to The Point. At the general store we were allowed to buy popsicles for the final stretch. More times than not we had to wait as the bridge over the Intra-coastal Canal opened for the long barges to pass through. With popsicles melting in our hands, we would visit with the other families waiting in line at the bridge.

Finally we would be on our way. The last few miles were treacherous. This was before air-conditioned cars, so we had a choice to make: keep the windows down in hopes of getting a breath of air and choke on the dust kicked up along the shell road, or roll up the windows and die of suffocation. We compromised: roll up the windows for a few minutes, then roll them down for very brief periods.

We looked like a tribe of wild Indians by the time we arrived at the camp. Along with hands made red and sticky by the popsicles, our faces were coated with white dust streaked with perspiration, and we had great mosquito bites all over our bodies. But who cared? We were in paradise!

After we unloaded the car, we would drag the crab nets out of storage and quickly bait them with chicken necks. After all, Mama and Aunt Eva said we had to hurry and catch our supper. They knew how to get us out of their hair while they transformed the camp into our home away from home.

In a matter of hours we caught several dozen crabs, despite losing one of the younger children off the end of the pier and getting splinters in our rear ends.

While we hacked away at our boiled crabs, Mama and Aunt Eva would sip on their cold beers and peel the biggest crabs so that we could have crab chops the next day. I can't tell you which meal we liked best. You can decide after you try these.

Crab Chops

Makes 6 servings

3 tablespoons of butter
3 green onions, minced
2 tablespoons of all-purpose flour
1 cup of milk
1 pound of crabmeat, picked over for shells
   and cartilage
20 saltine crackers, finely crumbled
1 egg, beaten
½ teaspoon of salt
¼ teaspoon of cayenne pepper
2 dashes of hot sauce
Cracker meal or bread crumbs for dredging
Butter and vegetable oil for frying
Boiled crab claws for garnish (optional)

Heat the butter in a large saucepan over medium heat. Add the green onions and cook, stirring, for two minutes. Add the flour and cook, stirring, for one minute. Slowly add the milk, stirring constantly, until the mixture thickens.

Remove from the heat and add the crabmeat, cracker crumbs, egg, salt, cayenne and hot sauce.

Mix gently and set aside to cool completely. (The mixture can be chilled in the refrigerator for about an hour.) Shape the mixture into six patties.

Dredge the patties in the cracker meal or bread crumbs, coating evenly. Put about one-half inch of equal parts of vegetable oil and butter in a skillet over medium heat. Fry the patties until they are golden brown, two to three minutes on each side. Drain on paper towels.

At Cypremort Point we ate our crab chops on paper plates as we sat on the pier. Every person had his own garnish. My sister doused hers with ketchup. I daintily spread mine with tartar sauce. My brother sandwiched his between two chunks of French bread spread with mustard. We all agreed they went well with shoe string potatoes. Ah, the good old days.

Spring Alfresco

When the first warm spring breezes ripple through the trees, I find myself making any excuse to be out in the open air. Since I love this time of year, I roam the countryside, either on foot or by car, looking for the first signs of blackberries, checking crawfish ponds, and watching for the purple thistles that grow in abundance in fallow fields and pastures or in open ditches in rural areas.

The purple thistles, called *chardrons* by the natives, are delightful to eat. Although I had seen them throughout my childhood, it wasn't until some years later that I learned from a friend that parts of them are edible.

Having lived all her life near Bayou Boeuf and Lake des Allemands, she had a great knowledge of the land. She knew which swamp mushrooms are edible, when it is time to harvest *graine a volers* (edible seeds from certain water chinquapins) and, of course, she knew all about *chardrons*.

She brought the thistles to me in a large brown paper bag and proceeded to tell me how to handle these gigantic purplish-green thistle bushes.

"First of all," she explained, "if it doesn't have a large prickly head on it, it's not ready to pick. It *must* have a big head."

I nodded and promised I wouldn't dare pick one if it didn't have a big head.

"Be sure to wear boots that go up to your knees, and arm yourself with a big knife," she continued.

I had a great picture of myself stalking a pasture wearing big rubber boots while wielding a big knife.

"With the long knife, cut the *chardron* down at the base near the ground. Let it fall away from you and carefully pick it up with your fingers. Use gloves if you must. Then, with a knife, scrape off the stickers and chop off the head at the top. Put the stalk in a brown paper bag. Plastic bags won't do."

I didn't dare ask why. I rather like brown paper bags anyway. They have more character than plastic.

What she then pulled out of the paper bag was the *chardron* up to that point.

"Now, with a sharp knife, scrape off the

strings, much like you do with celery."

What she held up to show me was a cone-shaped stalk, light green in color, which looked like an odd piece of celery.

She went on.

"Trim off both ends and chop into half-inch pieces. Put the pieces in a colander and rinse with cold water. Drain. Place the pieces in a bowl and season with vinegar, salt and black pepper."

With the bowl before me, I chomped away. The *chardrons* were crunchy and had the taste of celery, cucumber and hearts of palm. I managed to salvage some to take home for supper. They would be perfect with some French bread and a chicken liver *pâté* made the night before.

Chicken Liver *Pâté*

Makes 8 to 10 appetizer portions

1/4 cup of chopped onions
4 tablespoons of butter
1½ pounds of chicken livers
2 hard-boiled egg yolks
4 tablespoons of softened butter
1/3 cup of heavy cream
1/3 cup of Cognac
1/4 teaspoon of nutmeg
Salt and freshly ground black pepper, to taste

Cook the onions in the butter over medium heat until soft and golden, about five minutes. Add the chicken livers and cook just until the pink disappears. Purée the mixture in a blender or food processor.

Put the egg yolks through a sieve and add to the chicken liver mixture, together with the four tablespoons of softened butter, the heavy cream, Cognac and nutmeg. Season with salt and pepper.

Blend together until smooth. You may also add a handful of chopped chives or green onions for a little extra taste and color.

Chill the *pâté* before serving with toast points or crackers.

Those warm, velvet evenings of spring make me pull back the curtains, throw open all the French doors opening onto the patio, and take deep breaths of jasmine-scented night air.

The evenings are perfect for *alfresco* dining. Quick, simple dishes are in order. One of my favorites is from Commander's Palace in New Orleans. The dish can be elegantly prepared tableside, but can also be done in a skillet on the stove. It's easy, delicious and versatile.

Singing Shrimp

Makes 2 servings

6 to 8 large shrimp per person, peeled and deveined
8 tablespoons (1 stick) of butter
½ cup of chopped green onions
1 teaspoon of minced garlic
½ cup of sliced fresh mushrooms
1 ounce of brandy
Several dashes of Worcestershire sauce
Salt and cayenne pepper, to taste

Heat the butter in a large skillet over medium heat. Add the green onions, garlic and mushrooms. Cook, stirring, for three to four minutes.

Add the shrimp and cook slowly until they turn pink. Add the brandy and Worcestershire sauce and season with salt and pepper. Cook for three to four minutes.

Serve over toast points, in pastry shells, or with pasta of your choice.

Note: For a variation on this recipe, add one-half cup of chopped tomatoes with the brandy and proceed as directed. Season with a tablespoon of chopped fresh sweet basil to give the dish another dimension.

Any way you serve this dish, eating outside will make it all taste just a little bit better.

Strawberry (or Raspberry) Romanoff

Makes 2 servings

2 cups of French vanilla ice cream
1 cup of fresh strawberries or raspberries
1 tablespoon of sugar
3 ounces of Grand Marnier
½ cup of whipping cream

Place everything in a blender and blend until smooth.

Serve in large wine glasses. (It's also good served over cubed pound cake placed in a small bowl.)

Garnish with a sprig of fresh mint.

When spring is in the air, so is the heady smoke of outdoor grilling. Late in the afternoon, when the humid heat begins to subside, people are either in their back yards, on patios or even on small French Quarter balconies, lighting up their grills. Some families opt for tree-shaded parks. But wherever one goes, the aroma of sizzling hamburgers, steaks, ribs and chicken fills the air.

When I lived in New Orleans (the third time around), all I had was a patio the size of a postage stamp. But it was fenced in, and I made it quite lush with potted palms, small flower beds filled with blossoming plants, and a selection of herbs and pepper bushes.

On many evenings my neighbors witnessed smoke spewing forth from my small grill. I often feared for my upstairs neighbors. I'm sure they kept a fire extinguisher close at hand when they heard me on the patio.

One of my favorite things to grill is a good hamburger. I like mine big and juicy; I guess everybody does. I don't think I've ever heard anyone say they like a small, dry one.

I also like my hamburger with bits of onion and bell pepper mixed into the ground beef. Others prefer a large thick slice of raw onion shoved between the burger and the bun. That's a bit too heavy for my taste.

The primary criterion, though, is that the hamburger is grilled over an open flame, rather than fried in a skillet or broiled in the oven. And I like mine medium-rare. I like to see a little blood ooze out when I bite into it.

I'm not much on shredded lettuce, and I don't particularly care for sliced tomato, unless it's a Creole tomato, fresh from the garden. And cheese? Well, I've been known to put a couple of slices of American or Swiss on my burger, but what I like best is a big chunk of bleu cheese spread over the burger just as it comes off the grill. I'm not picky about mustard and mayonnaise, but if I have homemade mayonnaise flavored with a little garlic, I'll choose that over the commercial kind.

But the crowning touch is the bun. I like it hot, but not toasted, and it has to be big enough to cover the burger. I don't like a hamburger on an onion roll or French bread, even less on regular old white sliced bread. It has to be a real hamburger bun.

Marcelle's Big & Juicy Hamburgers

Makes 6 hamburgers

2 pounds of lean ground beef
2 tablespoons of minced onions
2 tablespoons of minced green bell pepper
1 tablespoon of soy sauce
½ teaspoon of cayenne pepper
1½ teaspoons of garlic powder
1 tablespoon of Worcestershire sauce
1 tablespoon of olive oil

Mix all the ingredients together except the Worcestershire and olive oil.

Let stand in the refrigerator, covered, for at least one hour.

Shape the mixture into thick patties. Place them on a platter and drizzle with the Worcestershire and olive oil. Let the patties come to room temperature before grilling.

Cook until desired degree of doneness, turning only once.

WARM BUNS

In a large heavy skillet, melt one tablespoon of margarine or butter per bun.

Add a few dashes of Worcestershire sauce and place both halves of the bun, inside down, in the skillet and heat quickly over medium heat.

At another time of my life I lived at Oak Alley Plantation, a wondrous place, quiet and serene. My cottage was nestled in a spot surrounded by an old wooden fence draped with honeysuckle and shaded by ancient crape myrtle and live oaks.

Friends from New Orleans often wound their way along the River Road to Oak Alley to get away from it all. One evening we huddled around a fire we built in the yard, listening to a portable radio and sipping red wine. Someone came up with the idea of having a camp-out in the clearing near my cottage.

There were to be certain rules for the camp-out. No electrical equipment would be allowed, and everyone would have to cook their own supper on an open fire.

On the appointed day, we were there early setting up tents and cots. Ice chests held food and beverages. By late afternoon, the barbecue pits were being readied. And, needless to say, there was a lot of tasting of one another's dishes. But we were all in agreement the best of the lot was the pork and beans prepared by an old friend, Jet Smith.

My brother Henri Clay and I on Easter Sunday in St. Martinville in 1948...

Jet's Mean Beans

Makes 10 servings

1 pound of sliced bacon
2 large onions, thinly sliced
2 garlic cloves, minced
6 tablespoons of fresh lemon juice
4 (16-ounce) cans of good-quality pork and
  beans
2 cups of dark brown sugar
½ cup of barbecue sauce
Salt and black pepper, to taste

Fry the bacon in a large, heavy pot over medium heat until crisp. Add the onions and garlic, and cook, stirring, until the onions are soft, about six minutes. Add the lemon juice and stir for a minute or two. Then add the pork and beans, brown sugar and barbecue sauce. Season with the salt and pepper.

Simmer, stirring occasionally, or bake in the oven at 250 degrees for 1½ hours, or until, as Jet says, the onions are well-smothered in the beans. He also suggests that you cook them the day before serving and let them stand in the refrigerator overnight. Reheat to serve.

Another friend from Texas cooked the best ribs that night.

Country Ribs

Makes 6 servings

4 pounds of country-style pork ribs
1 teaspoon of garlic powder
1/2 teaspoon of Tabasco
1/3 cup of soy sauce
1/2 teaspoon of black pepper
1/2 cup of catsup
1 tablespoon of yellow mustard
1 tablespoon of cane syrup or honey
1 tablespoon of bourbon

Place the ribs in a baking pan.

Make the marinade/basting sauce by combining all the remaining ingredients. Pour the mixture over the ribs and let stand at room temperature for at least two hours.

Grill the ribs over slow coals, about six inches above the fire. Baste with the sauce and turn the ribs every 15 minutes. Continue basting. Grill until the juices run clear.

Some of my favorite side dishes for barbecues are new potatoes, boiled and tossed with butter and fresh parsley, or corn on the cob, dripping with butter. And my all-time favorite dessert is a good LEMON PIE.

Lemon Pie

Makes one 9-inch pie to serve 6

1 1/3 cups of sugar
6 tablespoons of cornstarch
Pinch of salt
1 1/4 cups of boiling water
3 egg yolks, beaten
1/3 cup of fresh lemon juice
2 tablespoons of butter
2 tablespoons of grated lemon zest
1 baked 9-inch pie shell

Combine the sugar, cornstarch and salt in a saucepan over medium heat. Gradually add the water, whisking to blend. Bring to a boil, stirring constantly. Cook until the mixture becomes clear and thick, about one minute.

Stir a small amount of the hot mixture into the beaten egg yolks and return to the hot mixture. Cook over medium heat for about three minutes, stirring constantly. Stir in the lemon juice, butter and lemon zest.

Pour into the pie shell.

Preheat the oven to 250 degrees.

TOPPING

3 egg whites
Pinch of salt
1 (7-ounce) jar of marshmallow cream

Beat the egg whites in a large mixing bowl with the salt until soft peaks form. Gradually add the marshmallow cream, beating until stiff peaks form.

Spread the mixture over the lemon filling, sealing to the edge of the crust.

Bake until the top is lightly browned, 12 to15 minutes. Cool and serve.

It was one of those perfect spring days. There was a light breeze blowing off the river. Wild clover covered the levee, and the fragrance of sweet olive trees filled the air. I decided it was a day to play hooky from work. Two or three hours away from the office might be just what I need to clear my overloaded brain.

As I pulled out the picnic hamper I knew tuna fish sandwiches were out. I wanted a gourmet picnic lunch. Fortunately, I had stopped the day before at a roadside vegetable and fruit stand and picked up fresh produce. And the night before I had experimented with an idea given to me by a friend, so I had six cold garlic-stuffed meatballs I could use to make po-boy sandwiches. I was on a roll!

Since I felt like I was going on a mini-vacation, I packed my basket with linen napkins, china and crystal. I threw in several magazines I hadn't had time to read.

All I needed now was a convertible so I could feel the sun on my face. But, alas, I had to settle for an old army jeep, which turned out to be great. I could ride up and down the levee in search of the perfect picnic hideaway.

I found a small grove of cypress trees, turned on a portable radio, and spread out my goodies. There wasn't a soul around. Ah, sweet solitude.

Garlic Meatballs for Po-Boys

Makes 2 large po-boy sandwiches

½ pound of ground chuck
¼ pound of ground veal
¼ pound of lean ground pork
½ teaspoon of salt
¼ teaspoon of cayenne pepper
¼ teaspoon of freshly ground black pepper
1 tablespoon of Worcestershire sauce
¼ teaspoon of oregano leaves
6 large garlic cloves, split in half
3 tablespoons of vegetable oil
½ cup of water or beef broth

Combine the ground meats with the salt, cayenne, black pepper, Worcestershire and oregano in a large mixing bowl. Shape the meat mixture into six large meatballs. Carefully poke the split garlic pods, two to each meatball, into the center of the meatballs.

Heat the vegetable oil in a large skillet over medium heat. Add the meatballs and brown evenly on all sides. Add the warm water or beef broth, cover and simmer over medium-low heat until the juices run clear, 20 to 30 minutes. Remove from the heat and cool.

Split the meatballs in half and make a po-boy, dressed to your taste, on French bread.

I had crisp munchies to go with my splendid po-boy.

Marinated Green Beans & Cherry Tomatoes

Makes 4 servings

8 cups of water
1 pound of fresh green beans, trimmed
1 teaspoon of salt
8 cherry tomatoes
1 tablespoon of olive oil
1 tablespoon of tarragon vinegar
1 teaspoon of Dijon mustard
1 medium-size onion, thinly sliced
Salt and freshly ground black pepper, to taste

Bring the water to a boil in a large saucepan over medium-high heat. Add the salt and green beans. Boil until tender-crisp, five to seven minutes (depending on size).

Drain in a colander and cool the beans in a bowl filled with ice cold water.

Toss the beans in a large salad bowl with the tomatoes, olive oil, vinegar, mustard and sliced onion. Season with salt and pepper.

To complete my picnic lunch, I filled a thermos with cold tea and added a few crushed mint leaves and fresh-squeezed lemon juice. To satisfy my sweet tooth, I rolled some strawberries in brown sugar and sour cream.

It's amazing what a couple of hours in the fresh air and Louisiana sunshine can do for your state of mind.

Lazy, Crazy May

By the middle of May, the foliage is so dense along the highways, yard fences and bayou banks that it is like a heavy curtain enclosing the countryside.

Just a few weeks before, you could spot a neighbor working in his garden. Now, you can barely see him as he hoes, weeds and mulches.

Today, I have to fight my way through a tangle of vines and bushes with a machete if I want to watch him at his work.

Ligustrum bushes along fence lines blossom with sweet flowers that attract hordes of bees and bring on sneezing attacks. Magnolia trees with their shiny dark leaves and glorious blossoms are at their peak. People work fanatically in their yards trying to keep lawns mowed, bedding plants watered and hedges trimmed. Late afternoon showers send the leaves of the banana trees reaching for the sky.

June is fast approaching and children are getting restless in classrooms all over the state. Everyone wants to head for the nearest swimming hole. Summer is creeping in.

Mama says the month of May makes her crazy. There is Mother's Day, First Communions, graduations, and pre-nuptial parties for June brides. She is tired of her linen dresses even before the slew of weddings begins. We try to get her in an improved state of mind and plan a big celebration for Mother's Day. It's always our hope that if she can make it through that, she'll manage the rest.

All the children and grandchildren plan for days. Once we decided to arrive with all the trimmings and simply take over her house and yard. Since my sister Edna and her brood live next door to Mama, she bore the brunt of the work. But the rest of us thought it quite appropriate because Mama adores Edna's husband, who is fondly referred to by Mama as "Poor Al."

We've never figured out why Mama calls him that because we believe that while he's not rich, he's the only one in our family who has a pool in his back yard. He also has a great sense of humor and doesn't appear to let anything bother him, despite the presence of four lively children who are always into everything.

We still laugh about the time one of his sons drove a brand new riding lawn mower into the deep end of the swimming pool, and all Poor Al did was shake his head and chuckle for hours.

Anyway, Poor Al takes good care of Mama – he trims her hedges, mows the yard, fixes fences and runs endless errands for her. And he always volunteers to cook for Mother's Day.

Poor Al prepares the main course, while the rest of us take care of all the other dishes. For many years he barbecued everything from chicken to ribs, but now his thing is to fry whole turkeys. Yep, the whole thing, not pieces.

Poor Al's Fried Turkey

Makes about 20 servings

2 fresh turkeys, 10 to 12 pounds each
1 large yellow onion, minced
8 to 10 garlic cloves, peeled
¼ cup of chopped green bell peppers
¼ cup of seeded and chopped jalapeño
  peppers (optional)
3 tablespoons of salt
3 tablespoons of cayenne pepper

Clean the turkeys well and rinse with cool water. Pat dry. Leave the skin flap at the neck on.

Combine the onion, garlic, peppers, and 1½ tablespoon each of salt and cayenne in a bowl. With a sharp boning knife, make slits in the breasts and upper thighs and stuff this seasoning mixture into the slits with your fingers. Pack it in well.

Season the outside of the turkeys with the remaining salt and pepper, rubbing well.

Place the turkeys in large plastic bags and refrigerate overnight.

Before you begin frying, you must do a little preparation. Al strongly recommends that you do not cook the turkeys in your kitchen. You will need a butane burner and a very large, deep, heavy pot with a cover.

Spread newspaper or thick cardboard beneath the burner to protect the area from

grease splatters. Have on hand two large paper bags and arm yourself with two long-handled forks, the kind used for barbecuing. I also suggest having barbecue mittens or large insulated pot holders.

Ready? Here we go.

Pour enough peanut oil or lard to fill the pot three-fourths full. The oil must be at 350 degrees before adding the turkey. Grab the turkey by the neck flap and gently submerge it into the hot oil. Be careful: The hot grease may overflow and splatter. Cover the pot. Turn the turkey every five to ten minutes, using the long-handled forks.

It will take 45 minutes to an hour to cook a turkey. When the legs begin to spread open, the turkey is done. Remove it from the grease and put it inside of a large brown paper bag; close tightly with a piece of twine or wire twist. Let the turkey stand for 15 to 20 minutes before removing from the bag and carving to serve.

I have another great turkey recipe I must share. My first encounter with my Aunt Git Broussard's famous baked turkey was at a family gathering held after a funeral. I spooned some of Aunt Git's famous rice dressing over several turkey slices. I can't tell you how good that turkey was.

It was juicy, well-seasoned and absolutely delicious. I hounded Aunt Git for the rest of the afternoon until we made a date for her to show me her secret. I couldn't wait.

I picked up a turkey, and armed with paper and pencil I met her in her kitchen for the demonstration.

The directions may seem complicated, so read the recipe carefully and have the turkey and ingredients ready at hand.

Aunt Git's Turkey

1½ sticks of butter
Salt and cayenne pepper, to taste
1 large onion, coarsely chopped
1 large green bell pepper, coarsely chopped
5 to 6 garlic cloves, peeled and cut into slivers
6 to 10 Cajun Chef brand "sport peppers" (small green hot peppers packed in vinegar)
2 tablespoons of vinegar from the pepper bottle

You can use any size turkey, but I recommend using one that is about 12 pounds. Remove the neck, gizzards and livers from the cavity. Rinse the turkey both inside and out and pat dry with clean dish towels. Place the turkey on a large tray or cutting board. Aunt Git says it's best if the turkey is not thoroughly defrosted, as it will make it easier to do what we are about to do.

Cut the butter into tablespoon-size slices. Place in a small bowl and season generously with salt and cayenne. Place the seasoned butter in the freezer for about an hour.

Combine the onion, bell pepper, garlic, sport peppers and vinegar in a small bowl and sprinkle lightly with more salt and cayenne. Allow this to stand for about an hour.

In a third small bowl, combine two tablespoons of salt and one tablespoon of cayenne or more if using a larger turkey. You will need a 6-inch boning knife and a small spoon with a thin rounded handle.

Be prepared to use your hands; you may want to wear a pair of surgical gloves if your hands are irritated by pepper.

Have all of the ingredients ready with the turkey on a tray or large cutting board. Go into the turkey's cavity and make a slit in the breast meat on either side of the center breast bone. Do not cut through the skin. Spoon in some of the salt and pepper mixture, and then, with your fingers, stuff in the onion, green pepper, garlic and sport pepper mixture. Insert two or three of the frozen butter slices into the slits. If you have a large turkey, you will be able to make two slits on each side of the main breast bone.

With the turkey lying breast side up with the legs facing you, gently pull the drumstick forward to expose the inner thigh. Pull the skin away from the meat. Make a slit following the bone line from the top of the leg. Use your finger to make a path and repeat the stuffing procedure described above. Where the skin has been loosened on the inner thigh, spoon in the salt and cayenne mixture. Repeat the procedure on the other leg.

Now, turn the turkey breast side up with the neck opening facing you. Lift the skin flap and make a slit down the wing from the shoulder, again following the bone line. Repeat the stuffing process on both wings.

Season the outside of the turkey with the salt and cayenne you mixed in the third small bowl.

Any leftover seasonings, vegetable mixture and butter pieces may be placed in the cavity. Secure the wings by folding the lower half back over the top of the wing. Tie the legs together with twine. Place the turkey in a roasting pan, preferably granite. Do not put oil in the pan.

Preheat the oven to 400 degrees. Put the turkey in the oven and cook for 15 to 20 minutes, just to get the browning process going. Reduce the oven temperature to 350 degrees and cover with the roaster lid.

BAKING TIMES

8-9 pounds: 2 - 2½ hours
12 pounds: 3 - 3½ hours
18-20 pounds: 4 - 4½ hours

Baste often with pan drippings. Do not overcook; the meat will dry out if you do.

It may sound like a lot of work and struggling, but the reward is great.

After you carve the turkey, return the meat to the pan drippings and allow it to soak for a few minutes.

Note: Any leftover meat may be used to make an incredible gumbo. Skim off any excess oil and add the drippings to the gumbo pot. Delicious!

I really have digressed. I was telling about our Mother's Day celebration. Poor Al fries the turkeys, and everybody else provides the rest of the meal. I usually prepare a dish given to me by an old friend, Henry L. Mayer Jr., who is known for his culinary expertise.

Henry's Field Pea Casserole

Makes 6 to 8 servings

3 cups of cooked field peas
2 large tomatoes, sliced
3 large white onions, sliced
3 large green bell peppers, seeded and sliced
Salt and freshly ground black pepper, to taste
½ cup of freshly grated Parmesan cheese
6 bacon slices

Preheat the oven to 400 degrees.

Layer the field peas, tomatoes, onions and bell peppers in a large casserole dish, seasoning with salt and pepper between each layer. Repeat until all of the first four ingredients are used. Sprinkle the cheese on the final layer and arrange the bacon on top.

Cover with aluminum foil and bake for one hour. Remove the foil and place the casserole under the broiler for a few minutes, until the bacon becomes slightly crisp.

Homemade ice cream is a must for Mother's Day.

Nick's Homemade Ice Cream

Makes about 8 servings

2 (14-ounce) cans of sweetened condensed milk
16 ounces of sour cream
2 (12-ounce) cans of evaporated milk
¾ cup of sugar
1 tablespoon of vanilla extract
2 cups of chopped fresh fruit, such as peaches, strawberries or bananas
Whole milk

Combine all of the ingredients in a bowl and stir to mix well. Add the mixture to the ice cream freezer container and add enough whole milk to come to the fill line on the container.

Freeze the ice cream according to the manufacturer's instructions.

On the last day of school, the minute report cards are handed out and reviewed by parents, my sister Edna loads her van with her brood and several of their friends and heads for the camp at Catahoula Lake. She figures they deserve a couple of days of running around in the fresh air, doing whatever they please.

One year she invited me to join them so she would have another adult to keep her company. I must have had a screw loose, because I agreed to meet her at the lake at noon on the appointed day.

Children of all ages were everywhere – playing volleyball, jumping off the wharf, playing hide-and-seek in the woods, fishing and eating everything put before them. It was late into the night when they finally settled into their sleeping bags and my sister and I had some peace and quiet. I was afraid to think what the next day would bring.

Fortunately, I was up before everyone. I carefully stepped over sleeping bodies and made my way to the kitchen, where I made a pot of coffee. I fixed myself a tray and headed down to the wharf with a fishing pole under my arm. There was a mist over the lake as I made myself a nest on the old wooden bench. I felt like I was the only one in the world and I was going to make the best of it.

I had nearly an hour to clear the cobwebs from my mind before being discovered. A group of children soon joined me on the wharf. My sister yelled at me to be sure everyone had on life preservers. A five-year-old insisted he needed my fishing pole, and two rambunctious teenagers managed to knock my coffee tray into the water. So much for peace and serenity.

After a couple of days, I was looking forward to some time with adult company.

When I got home I called an old friend who is an ace at cooking steaks. In a short time he was at my door with steaks in hand, along with a basket of fresh strawberries. I had put together a corn pudding and green salad, so I left the kitchen and told him to have at it.

Be forewarned: If you are a purist about steak, you're not going to like this recipe, because we're going to "goop it up" with lots of seasonings.

Get a fire going in the pit while you're getting the steaks ready. Select the steak of your choice. My friend, James, swears that a Porterhouse is best. Me, I prefer a rib eye. Whatever you choose, be sure the steaks are thick and of good quality.

James' Steak

Makes 2 servings

2 steaks of your choice
12 tablespoons of butter
4 garlic cloves, minced
2 teaspoons of fresh lemon juice
2 teaspoons of Worcestershire sauce
2 teaspoons of Italian salad dressing
1 teaspoon of garlic salt
1 teaspoon of black pepper
¼ teaspoon of ground oregano
½ teaspoon of basil leaves

Melt four tablespoons of the butter in a saucepan over medium-low heat. Add the garlic and cook until it starts to become fragrant and begins to brown. (Be careful not to let the garlic burn or you'll have a bitter taste.) Remove from the heat.

Add the rest of the butter to the pan and return to a low heat.

(The aroma of the garlic butter will make your mouth water. At this point, all I want to do is dab a chunk of bread into the butter sauce and forget about the steaks. Fight temptation and continue.)

Let the garlic butter simmer a bit, whisking constantly. When foam begins to rise to the top, add the lemon juice, Worcestershire sauce and Italian salad dressing and continue to whisk. Blend well for a couple of minutes, then remove from heat.

Rub the steaks well with the garlic salt, black pepper, oregano and basil leaves. The coals in your grill should be turning gray and should not be too hot.

Brush the steaks liberally with some of the sauce and place them on the grill. Continue basting with the sauce until steaks are cooked to desired doneness.

Any leftover sauce can be tossed with pasta or poured over French bread.

We ate like savages. After his departure and while I was cleaning up the kitchen, I realized we had forgotten about the strawberries. I sprinkled them with powdered sugar and munched on them while I sat on the dark porch. I wondered what the children were doing at the camp. The quiet was welcome.

Just before the long hot summer is at hand, I'm always eager to enjoy the sights, sounds and smells of the swamps and marshes that constitute so much of the lower half of my native state.

Skimming along in a boat down a bayou or canal leading to the Gulf, I can always tell when we're getting close to the coast because I catch a whiff of the salty sea air. Above the whine of the boat engine, I can hear the shrill calls of the birds as they swoop down to pluck shrimp or tiny fish from the water. Turtles, large and small, sun themselves on stumps and exposed roots along the route. After a good rain, resurrection fern flutters in the breeze.

It's a good time for a fishing trip. Early one morning I met a companion at a prearranged site. While he put the boat in the water, I scanned the shore for blue herons and ibis. Nothing moved. Perhaps it was too early.

Once we were in motion and the sun began to rise, we spotted movement. We communicated by pointing as we observed birds, a fish jumping at the bow of the boat, and the beady eyes of an alligator in the distance. The water was like glass as the sun rose to warm our faces. We had no real destination in mind, but had brought along an assortment of rods and reels just in case we decided to fish.

When we entered the Gulf it was almost anti-climatic. We chose to keep close to the shore, stopping here and there, casting our lines, waving to fellow fishermen as they sped out to the open water. It was a lazy day. No deadlines, no responsibilities, no nothing.

By the end of the day our ice chest held nothing more than a couple of leftover sandwiches and cold drinks. We weren't disappointed. We had enjoyed ourselves.

When we returned to the boat launch area, a fellow inquired about our luck and when we showed him the empty ice chest, he offered us some of his catch – several speckled trout. Heading home, my friend and I discussed various methods of preparation. Should we fry them or broil them in butter? Then in unison we both shouted, "Roulades!" We couldn't wait to get home.

Trout Roulades

Makes 6 servings

6 fillets of trout or redfish, 6 to 8 ounces each
3 tablespoons of fresh lemon juice
4 tablespoons of butter
4 green onions, finely chopped
1 garlic clove, minced
½ pound of fresh mushrooms, wiped clean, stemmed and chopped
1 pound of shrimp (peeled and deveined) or 1 pound of lump crabmeat (picked over for shells and cartilage)
1 teaspoon of dried basil leaves
Salt, freshly ground black pepper, and cayenne pepper, to taste
1 cup of chicken broth
1 cup of fine dried bread crumbs (more or less as needed)
½ pint of half-and-half

Preheat the oven to 350 degrees.

Pound the fillets a bit to make them lie flat. Sprinkle with lemon juice and set aside.

Heat two tablespoons of the butter in a large skillet over medium heat. Add the onions, garlic and mushrooms and cook, stirring, for two minutes. Add the shrimp or crabmeat and basil, and season with salt, black pepper and cayenne. Add three-fourths cup of chicken broth and simmer for five minutes.

Add the bread crumbs and stir so that the mixture binds together. Remove from the heat, and cool.

Place equal amounts of the mixture on top of each fish fillet and roll up like a jelly roll. (You may have to use a toothpick to hold the roll together.)

Place the roulades in a baking pan with the remaining chicken broth and the half-and half. Dot with the remaining butter.

Bake until the fish flakes easily with a fork, 20 to 25 minutes.

Top with Creollaise Sauce (page 27).

There's nothing like fresh fish cooked the same day it was caught in the Gulf!

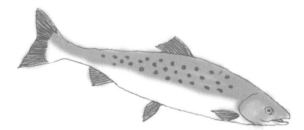

SUMMER

No questions about it, it's hot in Louisiana in the summertime. When June slips in after Memorial Day, the air becomes still and humid. With any luck, late afternoon thunder showers rumble in from the Gulf of Mexico, making life bearable for an hour or two before dusk. Summer is the time for cold food like deviled eggs, potato salad, cold fried chicken, homemade ice cream, watermelon and giant snowballs. It's the time of year to kick back, chill out and enjoy the longer days and some good food.

In the summertime, in late afternoon when the hottest part of the day had passed, family and friends would gather to visit on the patio in back of our house in St. Martinville. That's Mama in the plaid shirt in the middle of the group, circa 1955.

The Mystique of the Camp

Life moves more slowly in Louisiana than it does in the rest of the country. People come home earlier from work – or does it just seem so because the days are longer? Entertaining is less formal, and the days are planned not by the clock but rather by the position of the sun.

Cooking is best done early in the day or late in the afternoon. Ingredients come from home gardens and neighboring waterways rather than from supermarkets.

Families take long vacations at beach cottages in nearby Mississippi, Alabama or Florida. Often they opt for weekend jaunts to their camps, usually located on a body of water such as a lake, bayou or bay.

For as long as I can remember, my family has had a summer camp at Catahoula Lake. Folklore has it that the lake, situated just outside the Atchafalaya Basin levee system, was created by an earthquake.

Supposedly, the quake ripped open a huge cavern about 500 feet wide, two miles long, and more than 100 feet deep.

Cata-oula is an Indian word meaning "Lake of Sacrifice." Indians held the belief that the lake, which produces fine fresh fish and sweet-meat crabs, swallowed up an entire Indian village when the earth gave way. They also believed that the waters had magical powers, and they often came to bathe and make pilgrimages, asking the gods to keep them safe and protect them from evil spirits.

My father, an old Boy Scout leader known for his colorful campfire stories, chose a site for our first family camp in a clearing surrounded by centuries-old oaks, some of which leaned gracefully over the calm water. Muscadine vines clung to willows and swamp maple, and the hated poison ivy and sweet-smelling honeysuckle

My brother Henri Clay exhibits a string of fish caught in Catahoula Lake near our camp, while Mama and Papa fill an ice chest with soft drinks, circa 1950.

intertwined, forming a jungle-like wall around the clearing.

There Papa set up several army-issue tents with the inevitable mosquito nets and cots. A main tent, which was simply a large tarpaulin stretched over several big limbs of a huge live oak, served as the kitchen, or canteen, as he liked to call it. It was the heart of the camp, and it was here we gathered in the early morning for cups of dark, rich, hand-dripped coffee and crusty biscuits Papa managed to cook in a black iron pot over an open fire.

Large metal tubs filled with blocks of ice wrapped in sacks kept soft drinks, beer, lemonade and milk cool. We filled metal-lined boxes, the forerunner of what we now know as ice chests, with our daily catch from the lake – catfish, bream, *sac-a-lait* (white crappie), and huge blue point freshwater crabs.

The campfire never went out. It was fed regularly by Papa, for besides fishing, cooking was his next love. There were always large black cast iron pots of bubbling *courtbouillon* and his version of *bouillabaisse*. Late in the afternoon large skillets were dragged out to fry fish, and if we were lucky a pot of crabs steamed and hissed on the fire.

Today our camp is situated on a lovely spot, with moss-draped oaks, cypress and tupelos. It's now a compound comprised of several permanent buildings. Gone are the tents, mosquito nets and makeshift outdoor kitchen. There are a couple of wharfs to dock the fishing and ski boats. And, *mon Dieu*, air-conditioning and telephones. Shame on us! But we still have a campfire site and much of our cooking is still done outdoors.

The "season" for the camp begins Easter weekend and ends soon after Labor Day. Virtually every weekend in between these holidays the campsite is alive with family and friends. It has always been a place for each of us to find solace from a stressful world. It is here we can commune with nature, throw a fishing line baited with worms or crickets into the water, find a tree trunk to lean against to read a book, or watch the sun set through the dripping moss trailing from the limbs of the splendid oaks.

My father, Blackie Bienvenu, in his boat on Catahoula Lake, circa 1939...

Like Scarlett in *Gone With the Wind* I need only to pick up a handful of the dark earth to gain strength to face the world.

I remember a summer weekend when I was working at Oak Alley Plantation on the Great River Road and I had writer's block. I had decided not to join the family for that weekend because I was trying to make a deadline for my food column which appears in *The Times-Picayune* in New Orleans. It was the typical block – not one word would come forth from my mind, other than the name of the column and my own name. I tried a leisurely walk around the plantation grounds. Certainly inspiration would come forth.

But alas, after turning my dilapidated typewriter on and off so many times, I broke the switch. I tried using the office computer and managed to bungle it up. I resorted to a legal pad and several No. 2 pencils and ended up chewing off the erasers in a matter of minutes.

That was it! I felt that my days as a columnist were numbered. I had a lump in my throat and a pounding headache beginning at the nape of my neck. I thought of all the people who would be disappointed in me. My Mama wouldn't have my column to show off to her friends and my baby brother Bruce wouldn't have a desk blotter on Thursday. I hung my head and wept. I needed my Mama.

I knew she and the rest of the family were at the camp, so I packed up a couple of pairs of shorts, some T-shirts and my yellow flip-flops, grabbed my box of tapes and headed down the River Road toward the interstate. In a couple of hours, I was at the Henderson exit. I decided to ride along the levee to the camp.

It was late afternoon and fishermen were pulling their boats out of the water. Guys were leaning against pickup trucks with cans of cold beer clenched tightly in their hands. With faces glowing from sunburn, they were telling of the day on the water. I could hear bits and pieces of conversation, in half French and half English. In the distance I saw a water skier taking his last lap down the borrow pit before the sun went down.

I had visions of what the group was doing at the camp. Sitting around the campfire, they were contemplating supper. Was it to be fried catfish, or perhaps a crab stew? I couldn't wait as I turned off the levee and followed the dirt road that led to the camp.

When I pulled up and blew the horn to announce my arrival, little kids ran to greet me. Mama ran to get a drink for me, and Bruce gave up his seat on the swing for me. I was home.

When things quieted down, I turned to Mama.

"What's for supper? I need some inspiration for my food column."

She smiled and answered, "Liver and grits."

I went into shock. You don't eat liver and grits at the camp. No fish, no seafood gumbo? I can't even stand the smell of liver cooking. The group was adamant. They had taken a poll, and liver and grits had won hands down.

I thought they had all gone mad, but by the time I watched Mama prepare supper and then thoroughly enjoyed it myself, I, too, was sold on the idea.

Liver & Grits

Makes 6 servings

4 tablespoons of cold bacon drippings
3 pounds of calf's liver, membrane removed
Salt and cayenne pepper, to taste
2 large yellow onions, thinly sliced
Grits, cooked according to package directions (Don't use instant grits.)

Spread the cold bacon drippings on the bottom of a large black iron skillet.

Season the liver with salt and cayenne pepper.

Add the liver to the cold drippings, then turn on the heat to medium-high. When the liver begins to brown, turn a couple of times and add a little water and the sliced onions. Cook until the onions wilt. Do not overcook.

Pour the onions, gravy and liver over hot grits and serve.

Potato Croquettes

Makes 6 servings

3 to 4 pounds of red potatoes
1 cup of chopped onions
1 cup of chopped green bell peppers
Salt and freshly ground black pepper, to taste
Tabasco, to taste
3 eggs, beaten
2½ cups of bacon drippings or peanut oil
All-purpose flour for dredging

Boil the potatoes in lightly salted water until fork-tender. Remove from the heat and drain.

Cool, then peel and put them in a large bowl. Mash the potatoes, leaving some lumps. Add the onions and bell peppers, and season with salt, pepper and hot sauce. Fold in the eggs and mix well.

With your hands, shape the potato mixture into balls about two inches in diameter or, if you prefer, shape into three-inch "pancakes." Heat the oil in a skillet.

Dredge the balls or "pancakes" in flour and drop them into the hot oil. Fry until golden brown and drain on paper towels.

After supper the children went in search of gowns and pajamas and we grown-ups sat by the lake listening to the *cigales* (locusts) and talking about what tomorrow

Fred Beslin, a family friend, fries fish in our back yard in St. Martinville circa 1955, as my sister Edna Marie (who hated to wear clothes in the summer) looks on.

would bring. I knew that I could go back to Oak Alley and do my column, and that gave me a great sense of well-being.

Like the Indians who performed their pilgrimages and thought the lake to be magical, we, too, felt the mystical powers of Catahoula. Because we've spent such a great part of our lives there, we have developed some rituals of our own.

Every year when it's time to close down the camp, we throw a party. It's our way of saying farewell until next spring.

The cycle of the ritual actually begins in spring when we come armed with rakes, mowers, work gloves and wheelbarrows to get the place ship-shape for the season. The buildings are washed down and the wharfs are repaired. Mama, Aunt Lois and Cousin Cooney are wild with paint. With whatever colors they can find, they paint everything from swings to benches, flower pots and tables.

One year everything had a polka-dot theme. Because they had little cans of lots of leftover assorted colors, they splashed away. By Easter Sunday the place looked like a colored egg fantasy.

Bedding plants are put in and bird feeders are filled. Buttercups and other wild flowers bloom along the levee, and the first tiny green leaves of the cypress trees poke through. The fish are jumping and boats are taken down from their winter sheds and slipped into the water.

By Good Friday the place is in its glory. With our work done, some of us head for the levee for a couple of hours of crawfishing. If we have no luck, we go in search

of a commercial fisherman who has. Two sacks of live crawfish, about 40 or so pounds, will be our evening repast.

After the afternoon church services, huge pots are filled with crawfish generously seasoned with salt, cayenne pepper and lemons. Sometimes new potatoes and whole onions are pitched in for good measure.

When spring gives way to summer and school lets out, the camp looks like a disturbed ant hill. In the morning, the first person up makes a big pot of coffee. Slowly, like the sun rising, adults and children find their way to the stove and the cups of black liquid that will get the blood flowing. Still in robes and gowns, they sit on folding chairs and benches near the edge of the lake, sipping the hot brew and waiting for someone to make breakfast.

By midday, children are water skiing, teenagers are floating on inner tubes, and adults are at their favorite fishing spots.

But come late September it's time to close down for the cold months – and so, it's time for our party.

Mama, Aunt Lois and Cooney have put away their paint brushes and now wield cooking utensils. They issue invitations, plan the menu, and cook and cook.

The day before the party finds them running around arranging flowers, icing down cold drinks and making pitchers of spicy Bloody Marys. Sometimes we have *grillades* and grits, or baked egg pies, but one year we had a seafood brunch. Mama served this contemporary Louisiana crowd-pleaser.

Crabmeat & Shrimp Fettuccini

Makes about 12 servings

3 sticks of butter
3 medium-size onions, chopped
3 celery ribs, chopped
2 medium-size green bell peppers, seeded and chopped
½ to ¾ cup of all-purpose flour
¼ cup of chopped parsley
1½ pounds of shrimp
1½ pounds of lump crabmeat, picked over for shells and cartilage (peeled crawfish tails can be substituted)
2 to 3 cups of half-and-half
1 pound of Velveeta cheese, cubed
2 tablespoons of chopped jalapeño peppers
3 garlic cloves, minced
Salt and cayenne pepper, to taste
1 pound of fettuccini, cooked and drained
1 cup of grated Parmesan cheese

Preheat the oven to 350 degrees.

Melt the butter in a heavy, large pot or Dutch oven over medium heat. Add the onions, celery and bell peppers. Cook, stirring, until the vegetables are soft and lightly golden, about eight minutes.

Add the flour and stir for five minutes, blending well. Add the parsley and seafood, and cook for five minutes, stirring gently.

Add the half-and-half, cheese, jalapeño peppers and garlic, and mix. Season with salt and cayenne and simmer, stirring often, until the cheese has completely melted and the mixture is smooth and thick, about 10 minutes.

Add the fettuccini and toss gently. Pour the mixture into a three-quart buttered casserole and sprinkle with the Parmesan cheese. Bake uncovered until bubbly and heated through, about 20 minutes.

Serve with lots of French bread and a fruit compote of seasonal fresh fruit drizzled with dark rum and topped with fresh mint leaves.

One year as I bade everyone *au revoir* I took one last glance around the campground. People had pulled chairs close to the bank of the lake and were taking in the glories of the setting sun. That memory and others of past summers made my trip back to the city an easy one.

I remember one year when I was unable to attend the "close down the camp" party because the date fell on the same weekend that I planned a house party of my own.

When I informed Mama of my previous engagement, she was so disappointed she called several times.

"I can't believe you're not going to be with us. We have a fabulous menu planned – chicken pies, spinach casserole and Cousin Cooney's special bread."

She tempted me and then tried the old guilt trip.

But I, too, had what I thought to be a no-slouch menu – chicken *fricassée*, potato salad with homemade mayonnaise, lima beans that make you cry they're so good, and creamy bread pudding with whiskey sauce.

She telephoned again.

"We're putting balloons and palmetto leaves everywhere!"

"I have hundreds of little white paper bags with candles plus large torches to light up the yard," I shot back.

I didn't want to rub it in, but I planned to serve mint juleps at dusk under the alley of 28 oak trees that lead up to the main house at Oak Alley Plantation.

Her final call was to suggest that we all come after my party and watch the sunset with them. Exasperated, I told her that sounded divine, but a two-hour drive was out of the question. Amen.

I bid her good-bye once again and told her I would be there in spirit if not in body. As I hung up the phone, I heard my guests arriving.

I hurriedly showed them to their respective cottages and told them to meet back at the Big House. There we watched the sky turn pink and purple, listed to the sounds of the traffic on the Mississippi River, sipped our mint juleps from silver goblets, and exchanged ghost stories as the sun slipped down behind the levee.

When goose bumps and mosquitoes began to take their toll, we headed for my cottage, where the yard was dancing with shadows from the torches. The aroma of the *fricassée* bubbling in the pot greeted us. French bread was coming out of the oven and the smell of whiskey sauce wafted out over the deck.

Chicken *Fricassée*

Makes 8 servings

1 hen (4 to 5 pounds), cut into frying pieces
Salt, freshly ground black pepper, and
   cayenne pepper, to taste
2/3 cup of vegetable oil
1/2 cup of all-purpose flour
2½ cups of chopped onions
1 cup of chopped green bell peppers
2 quarts of chicken broth or warm water
1/4 cup of chopped parsley
1/4 cup of chopped green onions

Season the chicken pieces with salt, black pepper and cayenne.

Combine the oil and flour in a large, heavy pot or Dutch oven over medium heat. Stirring slowly and constantly, make a roux the color of chocolate.

Add the chicken pieces and turn them to coat evenly with the roux.

Add the onions and bell peppers, and cook, stirring gently, until they are very soft, about 10 minutes. Add the chicken broth or water.

Reduce the heat to medium-low, partially cover the pot and simmer, stirring occasionally, until the chicken is very tender, about two hours. Add more broth or water if it becomes too thick. Adjust seasonings to taste.

A few minutes before serving, add the parsley and green onions.

Serve in soup bowls with steamed rice.

Wet Potato Salad

I like potato salad made with lots of mayonnaise, preferably homemade. Mama was always heavy-handed with her homemade mayonnaise, so one of my cousins dubbed it "wet potato salad."

Boil some red potatoes and several eggs. Peel both and chop coarsely. I'm a purist, but you can add chopped celery, onions and olives, if you wish.

The secret to a good potato salad is the mayonnaise.

1 hard-boiled egg yolk
1 raw egg yolk
1 cup of vegetable oil
1 tablespoon of vinegar
   or fresh lemon juice
Pinch of sugar
Salt and cayenne pepper, to taste

Blend the egg yolks in a small mixing bowl. Slowly add the oil, about a tablespoon at a time, and beat well in between each addition with a fork or wire whisk. Add the vinegar or lemon juice, sugar, salt and cayenne – and, if you wish, a couple of dashes of hot sauce. Blend well.

Chill for an hour or so before adding to the chopped potatoes and eggs to complete the potato salad.

Our grandfather, "Pop-Pete" Broussard, and Henri Clay enjoy a visit in the yard at Banker Plantation, circa 1944.

Rhena's Bread Pudding

Makes 6 to 8 servings

½ loaf of day-old French bread,
  broken into small pieces
1 quart of whole milk
4 egg yolks, beaten
½ cup of sugar
2 teaspoons of vanilla extract
Meringue (Recipe follows)
Whiskey Sauce (Recipe follows)

Preheat the oven to 300 degrees.

Soak the bread in the milk in a mixing bowl for one hour. Then, with a fork, mash the bread well in the milk so that there are no lumpy pieces.

Beat the eggs, sugar and vanilla in another mixing bowl and add to the bread and milk mixture.

Pour the mixture into a baking dish and place the pan in another larger pan half filled with water.

Bake until the pudding sets, one to one and a half hours.

Remove from oven and top with meringue.

MERINGUE

8 egg whites
8 tablespoons of sugar

Beat the egg whites and sugar until the meringue is thick and forms stiff peaks.

Spread it evenly over the baked pudding and return to the oven. Increase the temperature to 425 degrees and brown the meringue. Watch carefully so it doesn't burn.

WHISKEY SAUCE

4 tablespoons (½ stick) of butter
½ cup of sugar
4 egg yolks, beaten
¼ cup of bourbon, rum, or brandy

Melt the butter in a double boiler over barely simmering water. Gradually stir in the sugar, beating with a fork or wire whisk, until it dissolves. (Do not allow mixture to become too hot.)

Add the eggs in a steady stream, whisking constantly.

Remove from heat and add your choice of liquor. Stir to blend.

Spoon the sauce over bread pudding and serve immediately.

After my guests had been served and satisfied and began drifting back to their cabins, I thought of Mama and the group at the camp.

I pictured them watching the sunset and listening to bull frogs croaking and the distant sound of an engine whining as a lone fisherman made his way through The Forks, a nearby fishing spot. The blazing fire was turning to glowing embers, and an empty black iron pot was probably dangling from a contraption fashioned by Papa.

Papa mastered the art of cooking over a wood fire. And it is indeed an art. There are no little knobs to turn to "simmer" or "medium." One has to be able to move the pot to that part of the fire that has a low or high flame. Papa had set up a metal swinging arm, which he could rotate around the fire to the desired heat area. He cooked everything from fried chicken and biscuits to *bouillabaisse* and *courtbouillon* over a wood fire.

The next two recipes are camp favorites. *Bouillabaisse* and *courtbouillon* both have more or less the same ingredients, but the difference is in how they are put together. These are not dishes that can be pulled together in a minute, so plan to make these when you have a leisurely day. The *bouillabaisse* of south Louisiana is somewhat different from the classic dish served in France.

Thackeray complimented the Acadian-Creole version in this tribute: "In New Orleans you can eat a *bouillabaisse* the likes of which was never eaten in Marseilles or Paris."

In New Orleans, and in the land of the Acadians, everyone has his own version of this delectable dish. Each is different, yet each is superb.

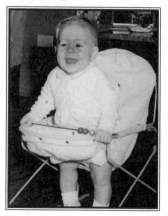

My brother Bruce was a happy child (circa 1953).

Aunt Lois' *Bouillabaisse*

Makes 8 servings

2½ pounds of fillets of firm white fish such as trout, snapper, grouper, or redfish
Salt and cayenne pepper, to taste
8 tablespoons (1 stick) of butter
3 large onions, coarsely chopped
2 large green bell peppers, seeded and coarsely chopped
2 celery ribs, coarsely chopped
3 garlic cloves, minced
2 (1-pound) cans of whole tomatoes with their juice, broken into chunks
¼ cup of dry white wine
1 pound of small shrimp, peeled and deveined
2 whole bay leaves

Cut the fish fillets into 2- to 3-inch chunks. Season with salt and cayenne and set aside.

Heat the butter slowly over medium-low heat in a large, deep, heavy pot. Layer the ingredients, beginning with the fish, then the onions, green peppers, celery, garlic and tomatoes; then the fish again, followed by the vegetables until all are used. Lightly season each layer.

Pour in the wine, down the side of the pot.

Arrange the shrimp and bay leaves on top of the final layer.

Cover and cook over a low heat for about an hour. (People question this cooking time, but you'll have to trust me on this. Restrain yourself from peeking in the pot, and do not stir the pot. Play a game of *bourrée* (a Cajun card game) or otherwise entertain your guests.)

The result will be a rich broth in which the fish has poached perfectly. Serve the *bouillabaisse* in deep bowls over steamed rice. Be sure to have plenty of hot French bread to sop up the juice.

Catahoula *Courtbouillon*

Makes 8 servings

As with the bouillabaisse, there are as many recipes for this dish as there are Acadians and Creoles. Papa's version is a thick soup, much like stew, and can be made with either freshwater or saltwater fish. If using the smaller freshwater fish, keep them whole; large saltwater fish can be cut into large chunks.

2/3 cup of all-purpose flour
2/3 cup of vegetable oil
2 medium-size onions, chopped
1 medium-size green bell pepper, seeded and chopped
2 celery ribs, chopped
3 cloves of garlic, minced (optional)
1 (1-pound) can of whole tomatoes, undrained and chopped
1 can of Ro-Tel tomatoes (the mild version)
1 quart of warm fish stock or water
1 tablespoon of salt
1 teaspoon of cayenne pepper
2½ pounds of fish, cleaned and dressed
1 bunch of green onions (green part only), chopped
1/4 cup of finely chopped fresh parsley

Combine the flour and oil in a large heavy pot or Dutch oven over medium heat. Stirring slowly and constantly, make a roux the color of chocolate.

Add the onions, bell peppers, celery and garlic. Cook, stirring, until the vegetables are soft, about five minutes. Add the whole tomatoes and Ro-Tel and stir to blend. Reduce the heat to medium-low and cook, stirring occasionally, until the oil forms a thin layer on top of the mixture, about 30 minutes.

Add the fish stock or water, the salt and cayenne, and cook, stirring occasionally, for one hour. The mixture should be slightly thick. (If the mixture becomes too thick, add more stock or water.)

Add the fish, cover and cook until the fish flakes easily with a fork, 10 to 15 minutes. Do not stir. Adjust seasoning if necessary with salt and cayenne.

Add the green onions and parsley. Serve immediately in soup bowls with steamed rice and plenty of hot French bread. (Note: I always have a bottle of hot sauce at the table in case guests want to add a little bit of "heat.")

You may not have the night sounds of the swamp around you, but close your eyes for a minute and make believe. Imagine the sounds of fish jumping in the water, of crickets chirping in the night, and the crackling of a wood fire as it burns down. There, now take a piece of crunchy French bread and dip it into your bowl. That first bite makes you feel like you're at the camp.

Living is Easy

Early on summer mornings, before the sun gets too high, I like to putter around in the kitchen, preparing odds and ends for the day. One never knows when a picnic may be inspired or an invitation to supper may be issued. And it's always nice to have goodies stashed around for impromptu excursions to the camp.

Spinach Bread

¼ cup of butter
3 eggs, beaten
1 cup of all-purpose flour
1 teaspoon of salt
1 teaspoon of baking powder
1 cup of whole milk
1 teaspoon of dried dill
4 cups of chopped fresh spinach
1 pound of grated Monterrey Jack cheese

Melt the butter in a 9½ x 13 x 2-inch baking pan in a 375-degree oven.

Meanwhile, combine the eggs, flour, salt, baking powder, milk and dill in a mixing bowl and whisk to blend. Add the spinach and three-fourths pound of the cheese, and mix well.

Remove the baking pan from the oven and spread the mixture in it. Sprinkle the top of the mixture with the remaining one-fourth pound of cheese. Bake uncovered until the bread sets, about 30 minutes.

Remove from the oven and cool slightly. Cut into squares to serve.

This is great to accompany a meal or to serve as *hors d'oeuvres*. (It can be frozen and reheated for later use.)

Fig Crunch Pie

Makes one 9-inch pie

CRUST

1 cup of all-purpose flour
2 tablespoons of sugar
1/4 teaspoon of salt
1/3 cup of slightly softened butter
1/4 cup of finely chopped pecans or walnuts

Preheat the oven to 350 degrees.

Combine the flour, sugar and salt in a mixing bowl. Add the butter and, with a pastry blender or fork, combine until the mixture resembles coarse crumbs.

Add the pecans or walnuts and mix again.

Press the dough into a 9-inch pie pan and bake until just golden, about 20 minutes. Remove from the oven and cool.

FILLING

2 cups of orange-pineapple juice
10 dried figs, cut in half
1/2 cup of dark brown sugar
2 tablespoons of cornstarch

Heat the orange-pineapple juice and dried figs in a saucepan over medium heat.

Combine the brown sugar and cornstarch in a small bowl, then add to the saucepan. Cook, stirring, until the mixture thickens, two to three minutes.

Pour the mixture into the baked pie shell, and serve as is or topped with chilled whipped cream.

Depending on the weather, blackberries can be picked from late April to early June. I love them so much I call my sister regularly to get picking reports. When she tells me they are at their peak, we make plans to go berry picking.

Edna organizes our foray into the blackberry patches she's had under surveillance. Her children hold paper bags and small pails, and are armed with long sticks. The long sticks are for poking around the underbrush to scare away snakes, and they are also handy for holding back the thorny blackberry trailers so one can reach the big berries nestled in hard-to-reach places.

We all head in different directions. Within a few minutes everyone is squealing in delight. I rarely fill my pail since I tend to pop every other one into my mouth – one for the pail and one for my mouth. I don't care if they're a bit dusty.

Once I wandered far from the crowd and my attention was focused on a patch of bushes laden with so many berries I picked three and four at a time. I was on my knees bending down near a barbed-wire fence when I felt a breath of warm air on the back of my neck. I froze. I slowly looked up and came face to face with a cow that had wandered over to investigate what was going on near her pasture.

When our containers were full, we walked home along the side of the road. Everyone had an idea of what to do with our pickings. We could make dumplings, or maybe a cheesecake topped with blackberries, or maybe some pies or a cobbler. We discussed the choices as we rinsed the berries in Edna's large outdoor sink. What about blackberry ice cream?

Blackberry Ice Cream

FOR THE SAUCE
2 quarts of fresh blackberries, picked over, rinsed in cool water, and patted dry
2 cups of sugar

Place the berries and sugar in a saucepan and cook slowly over medium heat. Don't add any water, because the berries release lots of juice. Cook long enough for them to soften and create a syrup. Cool and then strain the mixture through a fine-mesh sieve.

ICE CREAM
6 eggs, beaten
4 cups of whole milk
1 cup of sugar
1 tablespoon of vanilla extract
1 teaspoon of cornstarch

Combine the eggs and milk in a large mixing bowl. Add the sugar, vanilla and cornstarch and mix well. Transfer the mixture to a heavy non-reactive saucepan and cook slowly over medium heat until it thickens enough to coat a wooden spoon. (Do not allow it to come to a boil.)

Add one cup of the berry sauce and freeze in an ice cream freezer according to manufacturer's directions.

When serving, you can add a couple of drops of creme de cassis liqueur to each serving.

Blackberry Cobbler

Makes about 8 servings
3 cups of blackberries, rinsed and patted dry
2 cups of sugar
1 cup of all-purpose flour
1 egg
¼ pound of melted butter
1 teaspoon of vanilla extract
1 teaspoon of baking soda
1 teaspoon of baking powder
1 teaspoon of salt

Preheat the oven to 350 degrees.

Place the berries in a 9 x 13-inch glass baking dish. Sprinkle with one cup of the sugar.

Combine the flour, the remaining cup of sugar, the egg, melted butter, vanilla, baking soda, baking powder and salt in a mixing bowl. Stir to blend.

Spoon the mixture over the berries and bake until the pastry sets and is golden brown, 30 to 40 minutes.

One of my all-time favorite summer treats is to spend a weekend with friends at a woodsy hideaway near Poplarville, Mississippi. It's fun to get away from bayouland and spend a couple of days in piney woods thick with wild magnolias and dogwood. The cottage is like a cool island amid the towering trees, and the Wolf River that runs along the property is perfect for wading, canoeing and tubing.

We take leisurely hikes and visit the blueberry farm nearby, where we can pick our own. Some guests curl up in canvas chairs and read the hours away. Others take turns on the old hammock strung between two giant pines. We hide all the clocks and let the stress drain away.

One thing we all do is eat well, but with a minimum amount of trouble. Everyone pitches in. Someone brings pies for desserts while others bring fresh fruit and croissants.

One Friday, upon our arrival, we put on a pot of shrimp and ham jambalaya and let it simmer while we settled in.

On Saturday we packed sandwiches and spent the day on the sand and gravel beach by the river. That evening we enjoyed grilled fresh tuna, brought in from the city, along with baked onions and Creole tomatoes.

Grilled Tuna

Makes 10 servings

5 pounds of fresh tuna, trimmed and cut
  into 1-inch-thick steaks
3 tablespoons of olive oil
3 tablespoons of fresh lime juice
Salt and fresh ground black pepper, to taste
Lime wedges

Rub the tuna with the olive oil and lime juice, and then season it with the salt and pepper. Let stand for an hour.

Grill the steaks on a fairly hot barbecue grill until the fish flakes easily. (Do not overcook or else it will become dry.) Serve with lime wedges.

Baked Onions

Makes 10 servings

10 medium onions (Regular yellow onions
  will do, but if you can get your hands
  on some Vidalia onions or other sweet
  onions, they're even better.)
½ cup plus 1 tablespoon of olive oil
1 teaspoon of chopped garlic
4 tablespoons of puréed green onions
1 teaspoon of cayenne pepper
4 tablespoons of water
Salt and freshly ground black pepper
2 tablespoons of apple cider vinegar

Preheat the oven to 300 degrees. Brush a baking pan (large enough to accommodate the onions) with one tablespoon of the olive oil.

Cut off the ends of the onions so that they will sit flat in the baking pan. Leave the skins on. Bake until the onions are tender, about one hour. Turn the onions over with a spatula and continue baking for 30 minutes longer. The onions should turn slightly brown, but not burned.

Transfer the onions to a shallow serving dish. Remove the skins and any dried out rings.

Combine the remaining olive oil with the garlic, green onions, cayenne and the water. Spoon the mixture over the onions, sprinkle with salt and pepper, and drizzle with the vinegar.

Serve at room temperature.

Sliced Creole tomatoes, slightly chilled, made the meal a true feast.

After dinner, we retired to the screen porch with slices of blueberry pie to enjoy the night sounds.

On Sunday afternoon my friends each found a comfortable lounge chair and thumbed through a stack of magazines and newspapers, occasionally making comments on their reading.

I was content in the kitchen, slicing red and green peppers, yellow squash and eggplant. I had also come across a pound of shrimp and a pound of pasta. I was humming and tapping my feet to the sounds of Glenn Miller's big band when one of my hosts joined me in the kitchen. He busied himself making garlic bread and a dessert that looked absolutely divine.

As dusk fell, a thunderstorm rolled in with gusty wind and flashes of lightning. We sat down to dinner in our glass-enclosed room lit only by many candles.

Pasta with Garden Vegetables & Shrimp

Makes about 6 servings

4 tablespoons of butter
4 tablespoons of olive oil
1 medium-size green bell pepper, seeded
  and cut into thin strips
1 medium-size red bell pepper, seeded and
  cut into thin strips
1 medium-size yellow summer squash, cut
  into thin strips
1 medium eggplant, peeled and cut into
  thin strips
1 bunch of green onions, finely chopped
1 pound of shrimp, peeled and deveined
Salt, freshly ground black pepper, garlic
  powder, and dried basil, to taste
Tabasco, to taste
1 pound of angel hair pasta, cooked and
  drained
Freshly grated Romano cheese

Heat the butter and oil in a large skillet or shallow casserole over medium heat. Add the vegetables and shrimp, and stir fry quickly until the shrimp turn pink. Season to taste.

Toss with the pasta and cheese in a large serving bowl.

Serve immediately with hot garlic bread.

As the thunderstorm turned into a misty drizzle, we devoured dessert – thin slices of rum cake layered with blueberries that had been cooked in orange liqueur and port wine, topped with freshly whipped cream.

The blueberries we ate came from the Pearl River Blueberry Farm near Poplarville. Since most summer trips to Wolf River result in my bringing home lots of hand-picked berries from the farm, I asked owners Angie and Cas Larrieu to share their collection of blueberry recipes with me. One of Angie's favorites is one she calls JAR BREAD. It's cooked in jars, an idea which intrigued me.

Jar Bread

Makes 8 jars of bread

2/3 cup of vegetable shortening
2 2/3 cups of sugar
4 eggs
2/3 cup of water
3 1/3 cups of all-purpose flour
1/2 teaspoon of baking powder
2 teaspoons of baking soda
1½ teaspoons of salt
1 teaspoon of ground cinnamon
1 teaspoon of ground cloves
2/3 cups of chopped nuts
2 cups of blueberries, rinsed, picked over and patted dry

Preheat the oven to 350 degrees.

Cream together the shortening and sugar in a large mixing bowl. Beat the eggs and water into the mixture and set aside.

In a separate bowl, sift together the flour, baking powder, baking soda, salt, cinnamon and cloves.

Add the dry ingredients to the creamed mixture and mix well. Add the nuts and blueberries. Mix gently.

Spray eight wide-mouthed pint canning jars with cooking spray. Fill the jars half-full and place on a baking sheet. Bake 45 minutes.

Remove from the oven and cool slightly. Seal tightly with sterilized lids. Incredible!

Note: Angie notes that you can substitute the blueberries with the same amount of figs, pumpkin, carrots or zucchini. You can cut off the tops of cotton socks, dampen them slightly, and slip them over the jars before baking. This off-beat method helps to keep the bread moist.

Summer has always been a time for an excursion out-of-state. The Mississippi Gulf Coast is close enough for south Louisianians, and I've long been a fan of that area.

At age seven, along with Mama and Papa and siblings, a Mississippi beach was the first sand beach my little Cajun toes had ever touched. Until that time I knew only the squishy, muddy bottom of Bayou Teche. We went back every year until I was 12, when we graduated to Pensacola, Florida, where I was indeed overwhelmed with the crashing waves and bright blue water of the Gulf.

Every summer during high school, my best friend Cathy and I journeyed with her mother for a week-long stay in Biloxi. We always stayed at a gracious old hotel, complete with a huge veranda, where the older guests sat on rocking chairs and visited the day away.

Cathy and I were allowed to spend the day on the beach, where airmen from nearby Keesler Air Force Base entertained us for hours. Cathy's mother asked only that we return to the hotel before sundown, dress, and be with her for dinner. After our meal we were allowed to return to the beach for moonlight strolls with our airmen. From a perch on the seawall, we watched youngsters armed with kerosene lanterns and spears fishing for flounder.

I recounted the story of how I did the same thing with my brothers in previous summers and once accidentally speared my own foot, thinking it was a small flounder.

One summer I joined my sister and her family for a few days of fun in the sun on the same coast. As I drove through Waveland and Bay St. Louis, then headed for the highway that would take me past Henderson Point, Long Beach, Gulfport and Biloxi, the passing landscape reminded me of both the red-necked earthiness of Bonnie and Clyde and the romantic elegance of the Great Gatsby.

When I pulled into the driveway at the rented cottage, I was greeted by my frazzled sister, who quickly told me it was my turn to take the children to the beach. She and her husband were headed for a sand-free pool.

With five children in tow, all shod with

flip-flops, we dashed across busy Highway 90. The 2-year-old informed me he loved the "snow" – actually, the sand. Never having seen sand or snow, he was enthralled. Oh, well. The 15-year-old nephew wanted to know where all the women were. The 12- and 13-year-old girls oiled themselves down and settled in on their beach towels to watch the boys. The 8-year-old amused himself by making a sand castle. By late afternoon everyone was ready for a shower except for the baby, who wanted to stay and play in the snow.

By sunset we were back on the beach armed with lanterns, spears and a small ice chest. It was floundering time.

As luck would have it, the older children managed to spear several fish, and I was appointed keeper of the catch and had to promise to cook them for supper the following night.

Stuffed Flounder

Makes 4 servings

8 tablespoons (1 stick) of butter
1 cup of chopped onions
½ cup of finely chopped green onions
1 cup of seasoned bread crumbs
1½ cups of boiled shrimp, finely chopped
1½ cups of crabmeat, picked over for shells and cartilage
2 tablespoons of chopped parsley
1 egg, beaten
Several dashes of Tabasco
1 teaspoon of salt
1 teaspoon of cayenne pepper
4 medium-size flounders, cleaned and gutted
2 tablespoons of melted butter
2 tablespoons of fresh lemon juice
4 lemon wedges

Heat the butter in a large skillet over medium heat. Add the onions and cook, stirring, until just soft, two to three minutes. Add the bread crumbs, shrimp, crabmeat, parsley and egg, and mix gently. Add the seasonings and remove from the heat.

Cut each flounder down the center, from tail to head, on the dark side of the fish.

Carefully slit each fish crosswise. With a sharp pointed knife loosen the meat from the bone to form a pocket.

Lightly season the inside of the pocket with salt and cayenne. Stuff the pocket with the seafood mixture. Drizzle the melted butter and the lemon juice over the stuffed fish.

Place the fish in a shallow pan with about one-fourth cup of water and broil until the fish flakes easily with a fork. To prevent the fish from becoming dry, baste with pan drippings.

Garnish with the lemon wedges.

Note: Make it a simple meal and serve boiled new potatoes drenched with butter and tossed with fresh chopped parsley. Ice cold watermelon is great for dessert.

When we were children, fried seafood was a staple of summer suppers. More often than not, Papa opted to travel the few miles to the camp at Catahoula Lake and cook out in the open over a hot wood fire in one of his many well-seasoned black iron pots.

Small whole skinned catfish was the family favorite, fried to perfection, and easy to consume because it has few bones. Sometimes Mama also brought along a couple of pounds of shrimp and a carton of freshly shucked oysters for added treats. There were always either French fried potatoes or potato salad, and maybe some crunchy coleslaw tossed with raisins and mayonnaise.

Papa made a big production out of getting his cook station organized. He had to have several brown paper bags, a couple for shaking the seafood in the cornmeal or flour and a couple on which to drain the fried food.

As we all huddled around his fire, sitting on folding canvas stools, he explained how the oil had to be heated to just the right temperature. Mama, forever at his elbow, was instructed on seasoning everything to his taste.

We all love to tell the story about how we asked Papa when he knew the fire was hot enough, and he explained that Mama would stick her finger in the hot oil and if she said it was hot enough it was time to begin frying. Of course, as far as we know, she never actually did this, but I wouldn't have been surprised since she usually went along with all of Papa's shenanigans.

But despite watching many fish, shrimp and oyster fryings, I never seem to succeed in this art. My oysters come out like rocks and my fish are usually soggy. When I have an *envie* for fried seafood, I usually take myself to seafood restaurants specializing in these dishes, or at least make sure Mama or Aunt Lois is around to assist me in my kitchen or at the camp.

On one occasion I was confronted with a challenge. I had been given several pounds of fresh catfish fillets, some shrimp and oysters, the last of the season. I decided it was time that I master the art of frying, so I talked to some of the best in the business.

My first encounter was with Bryan Bourque at Black's, the famous oyster house in Abbeville. Besides having wonderful cold, salty oysters on the half shell, Bryan served some of the best fried seafood to pass my mouth.

While sitting in his tiny office watching the crowds come in for lunch he gave me his secrets.

Black's Fried Seafood

FISH
Always season the fish one day in advance of cooking. Season well with black pepper, cayenne, white pepper, salt, and Louisiana Hot Sauce (his choice in hot sauces). He fries his fish only in a black iron pot in LouAna cottonseed oil heated to 375 degrees. He dredges the fish in Aunt Jemima fine white cornmeal right before frying. When the fish pops up to the surface, he drains and serves immediately.

SHRIMP
Season peeled and butterflied shrimp with black pepper and salt. Then dredge in a batter made with eggs and milk (2 egg yolks, 2/3 cup of milk) and seasoned with a little salt and pepper. Then dredge in all-purpose flour and shake off excess batter and flour.
Deep-fry in 375-degree cottonseed oil. Drain on paper towels, and serve immediately.

OYSTERS
Bourque drains them well before coating them in Aunt Jemima fine white cornmeal seasoned with salt and pepper. Some of his customers ask that the oysters be coated in flour rather than cornmeal, and he accommodates these requests.

My next call was to Don's Seafood and Steak House in downtown Lafayette. Randy Hamilton, the kitchen manager, parted with their secrets.

Don's Fried Seafood

FISH
Season fish and fine cornmeal with salt and cayenne and fry at 350 degrees in peanut oil. (He referred to the cornmeal as cream meal since it's fine like flour.)
Drain and serve immediately.

SHRIMP
Dredge peeled and butterflied shrimp in flour, then in an egg-and-milk bath, then in a mixture (half and half) of bread crumbs and cracker meal seasoned with salt and pepper.
Fry in 300-degree LouAna cottonseed oil. (Seems like the LouAna oil is preferred because it's a local product and works well.)

OYSTERS
Don's uses the same procedure as for fish.

My next inquiry was at Poor Boy's Riverside Inn, a Lafayette legend now located near Broussard. Curtis Chaisson gave me his tips.

Poor Boy's Riverside Inn Fried Seafood

FISH
Season fish with salt and cayenne, then dredge in an egg-and-water wash that is also seasoned with salt and pepper, then dredge in flour and bread crumbs before frying.

SHRIMP
The shrimp are seasoned, then go through the egg-and-water wash, then dredged in flour before frying.

OYSTERS
Oysters should be well drained, then dredged in cornmeal, or in flour and bread crumbs. Curtis says their customers specify which they prefer. They use peanut oil and fry at 350 degrees for all their fried food.

GENERAL TIPS FOR FRYING SEAFOOD:

1. Be sure oil is clean and at the desired temperature.

2. Do not fry in large batches; cook a few pieces at a time to prevent oil from dropping below the correct temperature.

3. Use enough oil to completely submerge the seafood.

4. Bread and/or batter the fish, oysters or shrimp right before frying; otherwise items will become gummy and hard.

5. Drain and serve fried foods immediately after cooking.

Aunt Lois and Mama often put a couple of pods of peeled garlic in their pot of oil. They claim this prevents the oil from burning and keeps the oil clean while frying. Aunt Lois uses butter-flavored shortening and adds a little of it to her oil because, she says, it makes the fish, shrimp and oysters come out a beautiful golden color.

Now that you know the secrets, you might want to experiment to see which method you prefer. With my new-found knowledge, I made a dish called Shrimp Benedict. You can also do it with oysters when they're in season. It's prepared like Eggs Benedict, but instead of eggs, fried seafood is used. Cut an English muffin in half, butter and toast it. Then put broiled Canadian bacon or ham on the muffin slices, pile on the fried shrimp or oysters, and top with hollandaise sauce. You might try adding a little Creole mustard to the hollandaise sauce for added zip.

Another popular vacation spot for us is Destin, Florida. Every year I join a group of college buddies (all ladies) and head for the Emerald Coast. There, for a week, we sit on the beach, comb the shops, read until we're cross-eyed, and talk ourselves into a stupor. Our cottage reminds me of dorm life. Bathing suits of every shape and size dangle from shower heads, door knobs and deck railings. Makeup, suntan lotion and magic formulas cover every inch of the bathroom countertops. Books on all subjects are piled on sofas, chairs and beds.

We talk in whispers late into the night, catching up on each other's lives. We do everything at our own pace. Some get up at the crack of dawn for tennis. Others take long walks on the beach. We give each other facials, manicures and pedicures. There's no set time for meals, nor are there any planned menus.

However, one night during the week we don sundresses to show off our tans and dine at one of Destin's chic cafes, believing ourselves to be the cutest things around.

When the week is over and we have gone through the eternally long Creole good-byes, we head to our respective homes.

It always seems too quiet in my car driving westward along the coast. To break the

My family spent much of the summer of 1955 at Cypremort Point, at Uncle George's and Aunt Eva's camp.

monotony and to give myself a "sussie" (a reward), I usually stop at a little seafood market in Biloxi to get some shrimp. The same fellow waits on me every year and knows to pack my purchase in a bag of ice so it will still be fresh when I get home.

After unpacking and shaking sand out of every article of clothing, I usually go into a minor state of depression. I already miss the companionship of the previous days, and it's difficult to face a meal alone. That's why I treat myself to the shrimp as I'm passing through Biloxi. I can always get out of depression by playing in the kitchen, rattling pots and pans. One experiment with my shrimp resulted in this recipe. Try it sometime when you're alone. It is fun to do, and I promise it will get you out of the doldrums.

This really makes one very large serving so you might want to invite someone to share it with you.

Bleu Cheese Shrimp

Makes 1 serving

1 pound of jumbo shrimp, peeled and butterflied
¼ teaspoon each of salt, cayenne pepper, and garlic powder
3 ounces of bleu cheese, softened to room temperature
Several bacon strips, cut in half
¾ cup of yellow cornmeal
¾ cup of all-purpose flour
1 egg, beaten with 1 cup of milk
Oil for frying

Season the shrimp with salt, cayenne and garlic powder and let stand for half an hour.

Spoon a little of the cheese in the split of the shrimp, wrap the shrimp tightly with the bacon and secure with a toothpick. Dredge the shrimp in a mixture of cornmeal and flour, shake off the excess, then dip in the egg-and-milk mixture, then again in the cornmeal-flour mixture.

In a deep pot, put enough cooking oil so that the shrimp can float and heat the oil to 350 degrees. Fry the shrimp, two at a time, until they pop to the surface and are golden brown. Drain on paper towels.

Note: A simple potato dish goes well with the shrimp.

Scalloped Potatoes

Makes 4 servings

2 large red potatoes, peeled and thickly sliced
1¼ cups of chicken broth
¼ cup of milk
Salt and white pepper, to taste
¼ cup of grated Romano cheese
¼ cup of grated sharp cheddar cheese

Preheat the oven to 350 degrees.

Simmer the potatoes in chicken broth just until they are tender. Drain and reserve the broth. Place the potato slices in a small baking dish. Pour in the milk and sprinkle with the salt and pepper. Add three to four tablespoons of broth, then top with the cheeses. Bake uncovered until the potatoes are very tender, about 30 minutes.

I set myself a tray and sat under a whirring ceiling fan on the porch. I wondered what my friends were doing.

I thought about Judy, who was with us on the trip. She loves to make sandwiches. My idea of a sandwich is a couple of slices of bologna and a dab of mayonnaise between two slices of white bread. On the other hand, Judy goes through great preparations for her sandwiches. Her enthusiasm and delight in making sandwiches can only be likened to someone writing a symphony.

She takes this business of making sandwiches very seriously. Watching her at work is like watching a symphony orchestra conductor. She wields her knife much like a conductor waves his baton. And she has to have just the right kinds of knives. One is for spreading on mayonnaise and

mustard, another for skinning and slicing tomatoes, and still another is for slicing meats.

One year Judy, along with a couple of friends, joined me at the camp at Cypremort Point. The usual daily schedule was fishing and sunning on the pier until noon. Then we would retire to one air-conditioned room – the kitchen – for lunch and an hour or so of soap-opera watching.

Judy always volunteered to prepare sandwiches. While the rest of us huddled around the television with our glasses of lemonade, Judy set up her assembly line. It became a ritual. After a half hour, we would begin screaming and yelling for our sandwiches.

She coyly ignored us, and humming away she leisurely continued her work. Excuse me, her play.

Finally she delivered our plates and set before us sandwiches with as much aplomb as a waiter bearing Beef Wellington.

We all doubled over in giggles. How were we ever going to get them in our mouths? Her concoction consisted of mounds of baked ham, thinly sliced purple onions, chopped avocados, shredded lettuce, herbed mayonnaise, Creole mustard and tomatoes on French bread.

But her all-time favorite is made with what she calls pepper beef. When she announces she's going to make pepper beef you can see visions of lettuce and pickles dancing in her head.

Because Judy is as honest as the day is long, she is quick to tell you that her pepper beef recipe is not her own. She got it from her friend Dinky, who hails from north Louisiana but has assimilated into the Cajun culture quite well.

Dinky's Pepper Beef

5 to 6 pounds of boneless beef roast
or eye of the round, trimmed

First Day: (A friend of mine told me once that whenever she sees instructions that say "first day" she knows she's in trouble.)

PEPPER MIX
½ cup of coarsely ground black pepper
½ cup of poppy seeds

Place the roast on a flat surface. Rub the pepper mix firmly into roast with the heel of your hand.

MARINADE
4 tablespoons of catsup
½ teaspoon of garlic powder
½ teaspoon of onion powder
1 teaspoon of paprika
1 cup of soy sauce
¾ cup of white vinegar

Combine these six ingredients in a bowl and whisk to blend. Pour the mixture over the roast in a roasting pan. Cover and refrigerate for 24 hours.

Second Day: Remove the roast from the marinade and place on heavy aluminum foil. Pour the marinade into a bowl and spoon about half of it over the roast. Close the foil tightly. Place in a baking pan and cook at 300 degrees for 2½ to 3 hours. (Do not overcook or the roast will crumble when sliced.)

When done, remove the roast from the foil and the marinade and cool. Reserve the marinade.

Third Day: Slice the roast and pour the reserved marinade over the meat. Refrigerate and let stand for at least one day before serving.

During the first week of June I begin stalking the stalls of the French Market in New Orleans, cruising slowly past the truck vendors and questioning neighborhood grocers. My mouth is primed for Creole tomatoes!

They're not real plentiful yet and everybody wants to know, "What's the rush?" One year I thought I was going to go into a panic when a friend called to say he had finally found some down in the Quarter. I sped down there to be greeted by the sounds of machinery tearing up the street that runs alongside the produce market. Parking was almost an impossibility but I was willing to risk a parking ticket and the tow truck if I could get my hot little hands on some Creoles.

I parked on the broken up street and yelled to one of the workmen that I would only be a minute.

I dashed down the aisle, shouting, "Who has some Creoles?"

I suppose the vendors have seen just about everything and were not shocked by my behavior. They didn't even look up or bat an eye. I guess they figured I was just another madwoman who had one too many Hurricanes at Pat O'Brien's.

Finally, after much waving and shouting, one gentleman looked up from his newspaper, pointed down the aisle, and said, "He has some, but not many."

I scooped up three basketsful and dashed back to my car that was still sitting amid the rubble of the street. The workmen were not too happy with me, but, what the heck, I had my Creole babies.

On the way home, I held one in my hand, taking a whiff now and then. Oh, I couldn't wait to get home and eat them all.

The first thing I did was slice one, sprinkle it with salt and pepper, and savor every bite. Then I began to figure out how I could use them all up in one meal.

I had a Vidalia onion, so I sliced it along with two Creoles, poured some mint-flavored vinegar over them, and shoved the bowl into the refrigerator. While I had the fridge door open, I pondered what was available and at hand that could be used with my tomatoes. Ah, a luscious garden-grown zucchini, some sour cream, a pound of shrimp I had purchased earlier in the day, and various other tidbits. The first thing I came up with was:

Shrimp & Creoles in a Minute

Makes 2 to 4 servings

1 pound of shrimp, peeled and deveined
4 tablespoons of butter
1 tablespoon of cream sherry
1 tablespoon of sour cream
¼ cup of chopped green onions
2 Creole tomatoes, peeled, seeded and chopped
1 teaspoon of soy sauce
Pinch of dried dill
Tabasco, to taste
Salt, to taste

Heat the butter in a large heavy skillet over medium heat. Add the shrimp and cook, stirring, until they turn pink.

Increase the heat to medium-high, add the sherry and stir for a minute or two. Reduce the heat to medium-low and add the sour cream. Stir gently until the sour cream dissolves into the pan juices.

Add the green onions, tomatoes, soy sauce and dill, and season with the hot sauce and salt. Cook for two or three minutes. (I didn't pour it over pasta or rice. I devoured it with some hot French bread.)

I also fixed something with the zucchini.

Zucchini-Tomato Casserole

Makes 2 to 4 servings

3 tablespoons of butter
1 tablespoon of olive oil
1 large onion, sliced
1 medium-size zucchini, sliced into rounds
2 Creole tomatoes, sliced
Salt and white pepper, to taste
½ teaspoon of dried basil
¼ cup of grated Romano cheese

Preheat the oven to 350 degrees.

Heat the butter and oil in a large skillet over medium heat. Add the onions and zucchini and cook, stirring until the vegetables are soft, about five minutes.

Pour the mixture into a deep casserole dish and top with the Creole tomatoes. Sprinkle with salt, pepper and basil. Top with the cheese and bake uncovered until heated through, about 20 minutes. Serve warm.

Here's yet another Creole tomato recipe!

Creole Tomato Casserole

Make about 8 servings

¼ cup of vegetable oil
2 cups of chopped onions
1 cup of chopped green bell peppers
½ cup of chopped celery
1 tablespoon of minced garlic
1 pound of ground chuck or 1 pound of
    shrimp, peeled and deveined
6 medium-size Creole tomatoes, peeled,
    seeded and chopped
1½ teaspoons of salt
½ teaspoon of cayenne pepper
1 teaspoon of dried basil
¼ cup of chopped green onions
3 to 4 slices of toasted white bread,
    crumbled*

Heat the oil in a large, heavy pot or Dutch oven over medium heat. Add the onions, bell peppers, celery and garlic. Cook, stirring, until they are very soft and lightly golden, eight to ten minutes.

Add the ground chuck and cook until browned. (If you are using shrimp, do not add now or they will overcook. Add the shrimp when the dish is just about finished cooking.)

Add the tomatoes, salt, cayenne and basil. Reduce the heat to medium-low and cook, stirring occasionally, until the mixture is thick and rich, 45 minutes to an hour.

Add the green onions and stir to mix. Remove from the heat and serve hot.

* Note: If you want to use this for a stuffing for tomatoes, bell peppers or eggplant, add crumbled toast to bind the mixture.

Every summer, Mama was fortunate to receive from her gardener and farmer friends sacks of fresh corn, okra and tomatoes. I remember her brewing up a pot of coffee for her visitors, and while they enjoyed the strong black liquid they would talk about the year's crop. She herself had come from a farming family so she was well versed in agricultural "shop talk." After they left, she would stand in the middle of the kitchen and say, "Okay, everybody. Let's get to work and cook all of this to put in the freezer."

Nannan and Tante May, my two old aunts, were summoned from next door. Children who were old enough to wield a knife or spoon were kept home from swimming lessons, and before long the kitchen looked like a canning factory.

There were mountains of onions, bell peppers and celery to be chopped. Corn had to be shucked and scraped. Okra had to be cut. (I used to pray I wouldn't be chosen to do okra because while I loved to eat it, I sure didn't like to fool with the slimy things.) Tomatoes had to be skinned and seeded.

Those who had been assigned corn would work at the old picnic table under the oak tree in the back yard. Before long, we had corn kernels on our faces and in our hair. Others, in the kitchen, would do their tasks sitting under the ceiling fan while they told stories of past canning days and gossiped about the neighbors.

Soon we could smell the aromas of stewed okra and *maque choux*. I can still see Mama at the stove showering the pots with salt, pepper and other herbs and spices. She reminded me of the Wicked Witch of the West, standing there intent on her task with corn kernels still on the tip of her nose.

By the end of the day we had packed and labeled what seemed like hundreds of containers. The larder was stocked for the coming winter months.

Today, while I'm not the recipient of complimentary sacks of corn and okra, I do have my friendly roadside market from which to buy.

Early one morning while returning from my walk, I spied a sign announcing "fresh corn." In a few minutes I was the proud owner of a sack of corn and a basket of tomatoes. I couldn't wait to get home to put on a pot of *CORN SOUP*.

Corn soup, you say, in the heat of the summer? My purpose for making soup is twofold. One, the aroma of the corn cooking brings back such wonderful memories and, two, I want something in the freezer to remind me of summer when the cold winter days are upon us.

Corn Soup

Makes about 3 quarts

6 ears of fresh corn, shucked and cleaned
1½ quarts of water
3 bacon slices, cut into 1-inch pieces
1½ cups of chopped onions
1 cup of chopped green bell peppers
¾ cup of chopped celery
½ pound of ham, cut into ½-inch cubes
3 Creole tomatoes, peeled, seeded,
   and chopped
1 quart of chicken broth
1 teaspoon of dried basil
1 teaspoon of dried tarragon
Salt and cayenne pepper, to taste

Cut the kernels from cobs, scraping the cobs to get the corn milk. Put the cleaned cobs in 1½ quarts of water and let simmer for an hour to make corn stock.

Fry the bacon in a large, heavy pot or Dutch oven over medium heat until brown but still soft. Add the onions, bell peppers, celery and ham and cook, stirring, until they are soft, about five minutes. Add the tomatoes and cook, stirring, until they throw off some of their juice, about 10 minutes.

Add the corn, one quart of the corn stock, and one quart of chicken broth. Add the basil and tarragon, and season with salt and cayenne. Simmer for two to three hours.

Now you have a choice. You can have some for supper or you can put it in the freezer and serve it later in the year when everybody comes over to watch a football game.

Earthy Food

There's just something therapeutic about working in a garden, especially a vegetable garden. When we were children, Mama always had a big garden practically all year-round. We had potatoes, okra, all kinds of beans, onions, tomatoes, cucumbers, eggplant, squash and watermelons.

Early in the morning and late in the afternoon, Mama would don her big straw hat, tie a scarf around her neck and, with basket in hand, go to check on the garden. She would hoe, weed and pick. It was her quiet time, she said. Sometimes we were invited along. And, boy, it was great fun having her point out the blossoms, the new leaves and the fruits of the harvest. You felt you could almost see things growing. The smell of the damp earth and the feel of the sun on your neck made you glad you were alive.

When the crops began coming in, Mama's kitchen (along with Nannan's and Tante May's) was always busy with chopping, cooking and canning. Such wondrous smells! My sister and I would sit on the patio late in the afternoon, shelling peas and snapping beans. Edna would much rather have been frolicking with the dogs, but I loved it. I called it mindless work. It was a perfect time to "stare." I call it "staring," but it really is daydreaming and fantasizing. I still do it sometimes. I get a few pounds of beans at the supermarket, get a colander and sit on the patio in the late afternoon and snap beans. It clears the mind.

I had a glorious treat one time when I was visiting in Lafayette. Several of us were sitting around talking about the different kinds of peppers. Friends popped up and said they had several kinds (some I've never heard of) in their garden.

"What garden?" I asked.

Before I knew it, Ronnie was shoving me into his Jeep and we were off to see *the garden.*

It was like stepping behind the garden wall into the magic land of all things good and green. There was that earthy smell I remember so well from my childhood. We ran up and down the garden rows. We were having a ball! We cuddled the squash and squeezed the melons. We dashed from row to row, then settled down and toured again at a leisurely pace.

It was late in the afternoon and a shower descended upon us, but we didn't care. With moisture on the tender leaves, the plants seemed to plump up as if they were preening. All we needed now to complete our voyage into the magic kingdom was a rainbow!

With my arms loaded down with tomatoes, peppers and zucchini, we headed to the kitchen.

That evening we had zucchini bread with dinner. It was so good we had it again the next morning for breakfast.

Zucchini Bread

Makes 2 loaves

3 tablespoons of butter
3 eggs
1¼ cups of vegetable oil
1½ cups of sugar
2 teaspoons of vanilla extract
2 cups of grated raw zucchini (unpeeled)
2 cups of all-purpose flour
2 teaspoons of baking soda
1 teaspoon of baking powder
1 teaspoon of salt
2 teaspoons of ground cinnamon
2 teaspoons of ground cloves
2 teaspoons of grated nutmeg
2 teaspoons of ground ginger
1 cup of chopped pecans or walnuts

Preheat the oven to 350 degrees. Lightly butter two loaf pans.

Beat the butter, eggs, oil, sugar and vanilla in a large mixing bowl until light and thick. Fold in the zucchini.

Sift together all the dry ingredients and fold into the zucchini mixture. Add the nuts and pour the mixture into the prepared pans.

Bake until a tester inserted in the bread comes out clean, about an hour and 15 minutes. Remove from the oven and cool a bit in the pans before turning out on a wire rack to cool longer.

The bread can be served warm or at room temperature.

Mama and Daddy leave St. Martin de Tours Catholic Church in St. Martinville after their wedding, in 1940.

Mama is a mirliton freak. She likes them better than I like my Creole tomatoes. When it's time for them to come into season, she begins her hunt and usually finds someone to give or sell her a bagful.

If you're not familiar with mirlitons, here's some information.

While they are sometimes referred to as vegetable pears, they are known by some other names. Mirlitons are a member of the gourd family and are close kin to squash and cucumber. Their original home is Central America, where they are called chayote. They are sometimes called cho-cho or mango squash and are found now on several other continents.

Some vegetable pears are pale green, while others are pearly white and can have smooth or prickly skin.

Being resourceful, the Creoles and Acadians have found numerous ways to prepare mirlitons. I've always said that when in doubt, stuff 'em.

Stuffed Mirlitons

Makes 4 servings

4 mirlitons
1½ cups of cubed day-old bread
4 tablespoons (½ stick) of butter
1 cup of finely chopped onions
1 teaspoon of minced garlic
½ cup of chopped celery
1 egg
Salt and cayenne pepper, to taste
1 pound of shrimp, cooked and peeled
  (or 1 pound of chopped ham)
½ cup of grated sharp cheddar cheese
  (optional)
Buttered bread crumbs

Wash and cut the mirlitons in half lengthwise. Cover with cold water in a large saucepan, bring to a boil and simmer until tender, about 30 minutes. Remove them from the water and cool until they are easy to handle.

Remove the seeds and discard. Carefully scoop out the pulp, leaving the skins intact. Set aside.

Chop the mirliton pulp. Soak the bread in a little water or milk until soft, then squeeze out the excess liquid.

Preheat the oven to 350 degrees.

Heat the butter in a large skillet over medium heat. Add the onions, garlic and celery. Cook, stirring, until the vegetables are soft, five to six minutes. Add the mirliton pulp, the soaked bread and the egg, and season with salt and pepper.

Add the shrimp or ham and the cheese, and cook, stirring, until the cheese melts completely and the mixture thickens, about five minutes.

Remove from heat and cool for a few minutes. Carefully stuff the mirlitons with the mixture, top with buttered bread crumbs, and bake uncovered until lightly browned, 20 to 25 minutes.

My brother Bruce has an undying love for pickled mirlitons. When Mama does these, she dares us to touch *his* jars and doesn't even offer us any.

"Those are for Brucie-Boy, so don't even think about taking any," she orders.

He's just as bad. He quickly packs them in his car and doesn't feel bad about being so selfish.

Mirliton Pickles

6 to 8 mirlitons, seeded and sliced
  like large French fries
2 large onions, sliced
2 large green bell peppers, seeded
  and thinly sliced
4 carrots, cut into thin strips
1 small head of cauliflower, broken
  into flowerets
3 garlic cloves, sliced
½ cup of salt
1 scant cup of sugar
1 tablespoon of mustard seeds
1 teaspoon of tumeric (optional)
2¼ cups of distilled white vinegar
Black, white or cayenne pepper, to taste

Combine the mirlitons, onions, bell peppers, carrots, cauliflower and garlic in a large bowl. Cover with cold water and cracked or cubed ice. Let stand for three hours. Drain well.

Combine the salt, sugar, mustard seeds, tumeric, vinegar and pepper in a large saucepan and bring to a boil. Stir to dissolve the sugar. Add the vegetable mixture and reduce the heat to medium-low. Cook for five minutes.

Remove from the heat and fill sterilized jars with the vegetables and liquid. Wipe the jars with a clean towel, put on the lids and cool.

Store in a dry, cool area until ready to use. Once the jar is opened, store in the refrigerator.

When Mama is finished with her mirlitons she starts on her figs. She watches her fig trees like a hawk, and usually right around the Fourth of July they're ready for picking.

She always says you have to be on alert. If you don't get to them quickly, the birds will get them.

The bride and groom, my parents, were all smiles on their wedding day, in 1940.

Fig Preserves, According to Mama

First of all, the figs have to be washed. Fill the kitchen sink or a container large enough for the figs to be submerged. To this water add some salt or baking soda and, with your hands, give them a good bath. Drain the water, then rinse again in clear water. Drain again.

Then measure the figs, either in a large pot or measuring cup. One year, I had so many I had to use a large saucepan. Then it's "two of figs to one of sugar," for example, two quarts of figs and one quart of sugar.

Place the figs and sugar in a deep preserving kettle or pot and simmer. Stir gently as they begin to cook. Raise the heat when a syrup forms and allow it to come to a gentle rolling boil. Cook, stirring often, until the mixture begins to thicken, one to two hours, depending on the amount of figs you have.

Sterilize jars and caps.

While the fig preserves are still hot, fill the jars, being careful to wipe the tops of the jars well to remove any syrup that may be on the area where the caps will screw on.

Screw on the caps tightly and cool to room temperature.

Store in a cool place.

Fig preserves are great with *beignets*, toast, biscuits, or corn bread, and they can be used to make fig cookies and cakes around Christmas time.

Holidays and Weekends

During the summer every day seems like a holiday and every weekend is like a vacation, but for some reason I always look forward to the Fourth of July.

In my hometown of St. Martinville there is still a parade and lots of family picnics. Old Glory waves from flag poles, balconies and storefronts.

For many years, the Fourth of July was celebrated much like Christmas, save for the exchanging of gifts. Cousins came from up and down the bayou, and everyone gathered either at the camp at Catahoula Lake or in our back yard.

The feast lasted from morning until evening, with tables piled with barbecued chicken and brisket, fried chicken, salads of all kinds and desserts for everyone's sweet tooth.

One year I was unable to make it to the family celebration, but wanting to keep up the tradition I gathered some of my friends and hosted a glorious Fourth.

My houseguests began arriving a couple of days before the Fourth bearing bushel baskets of eggplant, tomatoes, okra, cucumbers and squash. Out of their cars came an ice chest of strawberries, heavy cream and champagne. Another friend emerged from her car with bags of sugar cookies and macaroons. Just when I thought my kitchen would burst at the seams, there came a pot of jumbo shrimp. Loaves of French bread poked out of picnic baskets. A watermelon was iced down on the deck. There was not a chance we would go hungry.

By the time everyone had gathered on that first day, we sounded like a bunch of chickens: We were all talking at once. We decorated the deck with tiny American flags and tried to determine where we would have our very own fireworks display. For a few days, we ate like kings.

On the big day, brisket topped the menu.

My family enjoyed summer vacation on the beach at Biloxi, Mississippi, circa 1955. Left to right: Marcia Bienvenu, my mother Rhena, my sister Edna Marie, and my brother Bruce (standing). Behind Bruce is Marcelle Olivier Bienvenu with her daughter Geralyn on her lap and her daughter Babette (the small child standing to their right). In the rear, left to right: Louisette Bienvenu, my brother Henri Clay, me (with my hands in front of my face), an unidentified boy, and Herman Bienvenu.

Stuffed Baked Brisket

Makes about 10 servings

First, make a marinade. This one is from Aunt Nan and can be used on chicken, rib racks or thick pork chops.

MARINADE

2 cups of liquid margarine
1 cup of soy sauce
1 cup of fresh lemon juice
2 tablespoons of garlic powder
2 tablespoons of white or black pepper
1 tablespoon of cayenne pepper
3 tablespoons of ground basil leaves
1½ tablespoons of salt
1 tablespoon of liquid smoke

Mix all ingredients together and allow to stand at least two hours before using.

This marinade can be made and stored in the refrigerator for several weeks.

1 (8-pound) boneless brisket, trimmed
¾ pound of lean ground beef
¾ pound of lean ground pork
1 carrot, peeled and grated
5 large pitted green olives, chopped
½ teaspoon of salt
½ teaspoon of cayenne pepper
2 garlic cloves, minced

Have the butcher butterfly the brisket. Or, you can do it yourself using a sharp boning knife. Simply make a slit from end to end large enough to fit the stuffing.

Make the stuffing by combining the ground meats, carrot, olives and seasonings, mixing well.

Stuff the brisket with the mixture. Place the brisket in a pan with two cups of the marinade, then cover and refrigerate for at least four hours. Baste occasionally with the marinade or turn the brisket over several times in the marinade.

Preheat the oven to 275 degrees.

Wrap the meat in heavy-duty aluminum foil with the marinade and one-half cup of water. Seal tightly and bake in a roasting pan until the meat is very tender, three to four hours.

After removing from the oven, allow to cool slightly before slicing.

Hummingbird Cake

3 cups of all-purpose flour
2 cups of sugar
1 teaspoon of salt
1 teaspoon of baking soda
1 teaspoon of ground cinnamon
3 eggs, beaten
1½ cups of vegetable oil
1½ teaspoons of vanilla extract
1 (8-ounce) can of crushed pineapple,
    undrained
1 cup of chopped pecans
2 cups of chopped and mashed bananas
Frosting (Recipe follows)
½ cup of crushed pecans

Preheat the oven to 350 degrees.

Combine the dry ingredients in a large mixing bowl.

Add the eggs and oil, stirring until moistened. Do not beat. Stir in the vanilla, pineapple, pecans and bananas.

Spoon the batter into three well-greased and -floured 9-inch pans.

Bake just until the mixture sets, 25 to 30 minutes.

Remove from the oven and cool for 10 minutes in the pans. Then remove the cakes from the pans and cool completely on cake racks.

Spread the top of each layer evenly with some of the frosting. Stack the layers and frost the cake with the remaining frosting. Top with the crushed pecans.

FROSTING

1 (8-ounce) package of cream cheese,
    softened
½ cup of butter
1 pound of confectioners' sugar
1 teaspoon of vanilla extract

Combine the cream cheese and butter in a large mixing bowl and cream until smooth. Add the sugar, beating until light and fluffy. Stir in the vanilla.

Chocolate Cheesecake

24 chocolate wafers
¼ cup of butter, melted
¼ teaspoon of ground cinnamon
1 (8-ounce) package of semi-sweet
    chocolate
1½ pounds of cream cheese, softened
1 cup of sugar
3 eggs
2 teaspoons of unsweetened cocoa powder
1 teaspoon of vanilla extract
2 cups of sour cream

Crush the wafers in a blender or food processor to make a little more than a cup. Transfer the crushed wafers to a bowl. Add the butter and cinnamon and mix well.

Press the crumb mixture into the bottom of an 8-inch spring-form pan. Then buckle the sides and chill for one hour.

Preheat the oven to 350 degrees.

Melt the semi-sweet chocolate, stirring occasionally, over low heat.

In a large bowl, beat the softened cream cheese until fluffy and smooth, then beat in the sugar. Add the eggs, one at a time, beating well after each egg. Beat in the melted chocolate, the cocoa and vanilla, blending well. Beat in the sour cream.

Pour the mixture into the prepared spring-form pan. Bake for an hour and 10 minutes. The cake will be a little runny, but will become firm as it chills.

Cool at room temperature, then chill for at least five hours or up to eight hours.

Summer weekends are perfect for fishing excursions.

One year I was invited on an adventure I will not soon forget. Here is my fish story.

I've crossed it hundreds of times. I've walked along its banks and watched the ships ply its muddy waters. I've read Mark Twain's adventures of Huckleberry Finn. On a paddle wheeler, I've traveled upriver and downriver, but I've never been to its beginning and only once did I see where it ends. The Mississippi River is awesome.

As I traveled by car on the West Bank from Belle Chasse to Venice, I noticed numerous roadside vendors stocked with Creole tomatoes, okra, bell peppers, corn and eggplant. Citrus groves stretch from the road to the levees that contain the river.

My little sister Edna Marie mimics Nannan, as I look on in amusement, circa 1949.

The land is flat and rich, and in a deep breath I smelled the combination of earth and water.

At Venice, where many Louisianians say the world comes to an end, I met my friends whose boat would take me on the final leg of my adventure.

Traveling through Tiger Pass, we encountered sleek Bertrams armed with heavy-duty rods and reels mounted like trophies on the stern. Shrimp boats draped with nets put-putted to their docks, and crew boats roared past on their way to rigs in the open water.

Our destination was the New Orleans Big Game Fishing Club, situated right beneath an old lighthouse and across from the now-abandoned village of Port Eads in South Pass, which was once the primary entrance from the Gulf of Mexico to the Mississippi River.

For two days we trolled the blue water of the Gulf, bringing in a Gulf tuna and a white marlin. Although the engines never stopped and the lines stayed in the water, we enjoyed brunch, lunch and tea onboard.

In the evenings, the club crew served us hearty meals of red beans and rice, prime rib, meat loaf and mashed potatoes, rib eyes and baked potatoes, and, for dessert, coconut pralines and banana pudding. I wondered why we weren't having the catch of the sea until I learned that all edible fish had to be cleaned and packed for the anglers to take home for later use.

One evening as we sat on the porch in rocking chairs, with fiddler crabs scurrying across our feet, we watched a pink moon rise above the thick reeds that look much like bamboo. The light from the lighthouse above our heads flashed its beacon to the incoming boats. People whispered in the darkness, and it was then I realized the magic of this great river.

On my way home I stopped and bought shrimp at Port Sulphur and tomatoes, corn, okra and bell peppers at Myrtle Grove. I had all the ingredients for a week of feasting. I pulled out a recipe given to me by an old co-worker at *The Times-Picayune*, a person I worked with while on the staff of *Dixie*, the magazine section.

Pantry Shelf Paella

Makes 6 servings

3 tablespoons of butter
1 chicken (about 3 pounds), quartered
   or cut into frying pieces
1 cup of chopped onions
1 cup of uncooked white long-grain rice
¼ cup of tomato paste
2 cups of water
1 pound of shrimp, peeled and deveined
1 garlic clove, minced
Salt and cayenne pepper, to taste
1½ cups of early peas (canned or frozen)
Wedges of Creole tomatoes

Heat the butter in a large, heavy pot over medium heat. Add the chicken and brown well. (You may have to do this in batches.) Remove the chicken and transfer to a platter.

Add the onions and rice. Cook, stirring, to coat evenly, three to five minutes.

Combine the tomato paste and water and add to the rice with the shrimp and garlic. Season with salt and cayenne. Stir in the peas and return the chicken to the pot.

Cover and cook until the rice is tender, about 25 minutes.

Serve warm and garnish with the tomatoes.

The following is a simple recipe for a light supper. Fresh shrimp is essential.

Vermouth Shrimp

Makes 4 to 6 servings

4 tablespoons of butter
2 tablespoons of olive oil
2 pounds of medium-size shrimp, peeled
   and deveined
Salt, to taste
½ teaspoon of coarsely ground black
   pepper
2 ounces of dry vermouth
3 tablespoons of fresh lemon juice
Snipped chives or finely chopped green
   onions (green part only), for garnish

Heat the butter and oil in a large, heavy skillet over medium heat. Add the shrimp and toss with the salt and black pepper. Cook, stirring gently, until the shrimp turn pink, about five minutes.

Add the vermouth and lemon juice, and toss again for about a minute.

Serve on toast points or on pastry shells and garnish with chives or green onions.

To go along with the shrimp, serve thickly sliced Creole tomatoes layered with thin slices of green bell peppers, small chunks of avocados, and coarsely chopped sweet onions, sprinkled with crumbled bleu cheese and snips of fresh herbs, such as basil or dill. Drizzle with olive oil and balsamic vinegar. Garnish the salad platter with pickled okra.

The week after my fishing excursion, friends invited me on another boat trip to the Mississippi Gulf Coast. It was to be a leisurely weekend to include some easy fishing and island hopping, and, of course, good eating.

My friends do not consider ham sandwiches, boiled eggs and soft drinks good shipboard fare.

They have developed a repertoire of divine boat food that can be easily prepared on a boat equipped with a two-burner stove and a refrigerator. These recipes are just as suitable for smaller boats equipped with only an ice chest and warm sunshine.

The common factors these dishes share is that they are easy to prepare, either before leaving the dock or on board, are tasty and imaginative, and, above all, simple to serve and enjoy.

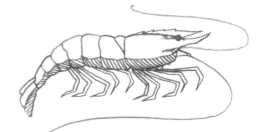

Southern Sausage Cake

Makes 8 servings

This can be prepared well in advance in a disposable 9x9x2-inch baking tin and either frozen or refrigerated until time to be served. Since it is best slightly warm or at "environmental" temperature, it is usually set in the sun for about 15 minutes. It can be just as good as a snack or an easy lunch. For an onboard brunch, serve Bloody Marys and chilled white asparagus tips sprinkled with lemon juice.

1 pound of hot bulk sausage
½ cup of chopped onions
1 cup of chopped red bell peppers
1 cup of chopped green bell peppers
¼ cup of grated Parmesan cheese
½ cup of grated jalapeño-flavored cheese
1 egg, beaten
¼ teaspoon of Tabasco
1½ teaspoons of a combination of salt, black pepper and garlic powder
2 cups of biscuit mix
¾ cup of milk
¼ cup of sour cream

Preheat the oven to 350 degrees.
Brown the sausage and vegetables in a skillet over medium heat. Drain off excess oil. Add the cheeses, egg, hot sauce and seasoning mix.
Make a batter with the biscuit mix, milk and sour cream.
Gently stir the sausage mixture into the batter and put into a greased baking tin.
Bake until lightly browned, about 45 minutes.
Remove from the oven and cool to room temperature. At this point, it can be frozen for later use. To serve, cut into squares.

Ceviche

Perfect for game fishermen, this recipe can be adapted to almost any firm seafood. In the Bahamas or southern Florida, where lobster is plentiful, break the meat from the tails and cut into bite-sized pieces. Fresh tuna (from the ocean, not from the can) and fresh shrimp right from the net are also ideal. The beauty of this recipe is that it requires no cooking at all and it is a delicious way to enjoy your fresh catches. It does require time for marinating, six to eight hours, but that just builds the anticipation.

It can be served as an appetizer with crackers and is excellent as a summer salad with fresh greens. Everything can be prepared ahead of time and carried in an airtight container. It is just as easy to prepare onboard.

3½ pounds of fresh firm seafood
Juice of 10 limes (Bottled lime juice may be substituted in a pinch.)
1 bunch of green onions, chopped
¼ cup of sliced jalapeños
¾ cup of extra-virgin olive oil
¼ cup of fresh lemon juice
¼ cup of chopped fresh parsley
½ teaspoon of dried oregano leaves
1 teaspoon of dried tarragon leaves
Salt and freshly ground black pepper, to taste
1 cup of sliced stewed tomatoes or fresh tomatoes, chopped

Mix all the ingredients in a plastic container and marinate in the refrigerator for at least six hours. Stir every now and then to make sure everything marinates evenly.

When at a fishing tournament, plan ahead for a celebration dinner. After a few days of hard fishing, there is a certain ambiance associated with dining dockside amid all the activity going on around you.
Your neighbors will watch with envy as they chomp down their cold bologna sandwiches.
A nutritious but delicious menu could include the following:

Anipasto Salad

Makes about 6 servings

1 (6-ounce) jar of marinated artichokes
1 (14-ounce) can of hearts of palm, drained and sliced
1 (3¼-ounce) can of pitted ripe olives
1 small jar of marinated mushrooms
½ cup of sliced summer sausage

Mix, chill and serve.

Summer Spaghetti

2 (14 ½-ounce) cans of sliced stewed
    tomatoes
½ cup of chopped onions
1 tablespoon of minced garlic
2 tablespoons of chopped fresh parsley
½ teaspoon of dried basil leaves
¼ cup of olive oil
Tarragon vinegar, to taste
12-ounces of angel hair pasta, cooked
    according to package directions and
    drained
Grated Parmesan cheese, for garnish

Mix together all the ingredients except for the pasta. Store in an airtight container or plastic storage bag and refrigerate until ready to use.

Store the cooked pasta in an airtight container or plastic storage and refrigerate until ready to use.

Before serving, bring the tomato mixture to room temperature. Rinse the pasta in tepid water, drain and mix with the tomato mixture. To serve, garnish with the Parmesan cheese.

Make a fruit compote of canned mandarin slices with their juice, canned grapefruit slices that have been drained, and grated coconut. Chill and serve.

With some French pistolettes, you've got a meal fit for champions.

My cousin Candy Broussard and my brother Bruce play on the floor at our camp at Cypremort Point, circa 1955.

Too Hot to Move

It's just been too hot to move. It's absolutely stifling. Not only is it hot, but extremely muggy. It's like breathing soup when one walks out of an air-conditioned building. My sunglasses steam up when I get into my hot car.

Just about every August I think of the term "the dog days of summer." There's not a breeze stirring under the oak trees and the ground is parched.

One August afternoon when I was living at Oak Alley Plantation a transformer blew during a thunderstorm. A European guest staying in one of the cottages came to my door ranting and raving. In French, he explained that he and his wife had been driving all afternoon in a rental car with no air-conditioning and had arrived to find his cabin in darkness.

In my best south Louisiana French, I explained that I had no control over lightning. And didn't they know about Acts of God? Didn't they have thunderstorms in France?

He didn't want to hear about Acts of God. He was hot, dripping with perspiration, and standing in a pool of water from the recent downpour.

I had to admit to myself I wasn't in such a good mood either. I, too, had been trying to keep cool and was worried about 50 pounds of shrimp that had been delivered that afternoon and stored in the cooler when the power went out. I had just returned from taking the shrimp out of the cooler, putting them in every ice chest I could find, and packing them in crushed ice. If the power went back on soon I would have to reverse the procedure.

I eyed his poor wife in the car fanning herself with their road map. I had to act fast. I couldn't let them think that we had no Southern hospitality.

In my broken French, I invited them in, offered them a glass of ice cold lemonade (I still had a couple of bags of ice in my ice chest.) and inquired if they had swimsuits. They nodded and looked at each other quizzically.

In a minute, dressed in our suits, I led them out to the back yard, where soon we were frolicking with my garden hose that has a wonderful nozzle with three speeds, much like a shower massager. I hung a large flashlight on a string in the trees and put a tape in my battery-operated radio and hung it in the trees, too.

The sun was setting and the electricity was still not back on so I figured I had to keep them entertained a while longer. I got out some old drink recipes, ran over to the shed and scooped up a couple of pounds of shrimp out of the ice chests and invited them to stay for dinner.

We were just going to have to make the best of it. While the shrimp were boiling, I made us a round of cool drinks. Thank goodness the stove was gas.

Green Cooler

1 (6-ounce) can of frozen limeade
   concentrate
1 (6-ounce) can filled with vodka
5 cans of crushed ice

I usually put all the ingredients in a blender and process until smooth, but without electricity I had to improvise. I put everything in a big jar and shook it to the sounds of the music.

Strawberry Egg Shake

1½ cups of frozen strawberries (thawed)
1 egg
1 tablespoon of fresh lemon juice
1 tablespoon of sugar
½ cup of crushed ice

Combine in a blender and shake. (Again, I used my jar.)

Scotch Frost

1½ ounces of Scotch whiskey
¾ ounce of fresh lemon juice
1 cup of crushed ice

Shake in a shaker (or blender) and serve.

Rum Flip

1 teaspoon of sugar
1½ ounces of light rum
1 egg
½ cup of crushed ice

Shake or blend and serve sprinkled with grated nutmeg.

Pineapple Passion

1 (13½-ounce) can of pineapple chunks
½ cup of light rum
¼ cup of lime juice
1 teaspoon of grenadine
Crushed ice

I guess you're getting the idea now.

After the boiled shrimp cooled I served them in a tray covered with ice, and we peeled and dipped them in a sauce I had made with mayonnaise, Worcestershire, a little ketchup, lemon juice, hot sauce and horseradish.

As we finished off our repast and licked our fingers, the electricity came back on. By the time I had walked them over to their cabin, it was cooling down. I gave them fans, the kind that are made of cardboard mounted on a stick, like the ones funeral homes used to give out at church, except these had Scarlett and Rhett faces on them.

I didn't see them the next morning at breakfast. Evidently they had gotten an early start. Hopefully, they had enjoyed the evening as much as I had.

It's not easy to be cool as a cucumber when the temperatures soar into the nineties and the humidity is knocking at 100 percent. The air is as thick as gumbo and just as hot. The only consolation I have when we hit the dog days of summer is that because of the moisture in the air, perhaps my skin won't wrinkle as quickly as our friends in dryer climates.

I knew it was some hot when, one day, as I sat in my car on the ferry crossing the Mississippi, my makeup dripped off my face and on to my freshly ironed white cotton dress.

Even the breeze off the river didn't

help. As I exited the ferry, I stopped at my friendly vegetable vendor and quickly bought up his Creole tomatoes, cucumbers and one big watermelon. With the car air-conditioner on full blast, I couldn't wait to get home to flop on an old canvas chair underneath a whirring ceiling fan. With a tall glass of lemonade garnished with fresh mint, I tried to get myself together before I entered my tiny kitchen.

There was no way I could even think about turning on a burner on the stove, much less the oven. A nice cool supper was in order.

I am a fanatic for homemade mayonnaise. Anything with homemade mayonnaise is a treat. There are many ways to make the stuff. Some people still make it by hand, others do it in a minute in a blender or food processor. I happen to have one of those gadgets Mama called a mayonnaise machine. It's a jar, about quart-size, with a concave cap with a hole in the center through which a plunger fits. I've had the thing for years and I don't know what will happen should I break it. Here are some recipes for mayonnaise:

Mama enjoys being out in the water at Cypremort Point in the summer of 1939.

Mayonnaise

USING THE 'MAYO MACHINE'

1 egg
2 tablespoons of fresh lemon juice
  or vinegar
1 teaspoon of dry mustard
1 teaspoon of salt
1 teaspoon of sugar
Dash of Tabasco
2 cups of vegetable oil or olive oil

Chill the "mayo machine" and the egg, oil and lemon juice, unmixed.

Next, put the egg, lemon juice or vinegar, dry mustard, salt, sugar and hot sauce into the jar. Screw the cap on with the plunger in place.

Pour a little oil at a time into the concave cap. Beat with up and down motion while the oil runs down the stem of the plunger. Repeat steadily until all the oil is mixed thoroughly. Keep refrigerated until ready to use.

BY HAND

If you want to make mayonnaise by hand, use one raw egg yolk and one hard-boiled egg, thoroughly blended, then add the dry mustard, salt and sugar. Mix well. Slowly add a cup of oil, one tablespoon at a time, beating with a fork or wire whisk. Season with black or white pepper or a few dashes of hot sauce, according to taste.

USING THE BLENDER

Take one whole raw egg and one raw egg yolk and blend at high speed for 30 seconds. Add one teaspoon each of dry mustard, salt and sugar. The sugar may be omitted if a tarter taste is desired.

Add 1 to 1½ cups of salad oil or olive oil, in a steady stream while the blender is on a high speed.

Finally, season with black or white pepper or hot sauce and blend for just a few seconds more.

For different mayonnaise variations try these suggestions:

For cold fish, hard-boiled eggs or boiled shellfish, combine one cup of mayonnaise, two tablespoons of anchovies (or one teaspoon of shrimp or lobster paste), one tablespoon of minced green onions and one-half teaspoon of curry powder.

For cold beef or poultry, combine one cup of mayonnaise, two tablespoons each of chili sauce and chopped green onions, two teaspoons of Worcestershire sauce, two peeled and seeded tomatoes, finely chopped, and a dash of dry sherry.

Try this on cold ham, pork, poultry or game: Combine one cup of mayonnaise, two tablespoons of softened currant jelly, one tablespoon each of dry sherry, grated orange and lemon rind. Use salt and pepper to taste.

For a sandwich spread or salad dressing, combine one cup of mayonnaise, four tablespoons of whipping cream, one tablespoon of Dijon or Creole mustard, and two tablespoons of vinegar.

For fresh fruit or green salads, mix together two cups of mayonnaise, and one-half cup each of sour cream and chopped walnuts or pecans, and two tablespoons of white wine or brandy.

Another idea for dressing salads: Combine one cup of mayonnaise, one cup of crumbled Roquefort or bleu cheese, one-half cup of sour cream, and one teaspoon of hot sauce.

For cold beef and vegetables, combine one cup of mayonnaise, puréed tomatoes, sliced pimientos, and one-fourth teaspoon of minced garlic.

For a dip for crudités – like blanched green beans, asparagus, broccoli and cauliflower, or fresh celery and carrots – combine mayonnaise, a purée of chervil, tarragon, watercress and minced garlic. Dill is also good.

The variations are endless. Go ahead and make a couple of batches of mayonnaise, and add your own herbs and spices.

For supper I had an assortment of cool vegetables with my mayonnaise and a sandwich, followed by a thick slice of cold watermelon.

I finally cooled down.

In August my garden is just about finished and it's time to tear it down and plow it under. I'm going to miss it. I planted it in April and since then I've visited it just about every day. I've weeded, watered, fertilized, sprayed, fought red ants, and run off birds and armadillos.

During May, June and July, I've had tomatoes, cucumbers, eggplant, squash, zucchini and fresh herbs. It's all coming to an end, and I'm sad.

With a basket in hand, I took a walk through the garden and gathered the last of the vegetables to prepare a memorial *RATATOUILLE*.

Ratatouille is a wonderful melange of vegetables that can be a main course or a side dish. It shouldn't be overcooked. I like the vegetables to have a little crunch to them.

Ratatouille

Makes about 4 servings

2 tablespoons of butter
1 tablespoon of olive oil
1 cup of chopped onions
½ cup of diced smoked ham (optional)
1 cup of coarsely chopped ripe tomatoes
2 cups of sliced okra (optional)
1 cup of coarsely chopped eggplant, peeled
½ cup of chopped green bell peppers
½ teaspoon of salt
¼ teaspoon of freshly ground black pepper
2 to 3 leaves of fresh basil, finely minced

Heat the butter and olive oil in a large, heavy saucepan over medium heat. Add the onions and ham and cook until the onions are slightly soft, three to four minutes.

Add the tomatoes, okra, eggplant and bell peppers, and cook, stirring often, for 10 minutes. Then add the salt, black pepper and fresh basil, and simmer for 10 minutes more.

Adjust seasonings to taste. Serve warm.

Another dish that is good for using up garden fresh vegetables is CAPONATA, an Italian favorite usually served as an appetizer. With the addition of lean ground beef or ground veal, it can become an entree served *en casserole* with linguine or your choice of pasta.

Caponata

Makes 6 to 8 servings

1/3 cup of olive oil
3 large eggplants, peeled and cubed
2 large onions, chopped
3 large ripe tomatoes, peeled and chopped
1/4 cup of tomato paste
4 celery ribs, cut crosswise into
    1-inch slices
5 garlic cloves, minced
3 teaspoons of salt
1/2 teaspoon of black pepper
Cayenne pepper, to taste
1 cup of pimiento-stuffed green olives,
    sliced and drained
1 (3-ounce) jar of capers, drained
1 pound of ground beef or ground
    veal (optional)
Pasta
Grated Romano cheese
Grated Parmesan cheese
Seasoned bread crumbs

Heat the oil in a large, heavy pot over medium heat. Add the eggplant and cook, stirring just until soft, three to four minutes.

Add the onions, tomatoes, tomato paste, celery, garlic, salt, black pepper and cayenne. Cook, stirring until the mixture begins to bubble. Add the olives and capers. Cover and reduce the heat to medium-low. Simmer for about an hour, stirring occasionally. Serve hot or cold with crackers or toasted slices of French or Italian bread.

If you wish to add the ground meat, brown the meat in a bit of olive oil and add to the vegetable mixture.

Prepare your pasta of choice, drain, and put into a buttered baking dish. Cover the pasta with the caponata, then sprinkle with grated Romano and Parmesan cheese and seasoned bread crumbs. Bake uncovered at 350 degrees for 20 minutes before serving.

Mama found a treasure while cleaning the camp at Catahoula Lake in preparation for one of our Labor Day celebrations.

She was cleaning out closets and cabinets like a madwoman. Dust was flying and she was mumbling to herself about how she hates this task. We tend to ignore her rumbling and mumbling, because once everything is gleaming, she's happy as a lark.

She was attacking a small storage closet when she let out a yell. We all came running. I didn't know if she had hurt herself, found a snake (which she loves to do) or a dead mouse, or if the mess was so great she had reached the end of her rope.

She had crawled into the closet on all fours, so we had to yank her out by her belt. She came flying out holding several black books we recognized as being her old travel diaries. Assured she was okay, we left her sitting on the floor going through her little black books. We occasionally heard a chuckle, a sigh and a few groans. We knew it was best to leave her alone with her memories.

A few days later she handed over a couple of the diaries to me and told me to read them. She thought I might find her notes interesting.

The first one I chose to read was for the year 1969. I couldn't believe 20 years had passed so quickly as I began reading her notes.

Mama and Papa had just bought their first recreational vehicle and the Toledo Bend Reservoir had evidently just been opened. They appeared to have burned up the roads between St. Martinville and the huge reservoir situated on the Texas-Louisiana border. I remembered that Papa was ecstatic when he learned that the large body of water had been well stocked with bass, perch, *sac-a-lait*, better known as white perch or crappie, and the other freshwater fish he so loved to catch.

Mama's notes indicate they tried just about every campsite, fishing spot and park area. Paper-clipped to the cover of her book are receipts from most of the places they stayed. Her observations include descriptions of the area, names of people they met, a list of family and friends who joined them for weekends, and the food they cooked.

"Thursday, July 31. We're at Toledo Bend. Lois and children, Blackie and I, Brother and Pat and children are settled in. We've made ourselves a small compound with three camping trailers. All the children slept in ours. Mopped up fishing today and had fried fish, *courtbouillon*, potato salad and hamburgers. We were stuffed. No mosquitoes!"

"August 6. Multibreaker burnt. We were without lights, but still having fun."

On and on it went until June of 1970

because it was that summer we situated our camp at Catahoula on what Mama describes as "Truly beautiful property. We are roughing it because as yet we have no electricity. We are anxious to really fix it up."

Her notes continued in much the same vein. "Thursday, August 13. Fished all day. Caught 30 bream. No *sac-a-lait*. We cleaned them on the banks and then it began to pour down rain. A gang is coming to spend the day on Saturday. Hope to catch more fish."

A flood of memories came back to me. I remembered how Papa loved to fish in his beloved Catahoula Lake. He would spend hours in his small boat, paddling along the banks, stopping here and there, trying this and that for bait and coming back to the camp with a string of perch, green trout and *sac-a-lait* trailing alongside the boat. He liked saltwater fishing, but freshwater was his forte.

And he was a great cook. When he had a batch of catfish, he fried them to perfection. And while traditionally *courtbouillon* is made with redfish, his version with bream and perch was a masterpiece. And sometimes, when he had an abundance of any kind of fish, he would poach them, pick off the meat and make a divine fish salad.

Catahoula Lake Fish Salad

Makes 6 servings

6 cups of water
12 to 14 bream or perch, scaled and cleaned
1 large onion, thickly sliced
2 ounces of dry vermouth
2 lemons, sliced
1 teaspoon of salt
1 teaspoon of cayenne pepper

Bring the water to a gentle boil in a large pot over medium-high heat. Add the rest of the ingredients, and cook until the fish are fork-tender, 10 to 12 minutes.

Remove the fish with a spatula or slotted spoon. Cool and pick off the meat from the bones.

Then use your imagination. Papa mixed the fish with homemade mayonnaise, a little yellow mustard, chopped celery, chopped olives, sweet pickle relish, chopped hard-boiled eggs, minced parsley and minced green onions.

Serve your salad on a bed of lettuce. Papa liked to scoop his up with saltines. I prefer toast. Papa sprinkled his with hot sauce; I opt for a dash of peppered vinegar.

For variety, you may want to try cooking your fish on the grill.

Fish in a Bag

Makes 6 servings

1 large bass, 4 to 5 pounds, dressed (or several small ones equaling 4 to 5 pounds)
1 medium-size green bell pepper, seeded and cut into thin slices
1 large onion, thinly sliced
3 tablespoons of melted butter or olive oil
¼ teaspoon of dried thyme
3 tablespoons of fresh lemon juice
36 to 40 small shrimp, peeled and deveined
Salt and cayenne pepper, to taste
2 bacon strips

Prepare a medium-hot charcoal fire, or preheat the oven to 400 degrees.

Place the fish on a large sheet of heavy-duty aluminum foil. Arrange the bell pepper and onion slices on the fish. Drizzle with the butter or oil. Sprinkle with the thyme and lemon juice. Arrange the shrimp on the vegetables and season with salt and cayenne. Lay the bacon on top of the other ingredients.

Bring the edges of the foil together to make a loose "purse," rolling the edges to close securely.

Place the bag on the grill (or in the oven) and cook until the fish flakes easily with a fork, about 25 minutes.

Remove from the heat and carefully roll back the foil. Serve immediately.

"Friday, September 11. We're at Cypremort Point on Vermilion Bay. No boat, so fished off the wharf. Caught spade fish, small flounders and some croakers. Have enough for supper so we'll probably bake a few, fry a few and stuff a few."

And that's another story.

Summertime seems to go by quicker and quicker each year. Why, it seems I just returned from my four-day Memorial Day getaway. And although the Fourth of July weekend was a washout, I'd swear it was only yesterday. Can it be almost two months since, determined to spend the holiday at the camp, we withstood rain, rising water and mud-caked children?

It was a holiday that I will long remember despite the hardships. There were 20 of us trying to keep things festive despite the dampening weather. We couldn't put the boats in the water because our wharves were under water. Children were underfoot simply because there wasn't anywhere for them to play except the rain-filled ditches. And we adults spent most of our time under the tin-roofed patio reminiscing about more pleasant fair-weather holidays.

But now we have Labor Day weekend fast approaching and already Mama has sent word out that we are all expected again at the camp for our last full-fledged gathering before the camp is closed for the season.

She's making her menu list for the three-day extravaganza and has given us each assignments.

Aunt Lois is bringing fixings for a barbecue. My Baby Brother Bruce has been hoarding fish from his fishing expeditions so we can have a big *courtbouillon*. A couple of the cousins have volunteered to make a big pot of jambalaya, and Mama has already put aside the allotment of *maque choux*, smothered okra and eggplant dressing in the freezer. My sister and I are in charge of sweets and desserts.

Knowing how tiny Mama's kitchen at the camp is and how many mouths there are to fill, I have already placed my order at the bakery for assorted cookies, fudge cakes and éclairs. I will also take a few homemade treats that are both cool and easy to prepare.

Pound Cake

Here is a modification of the original pound cake in which a pound of each main ingredient was used.

1¾ cups of all-purpose flour
1 cup of sugar
2 teaspoons of baking powder
1 teaspoon of salt
1/3 cup of vegetable shortening or butter
1 teaspoon of vanilla extract
5 egg yolks, unbeaten
3/4 cup of milk

Preheat the oven to 350 degrees. Grease a 9x5x3-inch loaf pan.

Combine the flour, sugar, baking powder and salt in a large mixing bowl. Add the shortening or butter, the vanilla, egg yolks, and one-half cup of milk.

Using an electric mixer, beat for two minutes on medium speed. Scrape the sides and bottom of the bowl constantly while mixing. Add the rest of the milk and beat two more minutes.

Spoon the batter into the prepared pan. Bake until a tester inserted in the cake comes out clean, an hour to an hour and 10 minutes.

Remove from the oven and cool in the pan. Cut into slices to serve.

I prefer pound cake a day old or even a bit stale. Then I cut it into slices and toast for a minute or so in the oven, then spoon Bananas Foster Topping over it. Of course, a scoop of vanilla ice cream on top makes it a true delight.

BANNANAS FOSTER TOPPING

For a new twist on an old favorite, bring along the fixings for Bananas Foster: brown sugar, butter, ripe bananas, cinnamon, banana liqueur and rum.

Heat the butter and add the brown sugar and cinnamon and blend together. Add sliced bananas, then pour in banana liqueur and rum.

This can all be done easily in a large skillet – and don't worry about trying to flame the liqueur and rum like they do at Brennan's.

Make a big batch if you have a crowd. Then serve the warm bananas over pound cake.

Crazy Cake

1½ cups of unsifted all-purpose flour
1 cup of sugar
3 tablespoons of unsweetened
   cocoa powder
1 teaspoon of salt
1 teaspoon of vanilla extract
1 teaspoon of distilled white vinegar
6 tablespoons of vegetable oil
1 cup of water

Preheat the oven to 350 degrees.

Sift the dry ingredients together into an ungreased 8-inch square baking pan. Make three wells in the flour mixture. In one well, add the vanilla. In the second well, put the vinegar, and in the third, the oil. Pour the water over the mixture and blend all together with a fork.

Bake until the cake sets, about 30 minutes. Put it in an airtight container and chill in the refrigerator. When serving, top with whipped cream or a dab of cream cheese frosting.

This next recipe is an old childhood favorite. My Nannan used to make a batch of this and put it into ice trays, then pop a couple of cubes out when we came to her back porch screen door begging for a treat.

Frozen Cream Cheese

First of all, you can't use a product like regular cream cheese; it must be Creole cream cheese. It's available in some south Louisiana supermarkets. My method of making the frozen cream cheese is akin to that of the late Leon Soniat, a former Times-Picayune food columnist.

5 cartons of Creole cream cheese
1 quart of milk
1 quart of whipping cream
3 cups of sugar
3 tablespoons of vanilla extract

Mash the cream cheese through a colander set over a large bowl to remove any lumps. Add the milk, whipping cream and sugar and mix well. Add the vanilla and stir.

Freeze in ice trays or other container.

Nannan used to add chopped strawberries or crushed pineapple to hers. Use your imagination.

FALL

D eep in the swamps and along the bayous of south Louisiana, the leaves of baldcypress trees turn an earthy sienna and drop into the many murky waterways. Spindly pecan trees that flourish in the humid flatlands begin to shed their brown, brittle leaves. Only the giant graceful live oaks retain most of their foliage while showering the earth with thousands of acorns. Hunters, fishermen and trappers prepare their camps for the coming season, cleaning and oiling their guns, readying their decoys, and working on the small skiffs that have been in storage during the off-season. Flocks of waterfowl fly overhead as they find their way from Canada to the warmer waters of Louisiana.

Here in the Deep South, where many Northerners believe there is little change between seasons, autumn is creeping on *la prairie tremblante*, along the banks of the bayous that reach out like many fingers toward the Gulf of Mexico, and in the great Atchafalaya Basin, surrounded by its miles and miles of levees.

The Bienvenu and Broussard children, first cousins, seem to be enjoying a family gathering at our home in St. Martinville circa 1949. First row, left to right, are Billy Broussard, my little sister Edna Marie Bienvenu (in stroller) and me (sitting on the ground). My big brother Henri Clay is behind the stroller, and next to him is Curt Broussard Jr.

The Hunt: A Male Rite of Passage

The millions of acres of marshland that make up much of the coastline of Louisiana appear monotonous at first glance. The swaying marsh grass interspersed with serene water pools gives an illusion of sameness. The landscape is not broken by trees or solid ground. It's neither land nor sea, but a combination of both. An occasional whiff of sea salt and air wafts through as a gentle wind blows from the Gulf.

This seemingly desolate area lying between the swamps and the Gulf is actually a place of teeming wildlife – fish, crustaceans and waterfowl.

Long before the first brisk north wind of a cold front moves into the lowlands, avid hunters are preparing for the coming hunting season. Overhead, flocks of green-winged teal, mallards and pintails can be seen flying in loose V formations. By the time the cold winter winds blow through south Louisiana, honking blue geese and snow geese will join the migrating ducks, swooping down on the feeding grounds of the marsh.

To many men of south Louisiana, hunting is an important ritual of manhood. Even those who are not passionate about hunting will often find themselves part of a group that heads to the camp on any given Friday afternoon during the hunting season.

I have often wondered what is so magical about this time spent together in usually cold and primitive quarters. The lives of my father and brothers revolved around the duck camp. There seems to be a combination of special camaraderie and of sharing the spoils of the hunt in their makeshift kitchens. I have heard countless stories about the camp, the tales of the hunt, and the food prepared and eaten. Gather together a group of men and listen to them tell their stories. It's entertainment of the highest form.

A young man once tried to explain to me his experience, and I offer you his narrative:

"There are several rites of passage that every young man in south Louisiana must go through en route to manhood. Eating raw oysters, killing a buck, and mastering the art of frogging are, of course, all part of that ritualistic experience. There is one ritual, however, that many consider to be the most sacred of all – cooking supper for a group of men at the camp.

"First, it must be understood that people in south Louisiana, myself included, tend to associate everything with food.

"For example, I once heard a television anchorman ask his audience if they could remember what happened on November 22, 1963. My answer immediately sprang to mind: That was the day that my Aunt Tootie made the best turtle sauce piquante that I've ever tasted. I was humbled when I heard the anchorman continue. It seems that November 22, 1963 was the day President John F. Kennedy was assassinated. I was a mere youngster then, so I forgave myself.

"In case you haven't caught on to the food association game, let me explain further.

"One day, a friend of mine came to my office to ask if I wanted to go goose hunting with him at 'Shot's' camp in Lake Arthur. I was excited about the proposition, but rather than envisioning graceful flights of specks and snows, I wondered what we would eat the night before the hunt.

"Being a stickler for details, I began to plan a menu.

"First, I scanned my brain for a reference point. Like a newly made slab of hogshead cheese, a thought congealed in my mind. I remembered back to that cold December night when I crossed the sacred bridge that separated men from boys. It was at 'Goat' Romero's camp in Kaplan. The men had gone out for an afternoon hunt leaving me, a 15-year-old boy, with two feathered French ducks with which to make supper. I poked around the ice chests and pantry searching for familiar ingredients to make a gumbo. I found all of the ingredients I needed to make the following:

Duck, Oyster & Andouille Gumbo

Serves 6

2 ducks (which I cleaned and plucked)
Salt, black pepper, and cayenne pepper
1½ cups of all-purpose flour
1½ cups of vegetable oil
2 cups of chopped green bell peppers
3 cups of chopped onions
6 to 8 cups of hot water or chicken stock
2½ pounds of andouille sausage, cut
    crosswise into ¼-inch slices
2 dozen oysters and their liquor
1 bunch of green onions, chopped

Cut up the ducks (as you would cut up a chicken for frying) and season generously with salt, black pepper and cayenne.

Brown the duck pieces in a small amount of oil in a big black iron pot over medium-high heat. Transfer the ducks to a platter and set aside.

Pour out the pan drippings and wipe the pot clean with paper towels.

In the same iron pot, make a dark roux with the flour and oil. Once the roux is just the right nutty-brown color, add the bell peppers and onions, and cook, stirring, until they are wilted and lightly golden, about 10 minutes.

Return the browned ducks to the mixture and slowly add enough hot water or chicken stock to cover them. Add the andouille sausage and cook, stirring occasionally, on a very low heat for three hours.

The oysters, their liquor, and the green onions should be added just before serving.

"Before we left for the hunt, a reliable source told me that a meal is incomplete unless it includes at least four starches. With this in mind, I accompanied my Duck, Oyster & Andouille Gumbo with rice, potato salad, hot crusty French bread, and baked sweet potatoes. For those of you who don't adhere to the four-starch philosophy, the potato salad can be omitted.

"After the last bites of food were washed down with hearty burgundy I knew that the meal was a success and that I had entered the bonds of manhood, for Mr. Goat said out loud, *'Leon, tu n'es pas un petit bébé. Tu es un grand homme maintenant.'*"

O h, the sweet joys of arriving at man-hood.

The young man's story did give me a clue to the mystery of the hunt. Not long after he told me his story, I woke one morning just as the fog was clearing from the nearby marsh. In the distance I could see figures clad in various types of garb, including but not limited to tattered jeans, boots of rubber and canvas, and caps and hats of all colors and designs. There was a profusion of camouflage jackets and vests.

I ventured forth to investigate. I tread lightly on the fallen brown leaves and approached the group. Calling out a warm greeting, I realized, when their surprised faces turned my way, that I was intruding on the ritualistic building of duck blinds.

They waved shyly, and without a word, I retraced my steps. I felt like I had disturbed sacred ground.

On my walk home, I thought about these goings-on. These robust men haul out mud boats, air out and clean camps, and stock them with supplies. The old black iron pots used for cooking are oiled down. The assortment of eating utensils such as plates, mugs and trays – many of which sport a hunting scene, the face of a black lab, or a duck in flight – are dusted off.

Decoys are retrieved from canvas sacks, then they are tied, weighted and marked with the owner's identification. Shotguns are cleaned and oiled, and a small fortune is spent on ammunition – "shells" are the preferred word, I think.

This sounds like a lot of work, but the guys seem to love it. The truth is, they probably love getting ready for the hunt more than they do the actual hunt. I will never understand how it could be fun to get up before dawn in an ice-cold camp, walk through the wind, rain and mud, then sit in a wet duck blind. I know for a fact that I would go into deep depression if, after doing all of the above, I wound up not bringing in a bird. Yet hordes of men go through this week after week during hunting season.

And, if I've figured correctly, this is no cheap hobby. There's the gear, the guns, shells, licenses, decoys, the cost of the lease for the hunting land, boats, food and drink, and possible money losses at the card table. I'll bet many women have figured that the money spent on hunting season could very well pay for a full-length mink coat, a diamond necklace, or a trip to the Bahamas. Of course, there is the enjoyment of the spoils of the hunt. I am one of the first to say there's nothing better than a roasted duck dinner, or a good sausage and goose gumbo.

Because I come from a family of hunters I thought I'd had birds cooked just about every way possible. But one day an old neighbor who has always shared his catches from the sea – speckled trout, crabs, shrimp, flounder – stopped by with a real treat.

When I opened the door to his grinning face, he was holding up a carefully wrapped package. I gleefully asked him what might be in this beautifully wrapped brown paper bag. With a great flourish he opened the bag, and there between layers of wax paper were six fine duck breasts. I could see he had cut the breasts away from the bone as skillfully as a surgeon. In a minute he had taken over the kitchen, and I was directed to sit on a stool in the corner while he prepared our evening treat.

Grilled Duck Breasts

Makes 2 servings

8 tablespoons (1 stick) of butter
1 tablespoon of Worcestershire sauce
1 garlic clove, finely minced
¾ cup of thinly sliced fresh mushrooms
6 duck breasts, removed from the bone
   and skinned
Salt, black pepper and cayenne pepper,
   to taste
6 bacon strips

Melt the butter in a saucepan and add the Worcestershire, garlic, and mushrooms. Cook, stirring gently, until the mushrooms are slightly soft, about a minute. Remove from the heat.

Light a fire in the barbecue pit and allow the coals to get glowing red-hot. While you're waiting, rub the duck breasts generously with salt, black pepper and cayenne. Carefully wrap each breast with a strip of bacon, securing it with toothpicks. Let the breasts stand at room temperature. You might want to take this time to fix a green salad with a creamy spicy dressing and some wild rice cooked with a handful of chopped roasted pecans.

When the coals are ready, grill the breasts quickly, three to four minutes on each side if you like them juicy and with a little red in the meat. Grill longer if you prefer your meat well done. Baste with the butter and mushroom sauce.

To serve, place the breasts on toasted slices of bread and pour the remaining butter and mushroom sauce over each breast. You've never tasted better!

While my friend and I savored our dinner and watched the coals die down, I reminisced about my father's craze for hunting.

During the season, my father was a madman. I remember many times when Papa arrived at home, rushing from his newspaper office, crashing through the kitchen door as though a herd of wild horses were after him, shouting with glee, "A cold front is on the way. Perfect duck hunting weather!"

We would all dash off in different directions. Papa would go directly to the hall closet for his worn suitcase. Mama would throw down mothball-scented blankets kept in an overhead storage closet. My brothers would gather shotguns and shells from the gun cabinet, and my sister and I would stuff the gear into the tattered grip. By then, Papa was pulling on his long johns with one hand and stuffing shotgun shells into his hunting jacket with the other.

In short order he was climbing into his old red pickup truck, and with a grin on his face shouting, "I'll see y'all when I see y'all!"

That meant not to look for him until either he had shot his limit or the weather had turned into one of those clear bluebird days so common after a cold front moves through.

It was quiet in the kitchen after he departed. Mama would sigh and murmur, "Guess we'll be eating ducks and geese for the next few months."

It was a yearly ritual that announced hunting season was at its peak. I was always happy because I like few things better than the aroma of roasting ducks. Mama has a foolproof recipe. It's simple and can be cooked along with *topinambours*, otherwise known as Jerusalem artichokes, ground artichokes, or sunchokes. Her roast duck dinner usually includes potatoes of some kind and a Louisiana version of WALDORF SALAD. *GATEAU DE SIROP* (a syrup cake) is a must for dessert. It's a dinner she usually reserves for Sunday afternoon.

While she performs her magic at the stove, family and friends enjoy a cold beer or chilled wine and a few bites of boudin – a Cajun sausage made with ground pork, rice, herbs and spices.

Rhena's Roast Duck

Makes 4 servings

4 teal ducks or 2 mallard or pintail ducks, cleaned and rinsed in cool water
3 large garlic cloves, peeled and thinly sliced
Salt and cayenne pepper, to taste
3 cups of coarsely chopped green bell peppers
2 cups of coarsely chopped onions
½ cup of dry sherry
All-purpose flour
4 thick bacon strips
1 cup of chicken broth or water
8 ounces of fresh button mushrooms, wiped clean, stemmed and thinly sliced (optional)
1 pound of *topinambours* (Jerusalem artichokes), skinned

The night before you want to cook the ducks, make slits in the duck breasts with a sharp knife. Insert the slivers of garlic into the slits. Rub the outsides and the cavities of the ducks with a generous amount of salt and cayenne. Stuff the cavities with a mixture of the chopped green peppers and onions. Place the birds in a deep bowl or pan and add any remaining peppers and onions. Pour in the dry sherry. Cover and refrigerate overnight.

The next day, drain and reserve the marinade. Preheat the oven to 350 degrees. Dust each duck liberally with flour and set aside. Cook the bacon in a large iron pot or Dutch oven just until crisp and drain on paper towels. Set aside.

Over medium heat, brown the birds in the bacon grease (from the fried bacon), turning often until they are evenly browned. Add one cup of water or chicken broth and cook for 10 minutes. Lay the reserved bacon strips over the duck breasts.

Add the reserved marinade, cover and bake, basting occasionally with the pan drippings, until the ducks are tender, one to one and a half hours. (Note: Add more water or chicken broth if the pan drippings become too dry.)

Add the mushrooms and *topinambours*, cover, and cook until the *topinambours* are fork-tender, about 30 minutes.

Remove the ducks from the pan, carve and serve with the rich gravy that has accumulated in the pan.

Cajun Waldorf Salad

Makes 4 servings

1 Granny Smith apple, cored and chopped, skin on
2 Winesap apples, cored and chopped, skin on
1 cup of seedless raisins
½ cup of chopped and roasted pecans
1 tablespoon of fresh lemon juice
Mayonnaise
Shredded lettuce

Toss the first six ingredients together, using just enough mayonnaise to lightly coat the apples. Serve on a bed of shredded lettuce.

Gateau De Sirop

Makes 1 cake to serve 6 to 8

2 tablespoons of butter
1 large egg
1 cup of pure cane syrup
2 cups of all-purpose flour
1 teaspoon of baking soda
1 cup of boiling water
1 cup of pecan halves
Whipped cream

Preheat the oven to 350 degrees.

Put the butter into a 7x11x 2-inch baking pan. Put the pan in the oven just long enough to melt the butter. Remove the pan from the oven and tilt the pan to spread the butter evenly.

Beat the egg in a large mixing bowl. Add the syrup and the flour, and mix well to blend. Add the baking soda to the boiling water and then add this mixture to the syrup/flour mixture. Be careful when adding the baking soda/boiling water mixture as it will bubble.

Pour the batter in the pan, cover the top of the mixture with pecan halves, and bake for 20 minutes.

Serve warm with whipped cream.

Ducks and geese are not the only flying fowl that please the palates of south Louisiana. During early fall the highways between south Louisiana and south Texas are well traveled as sportsmen head for annual white wing dove hunts along the Texas-Mexico border. They return with enough doves to last the winter.

Each year I anxiously wait for someone to share his cache. One year I almost waited in vain, but I did not go without, as I was lucky enough to be invited to dinner by an old beau. Since we had not seen one another in more than ten years, we had a lot of ground to cover, and what better way, he said, than to really get into the nitty-gritty over dinner. It wasn't until we were about to end our telephone conversation and he began giving me directions to his home in Baton Rouge that I realized it was to be dinner *chez nous*, at his house.

Because he was a single parent with a teenager at the time, he thought it easier (for him anyway) for me to go there.

I headed for Baton Rouge in the middle of Hurricane Juan, and while driving through wind and rain I had visions of being drafted to cook dinner for the bachelor father and his son. When I arrived they announced they had defrosted a dozen doves. Well, at least they had gotten that far. And before I could get out of my rain gear they were propelling me to the car saying that we had to go to the grocery store to get the rest of the dinner fixings.

Oh, oh, I thought. I had done my own grocery shopping earlier that day and didn't think I could bear doing it all over again. But these guys had their act together. They told me that all I had to do was push the cart. To watch these two guys shop was entertainment in itself.

As I headed down the produce aisle they stood back and shook their heads with grins on their faces as if to say, "Poor thing just does it all wrong."

I let them take the lead, and in short order the cart was filled with the needed ingredients.

Back at the ranch, I watched them put everything away, something I hate to do. But father and son made a game of it. They played football with the groceries as they put things away. I was beginning to think

My grandfather Lazaire "Pop" Bienvenu, as he appeared circa 1952. Pop founded our family newspaper in 1886. My father Blackie Bienvenu took over after Pop died, and now my brother Henri Clay is editor and publisher of The Teche News.

we women just have the wrong attitude about domestic duties.

With that task out of the way, I was told to just sit back and relax. That sounded too wonderful to be true. My host handed me a drink and pulled out a chair, and I watched him as he chopped vegetables for salad and the dove dish. His son carved out a jack-o-lantern. The roles seemed reversed, but I reveled in this domestic scene. They even set the table.

I was getting a bit restless so I volunteered to fix corn pudding. I just had to show them that I, too, knew something about a kitchen.

I thought I had tasted these birds prepared in every possible manner, but my friend Rick pulled off the best dove dish I've ever had.

Rick's Doves

Makes 4 servings

6 tablespoons of butter
Breasts of 1 dozen doves (hopefully without any shot still in)
3 tablespoons of all-purpose flour
2½ cups of chicken broth, plus 2 cups of water
1 bunch of green onions, chopped
1 large green bell pepper, seeded and chopped
3 garlic cloves, thinly sliced
¼ cup of Worcestershire sauce
2 teaspoons of salt
1 teaspoon of Cajun seasonings (He had his own special blend, but there are several brands available in most markets.)
1 tablespoon of dried thyme leaves
1 teaspoon of Chinese red pepper (or cayenne pepper)
2 bay leaves
½ cup of cream sherry
1 pound of white button mushrooms, wiped clean and stemmed

Heat the butter in a large, heavy pot or Dutch oven over medium heat. Add the dove breasts and brown evenly. Remove the breasts and set aside.

Add the flour to the pot and blend into the pan drippings. Add the chicken broth and water; bring to a rolling boil and cook, stirring, until the mixture becomes thick enough to coat the back of a wooden spoon.

Add the green onions, bell pepper and garlic, and cook for five minutes or until, "It begins to smell good" (his words). Add the Worcestershire sauce, salt, Cajun seasonings, thyme leaves, red pepper, bay leaves, dove breasts and sherry, then reduce the heat to medium-low and cover. The heat has to be high enough so that the gravy makes "slow, tiny bubbles" (again, his words). Simmer until the breasts are fork tender, 40 to 50 minutes.

Add the mushrooms and a dash more of sherry, and cook for another 10 minutes.

Serve over rice.

While the guys dished up the doves, I pulled the corn pudding out of the oven. Dinner was fantastic. The gentlemen had done very well.

Ginja's Corn Pudding

Makes 6 servings

8 tablespoons (1 stick) of butter
2 cups of corn (canned or frozen)
3 tablespoons of all-purpose flour
2 eggs
1 cup of milk
Salt and cayenne pepper, to taste
Two to three dashes of hot sauce
Sweet paprika

Preheat the oven to 350 degrees.

Melt the butter in a saucepan over medium heat and add the corn. Cook, stirring, for 15 minutes. Pour the corn into an electric blender or food processor. Add the remaining ingredients except for the paprika. Blend at medium speed for 30 seconds.

Pour the mixture into a 9x12-inch baking pan. Place the pan into a larger pan containing about one inch of water. Bake until the pudding sets, about 45 minutes.

Remove the pan from the oven and sprinkle the top of the pudding with paprika.

Serve warm.

I also have a great fondness for quail. In fact, while I'm not so entranced about going duck hunting, I think quail hunting is quite civilized. Watching bird dogs with their master "flushing quail" is fascinating. I had occasion, while living and working at Oak Alley Plantation, to become acquainted with yet another aspect of quail.

After I moved into my small cottage on the plantation grounds, I noticed that every afternoon a pickup truck went slowly past my house on the gravel road. It stopped a few hundred feet away at a fenced-in compound consisting of several tin buildings. Out of the truck would emerge one, sometimes two or three ruggedly handsome gentlemen.

For a week or so I watched this recurring scene from my screened-in front porch. After their arrival the men would reach into an ice chest in the back of the pickup and pull out ice cold cans of beer. I thought the scene would have made a great beer commercial.

I watched the dark-haired men unlatch the gate and head for the buildings. And for about an hour or so, they would work quietly, sometimes talking good-naturedly with one another. Occasionally I'd hear a great roar of laughter.

One day I couldn't stand it. I had to investigate. I carried a few cold beers with me as a friendly gesture. I tapped at the gate and called out a greeting. Three tanned, brown-eyed faces peeped out from behind one of the doors and beckoned me to come in.

I walked into a warm room where hundreds – no, thousands – of tiny, tiny birds were contained in a low fenced-in pen. My new friends, the Rodrigues, with great sweeps of their arms, introduced me to their newly hatched quail.

What a sight! The chirping chicks were so little I could hold ten or so in my cupped hands. I leaned against the tin wall and watched these men gently checking the feeders, the heat lamps and the watering troughs. I learned this was a hobby of the father and his two sons. They are all bird hunters, so naturally they needed to work their dogs, and what better way than to have your own source of birds. They also supplied other hunters in Louisiana and Mississippi with birds with which to work their dogs.

Of course, too, when the quail were grown, the Rodrigues cleaned a mess of quail to bring home for supper. I was the lucky recipient of a few dozen several months later, and one of the sons gave me his recipe.

Keith's Smothered Quail

Makes 4 servings

1 dozen quail, dressed
Salt, black pepper and cayenne pepper, to taste
6 tablespoons of butter or vegetable oil
1½ cups of chicken broth or water
3 cups of chopped onions

Season the quail generously with the salt, black pepper and cayenne.

Heat the butter or oil in a large, heavy pot or Dutch oven over medium heat. Add the quail and brown evenly.

Add the water or chicken broth and the onions. Stir, then cover and simmer on medium-low heat until the quail are tender, two to three hours. Add more broth or water if the gravy becomes too dry.

Keith suggested serving the quail over rice, and I suggest having lots of hot French bread and cold beer to wash it all down.

Fried Quail

Makes 2 servings

4 quail, dressed
4 bacon strips
2 cups of milk
1/3 cup of all-purpose flour
1 cup of yellow cornmeal
1 teaspoon of salt
1/4 teaspoon of black pepper
1/4 teaspoon of cayenne pepper
Vegetable oil for deep-frying

Wrap the birds with the bacon and secure with toothpicks. Soak the birds in the milk for a couple of hours in the refrigerator.

Remove the quail from the milk and gently pat dry. Combine the flour with the cornmeal in a shallow dish and season with the salt, black pepper and cayenne.

Heat the oil in a deep, heavy pot (or electric fryer) to 350 degrees. Coat the quail evenly with the flour/cornmeal mixture, and deep-fry until golden brown. Drain on paper towels.

Serve them on a cold winter's morning with biscuits, cane syrup and hash brown potatoes spiced up with a few green onions, and you've got a winner.

Fried quail are wonderful for breakfast, but they are also great when served for dinner and accompanied by special side dishes. I particularly like wild rice with birds and game.

An excellent cook and a dear friend, Dick Torres, gave me his recipe for this delightful rice dish. A whole head of steamed cauliflower sprinkled with grated cheddar cheese is a nice complement to the wild rice and fried quail.

Wild Rice Torres

Makes 8 servings

1 pound of pork breakfast sausage, fresh pork sausage, or Italian sausage removed from the casings and crumbled
2 boxes of wild rice mix, cooked according to package directions
¼ cup of chopped green onions
1 cup of seedless raisins
1 cup of roasted pecans or walnuts, coarsely chopped
Salt and cayenne pepper, to taste

Brown the breakfast sausage, pork or Italian sausage in a large skillet, and drain off the excess fat.

Add the sausage to the pot of cooked wild rice mix along with the green onions, raisins and nuts. Season to taste. Mix well and serve warm.

Baked Cauliflower

Makes 6 to 8 servings

1 large head of fresh cauliflower, bottom trimmed
Boiling salted water
8 tablespoons (1 stick) of butter, melted
2 cups of grated cheddar cheese
½ cup of seasoned bread crumbs

Preheat the oven to 350 degrees.
Boil the whole head of cauliflower in salted water until slightly tender. Remove from the water and drain well. Place in a shallow baking dish. Drizzle melted butter on top of the cauliflower, then sprinkle with the grated cheese. Top with the bread crumbs.

Bake uncovered until the cheese melts, about 15 minutes.

Cut into wedges to serve.

One game bird we do not have in Louisiana is pheasant. A neighbor of mine in New Orleans hailed from upstate New York and was known as "The Avid Sportsman." He hunted in just about every state of the union, fished from Tennessee to Colorado, and came home with everything from wild turkey to bass, including some things I never heard of.

His freezer was a sight to behold. One evening as I dug around trying to find a bag of ice in his oversize appliance, I was hit on the head by a package containing pheasants. As he administered first aid to the bump on my forehead and begged forgiveness, he offered to share the unfamiliar birds with me.

It was more like a challenge.

"Take the six pheasants. Make a grocery list of what we'll need to prepare them, and we'll invite some friends to share a meal with us."

With the cold pack still on my head, I stumbled home with my gift. It wasn't until I came to my senses the next day that I realized I had no idea what to do with these things.

I pulled out one of my James Beard cookbooks. Mr. Beard had a few recipes, but they didn't strike me right. Julia Child had a couple, but one called for the "plumage" which, of course, I didn't have. Nor did I have the right accoutrements to "serve under glass."

I got out my stack of treasured *Gourmet* magazines and began flipping through the pages, book after book, since I don't have the indexes for any of my ten-year collection. After skimming through several months, I decided this was, both literally and figuratively, for the birds.

I was getting a little frantic. I then attacked a stack of cookbooks I had shoved on the top shelf of the guest room closet. Ah! Bingo! I found my old Albert Stocki *Splendid Fare*, which I remembered had a great venison recipe. Surely he must have a pheasant recipe. I turned to the index. Peas, pepper slaw, pepperoni, pheasant! Not one, but several recipes were listed. Broth, casserole, cream of – oh, please let there be the perfect one. My shaking fingers found "– with purée of chestnuts." Page 183. I turned the pages quickly – 181, 182, 183.

Page 183 was torn in half. I had the ingredients but no directions.

Time was getting short. Guests were expected in four hours. My friend was at the door ready to go to the supermarket, and pheasants weren't the only thing I had to cook. Plus the table wasn't set. *Help!*

"Marcelle," I said to myself. "You are going to have to wing it."

I jotted down a grocery list and shoved my friend out the door. I pulled myself together and eyed the pheasants lying in a pan on the kitchen counter.

"Okay, guys. You had better be wonderful."

The phone rang. It was my friend saying he couldn't find peeled chestnuts. To be honest, I wouldn't know one if I saw one. I told him to forget the chestnuts.

I then decided there wasn't anything mystical about pheasant. They were birds, they had the appearance of large Cornish hens, and I felt that with my basic knowledge of game we would get through this together.

When my friend returned I gave him the tasks of setting the table, arranging some flowers, putting the wine to chill, and selecting music for the evening while I prepared dinner.

Frantic Pheasant

Makes 12 servings

Six 2- to 2½-pound pheasants, dressed
Salt, black pepper, and cayenne pepper, to taste
3 tablespoons of chopped rosemary
12 bacon slices
¾ cup of dry sherry
3 cups of thinly sliced onions
3 celery ribs, chopped
1½ cups of chicken broth
1 cup of heavy cream

Preheat the oven to 450 degrees.

Rub the pheasants with generous amounts of the salt and peppers. Sprinkle the birds with the rosemary.

Wrap two strips of bacon around each bird and place in a roasting pan. Drizzle about half of the dry sherry over the birds and roast for 15 minutes.

Add the onions, celery and chicken broth and reduce the oven temperature to 400 degrees. Roast until the wings pull away easily from the breast, about 45 minutes.

Remove the pan from the oven. Transfer the pheasants to a platter and keep warm.

Place the roasting pan on top of the stove, add the rest of the sherry and the heavy cream, and bring to a boil. Reduce the heat to simmer and allow the sauce to thicken, stirring constantly.

Cut the pheasants in halves or quarters (depending on size) and pour the sauce over the birds before serving.

One of our guests brought some real honest-to-goodness wild rice, which we served along with BABY LIMA BEAN PURÉE.

Baby Lima Bean Purée

Makes 6 servings

4 bacon strips, cut into 1-inch pieces
1 cup of chopped onions
1 pound of dried baby green lima beans
6 cups of chicken broth
1 cup of sour cream
Salt and black pepper, to taste

Fry the bacon with the onions in a medium-size saucepan over medium heat until the bacon is slightly crisp and the onions are wilted.

Add the lima beans and chicken broth. Cook, stirring occasionally, until the beans are tender and creamy, about an hour and a half.

Place the beans and sour cream in a food processor fitted with a metal blade and purée until smooth. Season with salt and black pepper.

Dinner rolls with currant jelly and a slightly chilled *Beaujolais* rounded out our meal. I had become so frantic with the pheasants I had no dessert, so we settled on a bag of Oreos. My friends are easily pleased.

My sportsman friend is really quite generous. Not too long after the pheasant escapade, I came home to find a message on my answering machine. He related, at the sound of the beep, that he was off to the wilds for a few days and he anticipated returning with heaven only knew what, and would I like several pounds of venison sausage that was in his gargantuan freezer, since he would need the space when he returned.

I knew where an extra key to his house was hidden and I had the alarm combination, but I felt like a burglar, armed with my paper sacks. Once inside I filled my sacks with the sausage, re-alarmed, re-locked and ran home with my bounty.

The venison sausage would come in handy as I was expecting a house full of guests for the weekend and had been beating my brains as to what kinds of "pot" dishes I could dream up to feed the hungry hordes.

When the packages defrosted, I realized the sausage was not in links, but was simply the ground venison, seasoned, but not stuffed into casings. Not to worry, I could do lots of things with this. I had several pounds of lean ground beef so I decided to combine the two and make a couple of items that could be easily heated up during the weekend.

As most of my friends know, I am a "red gravy" freak. Any sauce made with tomatoes makes my heart throb. The mere thought of having a pot of red sauce blurping on the stove is my idea of ecstasy!

Venison Spaghetti

Makes 6 servings

1 pound of ground venison
1 pound of lean ground beef
3 tablespoons of olive oil
1½ cups of chopped onions
1½ cups of chopped green bell peppers
3 celery ribs, chopped
6 garlic cloves, chopped
2 cups of canned diced tomatoes
1 (6-ounce) can of tomato paste
1 (8-ounce) can of tomato sauce
½ cup of dry red wine
½ teaspoon of dried oregano leaves
½ teaspoon of dried basil leaves
Pinch or two of ground anise
Salt and cayenne pepper, to taste

Brown the meat in the olive oil in a large heavy pot or Dutch oven over medium heat. Add the onions, bell peppers, celery and garlic, and cook, stirring, until the vegetables are soft and golden, eight to ten minutes.

Add the tomatoes, tomato paste and tomato sauce, and cook, stirring to prevent sticking and burning, for 20 minutes. Add the wine and the seasonings, reduce the heat to medium-low, and cook, stirring occasionally, for two hours.

Add a little water or beef broth if the mixture becomes too dry.

Serve with your favorite kind of pasta.

I still had some venison left, so I kept going. I was on a roll!

Venison Chili

Makes 6 servings

3 tablespoons of vegetable oil
1 pound of ground venison
1 pound of lean ground beef
½ pound of lean ground pork
1½ cups of chopped onions
2 fresh jalapeño peppers, seeded and chopped (Wear rubber gloves to protect your hands.)
2 (15-ounce) cans of red kidney beans (Purée some in the food processor to give the chili a creamy richness.)
2 cups of canned diced tomatoes
1 (6-ounce) can of tomato paste
2 to 3 tablespoons of chili powder (use according to taste)
(I had a small jar of piquante sauce hanging around so I threw that in, too.)
Salt and cayenne pepper, to taste

Heat the oil in a large, heavy pot or Dutch oven over medium heat. Add the ground meats and cook, stirring, until all the pink has disappeared.

Add the onions and jalapeño peppers, and cook, stirring, until the vegetables are very soft, eight to ten minutes.

Add the kidney beans (both whole and puréed), the tomatoes and tomato paste. Season to taste with chili powder, salt and pepper.

Reduce the heat to medium-low and simmer, stirring occasionally, for about two hours.

During the weekend, one of my guests got creative and poured the chili over a thick bed of large corn chips in a deep baking dish. Then he topped it all with a pound of grated cheddar cheese and more chopped jalapeño peppers. Not bad for a midnight snack. Not so good for your stomach.

La Roulaison (The Sugarcane Harvest)

One fall night as I closed down the house for the evening, I heard the wind whistling as it raced through the narrow passageway between the patio and the hedges. Leaves whirled and bare branches clicked against the tin roof, making an eerie sound. I smelled the acrid smoke from nearby cane fields and in the distance I heard the churning sounds of the sugar mill. *La roulaison*, the sugarcane harvest, was in full swing in south Louisiana.

Early the next morning, at first light, I pulled on a warm-up suit and decided it was the perfect time to "make a little pass" through the countryside to investigate the harvest activity.

Workers were already in the fields. Cane trucks and wagons were being loaded to bursting with long stalks of cane. Men working the cranes warmed themselves by a small fire they built on the headland. Loaded trucks stood in line at the entrance of the St. Mary Sugar Co-op near Jeanerette. The smokestacks belched steam, and the sickly-sweet smell of the cane being processed made me remember the cold mornings I devoured biscuits, *PAIN PERDU* (lost bread), and *COUCHE COUCHE* (fried cornmeal) drowning in dark, rich cane syrup.

I also remember coming home from school in the afternoons and sharing with Mama a small bowl of *la cuite* into which pecans had been stirred. Sometimes we stuffed the "nose" of a French bread with it along with a glob of sweet butter. Ah, the good old days before we had to worry about too much sugar and too many calories!

As I watched the activity at the mill, I decided it had been much too long since I had been inside a sugar mill. Years ago, Papa took me along on his weekly excursions to the St. John mill near St. Martinville, where he would share a hot cup of coffee with the mill foreman while they talked about the year's crop. Sometimes the men who fed the cane crushers would peel me a piece of cane to chew on while Papa went on with his business. After chewing the stringy stick of cane and rolling it around my mouth to get every drop of sweet juice, I spit it out like the men taught me. Mama would have rolled her eyes for sure if she knew Papa let me do this in public!

I decided to call an old childhood buddy, Brannan B. "Burt" Beyt Jr., who was the general manager of the St. Mary mill. I asked him if he had time to take an old friend on a tour through the mill. He gladly agreed to meet me the next day. Before he hung up he reminded me to wear old clothes and old shoes.

Before we began our trek, he pulled out an illustration to show me on paper what we were to encounter. It is rather complicated, but basically what happens is this: The cane that is brought in from the fields is loaded onto a conveyor belt, where it is literally ground with sharp knives, then dumped into a powerful shredder that extracts the juice. Hot water is sprayed over the crushed cane to extract every bit of the sweet juice. The juice is funneled into the evaporator tanks for processing. The fiber and pulp, called *bagasse*, is fed into furnaces to create the steam to run the turbines in the mill.

The raw juice heads for the clarification process. There, in huge tanks, it is boiled under pressure to separate the juice from any solids. The clear juice comes off the top and goes into an evaporator and is boiled again under extreme pressure. A thick syrup emerges. It is at this point that, in extreme vacuum heat, the sugar crystals are extracted and the molasses is drained off. The raw sugar is carried off onto a conveyor belt to what Burt calls the "sugar palace," a building that can hold 32 million pounds of sugar. It was like walking through fairyland, because the mountains of light brown sugar sparkled and glistened as the natural light from the doors and windows bounced off the crystals. I wanted to jump right in.

From the sugar palace, the sugar is loaded onto barges, which takes the sugar to refineries, where it becomes what you use in your coffee, on your cereal, or to cook with.

As we walked away from the deafening

noises of the mill, Burt remarked that I looked a sight. I had *bagasse* in my hair, my hands were sticky from running them through the slightly moist raw sugar, and syrup and molasses dripped down my face. I almost had to be hosed down before I got into my car – but what fun it had been! I couldn't wait to get home to make a batch of something on which to put cane syrup, or find a way to use the wonderful *la cuite.*

I thanked Burt with a sugary handshake and drove off into the sunset, only to find myself behind a slow-moving, heavily loaded sugarcane truck. For once I didn't mind being slowed down in the traffic. It gave me some time to think of all the things I could do when I got home to my kitchen.

I made a stop at the grocery store to pick up several cans of that wonderful pure ribbon cane syrup made by the Steen family in Abbeville. I was even fortunate enough to find some of their *la cuite,* which is available only in limited quantities each year.

Gingerbread

Makes 12 servings

½ cup of solid vegetable shortening
½ cup of sugar
1 cup of pure cane syrup
2 eggs
2½ cups of sifted all-purpose flour
1 teaspoon of salt
2 teaspoons of baking powder
½ teaspoon of baking soda
1 teaspoon of ground ginger
1 teaspoon of ground cinnamon
1 cup of hot water

Preheat the oven to 350 degrees.

Line a 9-inch baking pan with parchment or wax paper. Set aside.

Cream the shortening in a large bowl. Gradually add the sugar and cream to the mixture until it is fluffy and smooth. Blend in the syrup. Beat in the eggs, one at a time.

In another large bowl, sift together the flour, salt, baking powder, baking soda and spices. Add the dry ingredients to the creamed mixture alternately with the hot water.

Pour the mixture into the prepared pan and bake until a cake tester comes out clean, about 40 minutes.

Remove the pan from the oven and cool for about 10 minutes before cutting into pieces to serve.

Fruit Cake

½ cup of vegetable oil
¾ cup of *la cuite*
2 eggs
1½ cups of sifted all-purpose flour
½ teaspoon of baking powder
1 teaspoon of salt
1 teaspoon of ground cinnamon
1 teaspoon of ground allspice
½ teaspoon of ground cloves
½ cup of fruit juice (apple, pineapple or orange)
1 pound (2 cups) of candied fruit and peels
1 box of dates, chopped
1 box of candied pineapple, chopped
½ cup of Muscat raisins
2½ cups of chopped nuts

Preheat the oven to 275 degrees.

Combine the oil, *la cuite* and eggs in a large mixing bowl and beat for two minutes.

Sift together one cup of the flour with the baking powder, salt and spices. Stir into the oil mixture. Add the fruit juice.

Mix the remaining one-half cup of flour with the fruit and nuts. Combine this mixture with the batter and mix well.

Pour the batter into loaf pans lined with wax paper. Use 8x4½x2-inch loaf pans or a tubular pan. Bake until the cake sets well, two and a half to three hours.

Remove from the oven and cool.

When cool, the cake may be decorated with candied fruit such as cherries or pineapple. The cake should be stored in an airtight container.

Broiled Grapefruit

Cut grapefruits in half. Cut around each section, loosening fruit from membrane. (Do not cut around outer edge of fruit; cut only within the membrane of each segment.)

Top each grapefruit half with one tablespoon of cane syrup.

Place on broiler rack three inches from heat. Broil until the grapefruit is slightly browned and heated through, about three minutes.

My aunts, uncles and mother took time out from eating and visiting at a family gathering at our home in St. Martinville sometime around 1949. Left to right are Curtis "Cowboy" Broussard, Grace Broussard, Mama (Rhena), A.P. Broussard, Lois Broussard and George Broussard.

The sun was setting as I finished my cooking project. I enjoyed my goodies as I listened once again to the churning noises of the nearby sugar mill.

The next morning I realized that I'd dreamed about sugarcane all night, so I decided to indulge myself by preparing my childhood breakfast favorites, *PAIN PERDU* (lost bread) and *COUCHE COUCHE* (fried cornmeal). Heaven on a chilly morning!

Pain Perdu

Makes 4 servings

2 eggs, beaten
1 cup of milk
½ cup of sugar
¼ teaspoon of vanilla extract
8 slices of day-old bread (I prefer French bread.)
½ cup of vegetable oil or butter

Blend the eggs, milk, sugar and vanilla together in a bowl.

Dip the slices of bread in the mixture, coating both sides evenly.

Heat the oil or butter in a skillet over medium heat. Fry the bread, one or two pieces at a time, until golden brown, turning once.

Serve warm.

You can be creative and top the *pain perdu* with powdered sugar, cinnamon or honey. My friend Cathy used to put all of the above plus fig preserves on her "lost bread." I think cane syrup is best!

Couche Couche

Makes 6 servings

½ cup of vegetable oil or lard
2 cups of yellow cornmeal
1½ teaspoons of salt
1 teaspoon of baking powder
1½ cups of milk or water

Heat the oil or lard in a large, heavy skillet. Combine the cornmeal, salt, baking powder and milk or water, and pour into the heated skillet. Give it a couple of good stirs, lower the heat, cover, and let it steam for 15 to 20 minutes.

My father loved his *couche couche* with hot coffee milk poured over it. Mama used salt and black pepper, Tante May used to put fried eggs on top of hers, and me, well, I just drown my *couche couche* in butter and cane syrup.

La Boucherie

Every year while my grandfather, whom everyone called Pop-Pete, was overseer at Burton Plantation near St. Martinville he held a *boucherie*. Translated literally, *la boucherie* means the slaughtering and butchering of an animal, usually a pig, which has been fattened for the kill. Sometimes there were several pigs to be slaughtered, and family members, friends and workers on the plantation gathered early in the morning, prepared to work until dusk.

Either the night before or just before dawn, the men killed the animal, slit its throat and tied it up by its hind legs to allow the blood to drain out. The blood was saved to make *boudin rouge*, a sausage made with ground pork, seasonings, rice and the blood. The pig was then shorn of its hair and cleaned well for the butchering.

The head and feet were kept to make *fromage de tête de cochon*, hogshead cheese. The fat outer skin was cut into cubes to fry as *gratons,* or cracklings. This was done in a large black iron pot under which a roaring fire was kept alive throughout the day. The cracklings were heavily seasoned with salt and cayenne pepper, and as soon as they were cool enough everyone grabbed handfuls to gobble up while they went about their work.

The butchers, with their large, sharp knives, went about cutting out the roasts and pork chops, passing bits of meat on to the women who then made the *boudin rouge* and the *boudin blanc*. The intestines were cleaned and stuffed with ground pork, spices and rice to make the spicy sausages so dear to the Cajun's heart. Even the stomachs of the pigs were used to make *chaudin*.

One of my favorites of the *boucherie* was *le reintier de cochon*, or BACKBONE STEW, which was served later in the day with rice, baked sweet potatoes or smothered turnips.

Late in the afternoon everyone was given his or her share of the pig to take home. By the glowing fires – for most of the work was done outside on long wooden tables – everyone would linger for a while, relaxing while listening to the music of the men who had brought along fiddles and accordions. Old French songs were hummed,

and those with any energy left would do a few jigs in the dust under the oak trees.

You don't have to go through all the commotion of having a *boucherie* to have some of these delights. Take heart and don't worry about having to slay a pig. You can stir up a classic pork stew in the comfort of your kitchen.

Backbone Stew (*Reintier De Cochon*)

Makes 10 to 12 servings

One 6-pound lean pork loin, with bones, cut into chunks
1½ teaspoons of salt
1/2 teaspoon of cayenne pepper
2/3 cup of all-purpose flour
1/2 cup of vegetable oil
2½ cups of chopped onions
3 celery ribs, chopped
2 cups of chopped green bell peppers
4 to 5 cups of beef stock or water
1/4 cup of chopped parsley

Season the pork chunks with the salt and pepper. Roll the pork in the flour to coat evenly. Shake off any excess flour.

Heat the oil in a large, heavy pot or Dutch oven over medium heat. Add the pork chunks and brown evenly. Add the onions, celery and bell peppers. Cook, stirring often, until the vegetables are soft and golden brown, eight to ten minutes.

Add the stock or water and bring to a boil. Stir and loosen any brown bits in the pot. Reduce the heat to medium-low, cover, and cook, stirring occasionally, until the pork is very tender and is falling off the bones, about two hours.

Serve over rice and sprinkle with chopped parsley.

There are some who say a backbone stew can be made like a *fricassée*. To do so, make a roux with equal parts of oil and flour (1½ cups of oil and flour), then add the vegetables (same amounts as above) and beef stock.

If a backbone isn't available, thinly sliced pork chops can be substituted. Add to the roux and vegetable mixture. Add two to three cups of beef stock or water, and allow to cook until the meat is tender.

If you are really interested in preparing *chaudin*, contact your butcher or slaughterhouse and ask for a pig's stomach.

Chaudin

Makes 6 to 8 servings

1 pig's stomach
2½ pounds of lean ground pork
1½ cups of chopped onions
1 cup of chopped green bell peppers
2 teaspoons of minced garlic
1 bunch of green onions, finely chopped
3 slices of bread, broken into pieces and soaked in a little milk
1 sweet potato (raw), peeled and diced
½ cup of chopped celery
1 egg, beaten
½ teaspoon of cayenne pepper
½ teaspoon of black pepper
1 teaspoon of salt
3 tablespoons of cooking oil
2 cups of water (or more as needed)

Clean the pig's stomach well, picking off any bits of fat clinging to the lining or surface. Soak it in enough cold water to cover, for two hours, then rinse and pat dry. Combine all the remaining ingredients, except the oil and water, in a large mixing bowl.

Use your hands to mix the ingredients together. You might want to fry a little of the mixture in a small skillet with some oil to check for seasonings. Stuff the stomach with the mixture.

With a large needle and heavy thread, sew up the openings. Place the stomach in a heavy iron pot with the heated oil and brown quickly, turning it two or three times.

Add the water and cook, covered, over low heat for about two hours. Uncover and allow most of the water to evaporate to allow the skin of the stomach to brown.

Remove the ponce. Add a little cornstarch to the remaining water to make a gravy. Slice the ponce along with the skin to serve.

I suggest having some hot crusty French bread around to eat along with it.

Louisianians are very particular about the pots and pans they use for cooking, and they take special pride in the heirloom cast-iron Dutch ovens, skillets and griddles that are passed down in families from one cook to another. I have a friend who came into possession of his grandmother's 75-year-old *boucherie* pot – a large, three-footed cast-iron cauldron used to make *gratons*, sometimes known as cracklings or fried pig skins. The making of *gratons* is becoming a lost art because fewer old-fashioned *boucheries* are held in modern south Louisiana.

The *boucherie* pot had been stored for many years in a wash house, where it fell prey to damp and rust. My friend was determined to restore the valuable pot. After many inquiries he found a sugarcane farmer who also had a machine shop and who agreed to clean the pot.

After the pot was cleaned, it had to be cured so that it could be used for cooking. First it was rubbed generously with mineral oil. Mineral oil contains no salt or impurities that can cause rusting. The next step entailed collecting enough oak firewood to make a large fire into which the pot could be placed so that the oil could burn off. The pot was then rubbed several times with more mineral oil applied with Spanish moss. I recommended using the moss because I remembered Papa curing his black iron pots this way.

The only thing left to do was to use the pot to make *gratons*. My friend found a butcher who agreed to cut up pork bellies into 2-inch pieces. We set a date for the *graton*-making and invited friends and family to join us in my yard on the banks of Bayou Teche.

An old-timer heard about my friend's project and came by that day. He brought with him a gallon of rendered hog lard and some advice. The day was gray, windy and chilly – perfect weather for gathering around an outdoor fire.

The work table in the cooking area held a large pan filled with cut up pork bellies. Plenty of salt and cayenne pepper was close at hand. Nearby was a wheelbarrow lined with paper bags on which to drain the *gratons*.

The men built a fire, and we were ready to christen the *boucherie* pot.

Gratons

50 pounds of pork bellies, cut into 2-inch
  squares
1 gallon of rendered hog lard
1 quart of water
Salt and cayenne pepper, to taste

Place the rendered lard, water and pork
bellies into an iron cauldron, stirring often
with a large paddle to prevent sticking.

When the *gratons* start to float and turn
golden brown, quickly remove them from the
oil with a large wire basket. Drain on brown
paper bags and sprinkle generously with salt
and pepper.

Gratons are best served fresh, but they can
be stored in a tightly covered container for
several days.

Note: Do not attempt to prepare *gratons*
on an indoor stove.

We did not want to waste the hot oil,
so into the pot were tossed ten pounds of
thinly sliced pork chops, which took only
a few minutes to cook up brown and crispy.

Fried Pork Chops

15 pounds of thinly sliced pork chops
Salt, black pepper, cayenne pepper, and
  garlic powder, to taste

Season the chops generously and allow to
stand for one hour.

Add the pork chops to hot oil, a few at a
time. Remove and drain on paper bags.

Next we fried 15 pounds of skinned,
thinly sliced sweet potatoes. Drained on
paper towels and sprinkled with cinnamon
and sugar, the sweet potatoes were a great
finale to a wonderful outdoor feast.

Because farmers continue to raise hogs,
pork dishes are often seen on the Sunday
dinner table. Trimmings are used for seasoning vegetables and for making dressings.

Pork is considered to be a delicacy and is
important to Cajun cooking.

Some years ago, after undergoing a
series of dental surgeries, I longed for the
time my mouth would be back in commis-
sion so I could chow down on a succulent
pork tenderloin.

I thought of little else during the several months of painful trips to the dentist's
chair. Everything into my mouth came
through a straw or from a spoon. I didn't
see a fork or knife at my table for weeks.

Mama, who stayed with me during my
convalescence, tried to keep my mind
off the pain. She put me to bed with ice
packs wrapped in fluffy white towels. She
propped me up with all the pillows in the
house and even threw in a couple of my old
teddy bears. She brought me beautiful trays
set with linen tea cloths, bud vases with
tea roses from the garden, newspapers and
magazines, and cups of broth or custard.
She even put my milk shakes in fine crystal
wine glasses. She fixed me creamed potatoes with cheese and soft poached eggs.

As I got better, she puréed pizza and
lima beans. But all I could think of was
pork tenders. To get my mind off food, she
entertained me with coloring books and
paper dolls, just like she used to do when I
was a child.

When I graduated to firmer foods, she
took her leave. When I hugged her good-
bye I asked her to come back in a few
weeks to fix me that pork tenderloin. When
she noticed the tears in my eyes, she promised to return when the dentist gave me a
clean bill of health.

She kept her promise. A month later she
returned with tenderloins tucked in her
basket. She even brought the fixings for her
famous CORN CREOLE. I was in ecstasy
as I gave her full run of the kitchen while I
cut out a new batch of paper dolls she had
brought with her.

She used the recipe from a dear fried of
ours, Adeline McEnery.

Pork Tenders Adeline

Makes 6 servings

2 pork tenders, about 1½ pounds each
1 package of dry zesty Italian salad
  dressing mix
2 tablespoons of olive oil
1 tablespoon of red wine vinegar
2 tablespoons of water
3 green onions, chopped

Combine the dry salad dressing mix, olive oil, vinegar, water and green onions in a blender and pulse several times to blend.

Pour the mixture over the tenderloins and marinate for at least an hour.

Grill over a slow charcoal fire for 25 to 30 minutes, basting with the marinade.

Corn Creole

Makes 6 to 8 servings

3 tablespoons of vegetable oil
1½ cups of chopped onions
1 cup of chopped green bell peppers
2 cups of cream-style corn
1 egg, beaten
2 cups of milk
½ cup of yellow cornmeal
Salt and cayenne pepper, to taste
Fine dried bread crumbs
3 tablespoons of butter, cut into chips

Preheat the oven to 350 degrees. Lightly grease a 9x13-inch baking dish and set aside.

Heat the vegetable oil in a large, heavy pot over medium heat. Add the onions and bell peppers, and cook, stirring, until the vegetables are soft and golden, eight to ten minutes.

Add the cream corn, beaten egg, and milk, and cook, stirring, for five minutes. Add the cornmeal, stir, and allow the mixture to thicken. Season with salt and pepper.

Pour the mixture into the prepared baking dish, sprinkle with bread crumbs and dot with the butter. Bake uncovered until the mixture bubbles and the top is golden brown, 30 to 40 minutes.

Whenever Mama roasted a big pork roast, she often reserved some of the pan drippings and stored them in an airtight jar in the refrigerator. The fat that rose to the top was skimmed off and the gravy was used to enhance this wonderful rice dish.

Dressed Up Rice

Makes 6 servings

4 cups of cooked long-grain white rice
2 celery ribs (with leaves), chopped
8 bacon slices, fried crispy, drained and
  crumbled
1 cup of sliced white button mushrooms
2 tablespoons of chopped pimientos
¼ cup of chopped green bell peppers
¼ cup of chopped green onions
½ cup (or more as needed) of pork gravy
Chopped fresh parsley for garnish

Combine all the ingredients except the parsley in a large saucepan over low heat, adding the pan drippings until everything is well moistened.

Sprinkle with freshly chopped parsley.

With my mouth in better condition than before the surgery, I went on an eating spree. All the weight I had lost was creeping back on, but I didn't care. The holidays were approaching, and I cast my fate to the winds.

I was invited to a round of cocktail parties, wedding receptions and open-house *soirées*. It goes without saying, I ate hundreds of finger sandwiches and pastry shells filled with everything imaginable, and I munched on mounds of chips smothered in a variety of dips.

With my mouth in such fine shape, I was really ready for the next country wedding I attended. I loaded up my small plate with a little dab of everything and found a quiet place to sit down to enjoy what looked like real food. Everything was recognizable except for a richly seasoned dressing-like item. It was easily the best thing on the plate. I determined it had bits of pork in it, but that was as far as I could go.

While I filled my plate with more of the delicious stuff, I asked one of the bridesmaids if she knew what it was. She answered nonchalantly that it was *fare*.

"*Fare?*" I never heard of it. "What's in it? How is it made, and can I get the recipe?"

"Well," she told me, "my mother makes it all the time for weddings. You can make sandwiches with it, too. You know, you can make a sandwich like this (She folded her hand like a pocket) or like this (She

As children, my siblings and I enjoyed going to Banker Plantation and riding in a cart pulled by "Red." Left to right are Henri Clay, me and Edna.

clapped both hands together)."

I caught her drift. I make bologna sandwiches with one piece of bread rolled in half. Major sandwiches I make with two slices of bread.

Anyway, I was enamored with this *fare*. She promised to get me the recipe. In the meantime, I looked up the word in my Ca-jun-French dictionary and found it spelled "*farre*," and it referred to a stuffing of rice dressing used especially with fowl. How-ever, in another section I looked up the word "dressing" and found it spelled *fare* and it referred to jambalaya.

When I questioned Mama, she said she remembered it being pork dressing. My sister-in-law Nancy also remembered the term and said her mother used to make it – and it was so good it rarely made it to the dinner table. She and her brothers used to make sandwiches with it. (I had heard this story before.) If and when it made it to the dinner table, rice was added and sometimes her mother used it for the stuffing of her boudin.

So, as far as I could determine, it can be a dressing, a stuffing, or a sandwich filler.

Mom's Dressing (*Fare* or *Farre*)

Makes about 8 servings

1 whole chicken (about 3½ pounds), skinned and deboned
20 chicken gizzards, cleaned
1 pound of chicken livers
1 bunch of green onions, coarsely chopped
1 cup of chopped onions
1 cup of chopped green bell peppers
1 medium-sized sweet potato (raw), peeled and chopped
1 pound of lean ground beef
1 pound of lean ground pork
¼ cup of vegetable oil
Salt and cayenne pepper, to taste

Grind the chicken meat, gizzards, livers, onions, green pepper and sweet potato in a meat grinder or food processor. Transfer the mixture to a large mixing bowl.

Add the ground beef and ground pork and mix well.

Heat the oil in a large, heavy pot or Dutch oven over medium heat. Add the mixture, stirring until it begins to brown.

When the mixture begins throwing off juice, reduce the heat to low, season with salt and cayenne, cover and cook, stirring occasionally, until the mixture is juicy-moist, 30 to 45 minutes.

At the wedding reception, I had it without any rice added; however, you can add cooked rice for a rice dressing with a different taste. The sweet potato adds just a hint of sweetness. Be creative and try mix-ing it with smothered eggplant or use it for stuffing sweet peppers. Marvelous!

Festival Time

When my hometown newspaper arrives each week, I usually sit right down and read it from front page to last. Like most small town weeklies, it gives the news of who died, babies born in the parish, local football scores, who got married, and who visited with whom. The *Teche News* also holds a very special place in my heart because it's our family newspaper, started by my grandfather Lazaire in 1886. My father took over after Pop died, and now my brother Henri Clay is editor and publisher.

Many afternoons after school found all of us proofreading, folding papers and updating subscriptions. This was where I learned to love the sounds of the presses rolling and how to use the linotype machine. I had printer's ink in my blood!

One week, as I hungrily read each line, I came across some photographs of the annual *chariot* (pronounced sha-ree-o) parade.

The parade has been a yearly event for as long as I can remember and is usually held late in September or early October. This is how it works.

Children of all ages may participate, creating *chariots* in categories which include "fancy box," "plain box" and "floats." For weeks prior to the event children begin raiding their mothers' closets, the local grocery store trash bins, and dry goods stores storage areas, looking for just the right box.

Mama's closet always yielded those fanciful round hat boxes. You know, the ones that are covered with painted pastel flowers and have silk or taffeta handles – very chic.

The grocery store had the big boxes, like the ones bathroom tissue comes in, or the funny boxes in which eggs are packed. At the dry goods stores, we sometimes found long flat dress boxes. The choices were endless. A regular old shoe box could become a box of enchantment.

Then, with the help of parents or older siblings, we would make cutouts on the sides, sometimes in the shapes of half moons, stars or flowers – you name it, whatever your heart desired. Then the cutouts were covered with crepe paper or colored cellophane begged from local florists. A candle was placed inside the box to illuminate the cutouts. Finally, we attached a ribbon or string to the box, enabling us to pull our creation along the sidewalk.

Older children, or children with clever parents, had more elaborate *chariots*. They were called floats. The creative ones would take little red wagons (the kind your parents put you in to go for a ride around the yard) and made them into floats, akin to the large floats usually seen in big parades.

One year I made a float to look like one in the New Iberia Sugarcane Festival parade.

I dressed up all my dolls in evening gowns (made by Mama), then put a box over my wagon, decorated it with colorful crepe paper and small stalks of sugarcane, put a small pocket-size flashlight on each corner, and off I went.

The parade begins at dusk at the church square in the center of St. Martinville, and it is indeed a sight to behold. First of all, it's tricky to keep candles lit if it's a windy evening. Then, if someone doesn't know how to ventilate the boxes, your *chariot* goes up in flames. One year all my sister had at the end of the parade was her string attached to a burnt piece of cardboard.

Another year, a friend of mine, whose father was a general contractor, made an elaborate float. It was a *papier mâché* replica of "The Old Woman Who Lived in a Shoe," and all the children (represented by dolls) fell off along the parade route.

I am glad the tradition has continued, and I read about it in the *Teche News* each year. One year the photographs made me laugh out loud. There was one of a float with what appeared to be a *papier mâché* replica of the Statue of Liberty, but I couldn't tell if the statue was really *papier mâché* or a real child atop the box!

When we were little, we would wait anxiously as the judges made their decision. It was rare that any of us came home with a prize, but, boy, we sure had fun. After the winners were announced, Mama would pile us in the station wagon, along with what was left of our *chariots* and take us home for a late night supper.

While we discussed so and so's *chariot* and lamented that we didn't win, Mama turned on the stove, waved her hands like a bewitching sorceress, and in a few minutes something piping hot was brought to the table.

One late night supper I remember well was WELSH RAREBIT. I remember it because I recall my brother Henri Clay yelling that he wasn't going to eat any purple rabbit. He must have been thinking of a rabbit the color of Welch's grape juice.

After I finished reading the paper, I went in search of a recipe for WELSH RAREBIT. I also had a great urge to make a *chariot*. I had a few shoe boxes hanging around my closet, so I set to work creating both a *chariot* and a comforting, satisfying meal.

Welsh Rarebit

Makes 8 servings

2 pounds of grated American cheese
1 (12-ounce) can of evaporated milk
2 cups of white asparagus, drained and cut into 1-inch pieces (If white asparagus is not available, green asparagus may be used.)
Salt and cayenne pepper, to taste
Saltine crackers or toast points

Melt the cheese in a double boiler over simmering water. Add the milk, a little at a time, stirring constantly until the sauce is smooth and thick.

Add the asparagus and season with salt and cayenne pepper.

Spoon the mixture over crackers or toast points. Serve immediately.

If we weren't treated to WELSH RARE-BIT, it was vegetable soup that Mama had put on the stove to simmer earlier in the afternoon, and it was just about right when we got home from the parade. Mama often made corn bread to go with the soup, and it was a nice change of pace from French bread.

We all grabbed for the chunk of home-made butter that sat on the center of the old cypress kitchen table. I still get an *envie* (yen) for homemade vegetable soup and corn bread when I think of the fun we all had together.

Old-Fashioned Vegetable Soup

Makes about 6 quarts

2 pounds of beef brisket, trimmed and cut into 2-inch cubes
Salt, black pepper, and cayenne pepper, to taste
½ teaspoon of dried basil leaves
3 to 4 bay leaves
2 to 3 quarts of chicken broth
1½ cups of chopped onions
2 carrots, coarsely chopped
2 celery ribs, chopped
2 cups of chopped cabbage
1 cup of cut green beans
3 cups of canned whole tomatoes
6 ounces of curly vermicelli (optional)

Place the brisket in a large soup pot with salt, cayenne pepper, black pepper, basil, bay leaves and the chicken broth (enough to cover all the ingredients). Bring to a boil, then reduce the heat to medium-low and simmer, partially covered, until the meat is tender, about an hour.

Add the vegetables and cook until tender.

Add the vermicelli and cook for five minutes more. If the soup stock reduces too much, add more broth or water.

Before serving, check seasonings and skim off any excess fat that rises to the surface.

Corn Bread

Makes about 6 servings

3 tablespoons of solid vegetable shortening
2 cups of yellow cornmeal
1 cup of all-purpose flour
4 teaspoons of baking powder
¾ teaspoon of salt
1 teaspoon of sugar
1 egg, beaten
1½ cups of milk

Preheat the oven to 425 degrees.

Put the shortening in an iron skillet or other oven-proof skillet, and put it in the oven to heat the grease.

Meanwhile, sift the dry ingredients together in a mixing bowl. Add the egg and milk, and mix well.

Remove the skillet from the oven (The grease should be hot but not smoking.) and pour in the batter.

Bake until golden brown, 25 to 30 minutes.

And so it goes. Each weekend throughout the fall there are festivals and celebrations. One of the festivals not celebrated in the cool autumn months is the Jambalaya Festival, held during the summer in the town of Gonzales. But I always think of jambalaya during cool months because it's such a great "pot dish," perfect for serving to the multitudes, thus being one of the favorite foods served at any of the festivals.

Jambalaya always reminds me of gatherings. Many times when my family gathers together for a project, such as cleaning up the campground, or when we're all in for a weekend to just be together, someone is bound to pull out our biggest black iron pot.

"Let's put on a jambalaya while we're doing what we're doing!"

The great thing about jambalaya is that you can make it with whatever is at hand. Like the Spanish paella, its basic ingredient is rice, which every good Cajun or Creole cook always has in stock.

It's fun to see what can be added. Let's see. Ah, some chicken or duck. Oh, and maybe some smoked sausage and ham. What about some shrimp? You can use all of this or you can be discriminating.

Just as everyone has his own version of gumbo, so, too, will you find no two jambalayas alike. Some will argue that jambalaya should be brown, while others will say no, it should be red, chock full of tomatoes. Of course, each is right. The type you prefer should be what your taste buds tell you. I can assure you, both kinds are eaten with much gusto, and there's usually not a grain of rice left in the pot when everyone is finished.

I like it best when it's cooked outdoors, but if you don't want to do battle with such an undertaking at least take your plate of jambalaya outside and sit under a tree in your back yard. The aroma of any jambalaya seems to enhance the scents of the earth, and vice versa. Eat it slowly and savor all the tastes that have come together in the pot.

I have my own version, just as everyone else does. But be creative and take some initiative. Don't be afraid to add a little of this, a bit of that. Make it your very own.

Jambalaya – My Way

Makes 6 servings

1/3 cup of butter
1/2 cup of chopped green onions
1/2 cup of chopped white onions
1 cup of chopped green bell peppers
1 cup of chopped celery with leaves
1 teaspoon of minced garlic
1/2 to 1 pound of raw shrimp,
    peeled and deveined
3 dozen raw oysters (optional)
1 cup of chopped ham
2 cups of canned diced tomatoes
1 cup of chicken broth
Salt and cayenne pepper, to taste
Pinch of dried thyme leaves
2 bay leaves
Hot sauce, to taste
1 cup of short-grain white rice (uncooked)

Heat the butter in a large, heavy pot over medium heat. Add the onions, bell peppers, celery and garlic and cook, stirring, until they are soft and golden, about eight minutes.

Add the shrimp, oysters and ham. Cook, stirring, for about three minutes.

Add the tomatoes, chicken broth, salt and cayenne pepper, thyme, bay leaves and hot sauce.

Add the rice, stir a bit, and cover. Cook until the rice is tender and the liquid has been absorbed, about 25 minutes.

Add a little tomato juice or chicken broth if the jambalaya becomes too dry.

A mixed green salad or a salad of fresh fruit, along with plenty of French bread, are musts with this meal.

It seems that each year a new festival is born. I've said it before and I'll say it again: Louisiana natives are always thinking of a new reason for a party. However, many of the festivals have been around for a while.

The Sugarcane Festival and the International Rice Festival are legends. One of my favorites is the Crawfish Festival, created in the 1950s in Breaux Bridge to promote the lowly but tasty crustaceans that are now the toast of the town.

And there's not one, but several shrimp festivals. Probably the most well-known is the one held in Morgan City, where Bayou Teche flows into Berwick Bay, at the

On the occasion of my christening in 1945, Tante May Haines (left) and Aunt Bell "Nannan" Judice were dressed up and looking sharp.

Barbecued Shrimp

Makes 4 to 6 servings

6 pounds of large shrimp, heads on (don't peel them)
2 sticks of butter
¾ cup of olive oil
¼ cup of Worcestershire sauce
6 tablespoons of fresh lemon juice
1 teaspoon of garlic powder
2 teaspoons of paprika
2 teaspoons of cayenne pepper
1 teaspoon of black pepper
1½ teaspoons of salt (or to taste)
½ teaspoon of hot sauce
1 tablespoon of dried rosemary leaves
1 teaspoon of dried oregano leaves

Rinse the shrimp in cool water, and drain. Spread the shrimp in a large shallow baking pan and set aside.

Melt the butter in a saucepan over medium heat, then add the rest of the ingredients. Mix well. Remove the butter sauce from the heat and cool for about five minutes.

Pour the sauce over the shrimp and let stand for an hour.

Preheat the oven to 325 degrees. Bake the shrimp for 15 to 20 minutes, stirring the shrimp around with a spatula a couple of times. Do not overcook.

Serve in soup bowls with lots of hot French bread to sop up the sauce. Be sure to have some trays around for the shells and such.

Be forewarned: This can be eaten only with your hands, and I would advise you not to wear your best outfit since it can get rather messy. I sometimes have plastic bibs for guests or, if nothing else, large napkins to tuck in the collar.

mouth of the Atchafalaya River. Because of close access to the Gulf of Mexico, the fleet of shrimp boats that tie up at Morgan City is a large one.

Each Labor Day weekend, a crowd gathers in Morgan City for a round of merrymaking. One festival highlight is the blessing of the fleet by a priest who sprinkles holy water over the elaborately decorated boats as they chug along the waterfront on their way to the Gulf for a season of trawling.

Holding po-boys (the Southern version of hoagies) piled high with shrimp battered and golden-fried to perfection, the crowds roar and wave as the gaily festooned boats pass in review.

It never fails to amaze me what wonderful things can be done with the succulent shrimp that are brought in from the Gulf.

The shrimpers go through their catches, sorting them by size, for the market. The teeny, tiny ones are perfect for stews and gumbos while the medium-sized ones are great for frying.

The large ones are usually chosen for boiling or barbecuing. The latter treatment is a great delight, but actually the term is wrong, for the shrimp are never put on a grill or pit.

"Shrimp boats are coming. Their sails are in sight. Shrimp boats are coming. There's dancing tonight." So the song goes. But let me make one point: I've never seen a shrimp boat with sails where I come from. They do have large nets that when hitched up out of the water look like giant butterfly wings, which I guess gives them an appearance of having sails. And it's a wonderful sight to see the shrimp boats coming into port late in the afternoon, moving like giant insects across Vermilion Bay silhouetted by the setting sun.

The scene is one I've enjoyed for many years. Aunt Eva and Uncle George have a camp at Cypremort Point, an area on Vermilion Bay that was largely undeveloped until the 1980s.

Many weekends have found us lounging on the large covered pier, fishing, crabbing and waiting for the shrimp boats.

One Friday afternoon I came home from work in New Orleans, dragging. I was beat up, tired, hungry and in dire need of some fresh air. On the edge of a crying jag, I called Mama.

With a crack in my voice, I asked her if she would like me to come in for a visit. Could we coerce Aunt Eva and Aunt Lois to join us for a weekend at Cypremort Point?

I must have sounded bad because without missing a beat, she replied they would meet me there in a couple of hours. I think I even heard her say "poor baby" before she hung up the phone.

It was a crisp, cool afternoon, and in a wink I was packed and humming along Highway 90. The sun was just going down when I arrived. The ladies were busy rolling up the bamboo shades on the large screen porch, icing down cold drinks and beer, and setting up my favorite cot with lots of pillows and cool sheets.

After our usual hugging and a fusillade of greetings, we pulled up the folding chairs to watch the last purple-golden rays of the setting sun. We could see the shrimp boats headed for the docks. I offered to go and bargain for a few pounds of shrimp.

I was in luck. The captain of the first boat I boarded had a good day and agreed to part with five pounds of his best. By the time I returned, the ladies were chopping onions and had started a roux. We were going to have a rich stew.

Shrimp Stew at the Point

Makes 6 to 8 servings

5 pounds of medium-size shrimp
8 cups of water
Salt and cayenne pepper, to taste
2/3 cup of cooking oil
2/3 cup of all-purpose flour
2 cups of chopped onions
1 cup of chopped green bell peppers
6 to 8 cups of shrimp stock
2 hard-boiled eggs, peeled and finely chopped
1/4 cup of chopped green onions

Peel the shrimp and reserve the heads and shells, being careful to keep the golden "fat" from the heads.

To make a shrimp stock, place the heads and shells with the "fat" in a large pot with eight cups of water seasoned with a teaspoon of salt and a teaspoon of cayenne pepper. Bring to a gentle boil and simmer for one hour.

Meanwhile, make a golden roux with the oil and flour in a large, heavy pot over medium heat. Add the onions and bell peppers, and cook, stirring, until the vegetables are very soft, about 10 minutes.

Drain the shells from the stock, pressing down on the shells to get all the liquid.

Add the stock, a cup at a time, to the roux mixture. The stew should be thick enough to coat a wooden spoon. Simmer gently for 30 minutes.

Then add the shrimp and cook for 10 to 15 minutes. Taste for seasonings.

To serve, sprinkle the stew with the chopped boiled eggs and green onions. Traditionally, the stew is served with rice, but I like mine without. I want to savor the richness by itself.

Aunt Tommy Broussard holds me and hugs my brother Henri Clay on the occasion of my christening in 1945. Looking on is my dad, Blackie.

After supper, the ladies refused to let me help them clean up the kitchen. I settled into my cot on the porch, and as I dozed off I could hear the lapping of the water underneath the camp. I knew my tired mind and body were already on the road to recovery.

The next morning my spirits were restored. I was ready to get into the camp spirit, which generally means do anything you want, but don't strain too much.

I planned to spend the day lolling around in the sun, watching the sailboats on the bay, and gossiping with Mama, Aunt Eva and Aunt Lois. Naturally, food – what we were going to cook, when we were going to eat, how we were going to cook it – was an important topic.

I was thrilled to learn that Mama had stopped at the fish market in St. Martinville for gaspergou, a fresh water drum with firm meat that is perfect for grilling. We were going to have the fish for supper along with smothered potatoes and bacon.

I vowed I would never return to the city.

Grilled Gaspergou

Makes 4 to 6 servings

One (4- or 5-pound) gaspergou, or several smaller ones, deheaded, gutted and with the scales left on
8 tablespoons (1 stick) of butter, melted
½ teaspoon of hot sauce
1 tablespoon of Worcestershire sauce
2 garlic cloves, minced

Split the gaspergou in half lengthwise. Place the fish halves, scale sides down, on the barbecue grill over a medium-hot fire.

Make a basting sauce with the butter, hot sauce, Worcestershire and garlic. Baste the fish well with the sauce, then close the lid of the pit.

Allow the fish to cook for 20 minutes or until the meat pulls away from the skin.

Baste with more sauce and serve.

Smothered Potatoes with Bacon

Makes 6 servings

6 bacon strips
4 medium-size red potatoes, skinned and thinly sliced
1 medium-size onion, thinly sliced
Salt and cayenne pepper, to taste
¼ cup of chopped green onions

Fry the bacon until crisp in a heavy skillet. Remove the bacon, drain on paper towels, and crumble. Set aside.

Add the potatoes and onions to the skillet and season with salt and cayenne. Cook over medium heat, stirring until the potatoes and onions are lightly browned. The potatoes will break up and become slightly crispy.

Reduce the heat, cover the pot, and allow the potatoes to continue cooking for 15 minutes or until they are cooked through.

Add the crumbled bacon and the green onions. Serve warm.

In Thanksgiving

For many years, with a few exceptions, the whole family gathered at Mama's for all holiday meals. First of all, her house was the only one that could accommodate the brood. Even when my brothers and sister began having children of their own, she had room to expand. She had a large patio, a huge garage with a brick floor, and a yard that didn't stop. She was also the only one who had a 6-burner stove with double ovens. Mama had silver service for 24, as well as enough matching china and crystal for all 20 of us. Mama also had a huge freezer where she stored many delicious goodies she prepared in advance.

But in more recent years, we children have come more or less into our own and have bravely offered to have some of the holiday celebrations at our humble abodes.

When I had a restaurant near Lafayette, I invited the whole family, plus a few friends, to join me at the restaurant (which I closed for a couple of days) for Christmas dinner. There was a huge Christmas tree, a large kitchen with plenty of cooking space, and a commercial-size dishwasher that could handle the mounds of dirty dishes and pots in a matter of minutes. The walk-in coolers and freezers were perfect for storing pre-made delights.

As luck would have it, it was the holiday season that south Louisiana was locked into below-freezing temperatures and an unforgettable ice storm. But we were undaunted.

Early Christmas morning, everyone cautiously drove from their homes to the restaurant and began lugging in bundles of gifts, trays of food, and children wrapped in blankets. We were well settled in when Baby Brother Bruce calmly announced that he had discovered the pipes were all frozen and we had no running water.

At first, we thought nothing of it. We were all together, a pitcher of warm eggnog took the chill out of our bones, and we began to see about the business of getting dinner ready. It was only then that we realized the lack of running water might put a damper on our festivities.

But my family members are troopers. We've all been camping together many times under fairly primitive conditions. Papa was an old Boy Scout leader who had trained us well. We just had to put our heads together and overcome a few problems.

Nancy, my sister-in-law, made the observation that we had tons of ice in the ice machine. She began melting ice in large pots so we could make coffee, cook rice and wash dishes. We had a good laugh watching her stir the pots of ice on the stove.

Somehow we made it through the day, but as I hugged Mama good-bye I suggested we keep with tradition and have Christmas dinner at her house from now on. She smirked but agreed it would have been a lot easier.

A couple of years later, I bravely invited the clan for Thanksgiving. I was living at Oak Alley Plantation and the director kindly suggested that since the "big house" would be closed for the day, we could all have dinner there. What an invitation! The house is one of the loveliest on the Great River Road, and the old kitchen was more than adequate to handle the crowd. And what a setting for the children to play football and ride bikes!

For days preceding turkey day, I had visions of what a grand day it would be to have a memorable dinner in the historic, gracious home.

It was memorable all right. The day dawned gray and wet. There went the idea of seating the children at a large table on the veranda. While the table in the grand dining room was large, it could hardly accommodate all of us.

I quickly reorganized and soon had my brothers hauling folding tables and chairs to the Big House. At first, the teenagers thought this quite an adventure, but after getting soaked to the skin, they went in search of a portable radio and huddled on the front gallery.

In the meantime, Mama and I were trying to get dinner together. For the first time in years, the ovens went on the blink, so for the next hour we transported dishes that had to be warmed to other available ovens on the grounds, then brought them back to the Big House. We lost Mama's creamed

At a family gathering at our home in St. Martinville circa 1949, three of my uncles posed with the children. The uncles are (left to right) A.P. Broussard, George Broussard and Curtis "Cowboy" Broussard. The children (left to right) are me, my brother Henri Clay, and our cousins Billy and Curt Broussard Jr.

spinach casserole in the melee.

The music emanating from the portable radio seemed to get louder and louder. The drawer containing the silver serving pieces was locked and we couldn't find the key. I became a nervous wreck watching small children running around the 150-year-old mansion filled with family heirlooms.

But somehow we got it all together and sat down to dinner. Brother Henri Clay had just finished saying the blessing when we heard voices at the front door. Lost and weary travelers had seen a light and heard voices. They were in search of a place to have a warm meal. I had no choice but to invite them to join us. We found more folding chairs and place settings. As I watched everyone chow down, I realized I was probably the only one who didn't think all of this was the cat's meow. I was close to tears and having *gros coeur* when a child seated next to me looked up and winked, whispering to me about how much fun he was having. I finally realized that my family can put up with anything and have a good time at it.

Later in the day, when all of us were cleaning and sorting things out in the kitchen, my sisters-in-law and I said at the same time, "Don't you just love the *grimilles*?"

One of the guests overheard our comment and questioned, "What is a *grimille*?"

We explained that it was the crumbs, or tiny bits of anything. In this case, it was the pieces of pork roast and turkey at the bottom of the pans. We told her how wonderful the *grimilles* are for sandwiches or just for picking at the next day.

Early the next morning as I bade everyone *au revoir*, Mama told me that she had put the *grimilles* in a container in the back of the fridge for me to enjoy after everyone was gone.

That evening the quiet was deafening, but not unpleasant. I poked around in the fridge looking for leftovers and discovered the *grimilles*. I decided to amuse myself and make a gumbo. I even had the turkey carcass to make a rich broth. I instinctively knew this was going to be one of the best gumbos I ever made. I was right. It was hearty and nourishing – perfect for a lonely rainy evening meal along with reheated dinner rolls and leftover fruit salad.

Grimille Gumbo

Makes 8 to 10 servings

1 cup of vegetable oil
1 cup of all-purpose flour
2 cups of chopped onions
1 cup of chopped celery
½ cup of chopped green bell peppers
2½ cups of *grimilles* (or cubed turkey or chicken)
6 to 8 cups of turkey or chicken broth
Salt and cayenne pepper, to taste
Pinch of thyme
¼ cup of minced fresh parsley
1 bunch of green onions, chopped

(I usually make my roux in the traditional manner – combining flour and oil in a heavy iron pot and, over a medium fire, stirring slowly until the roux reaches a rich golden brown, then adding the vegetables for a few minutes. But being a bit weary from the past few days' activities, I proceeded to make a roux in the microwave.)

Combine the oil and flour in a 4-cup measure. Microwave on high for six to seven minutes. Stir and return to the microwave for 30 seconds to one minute until the roux reaches a dark brown color. Add the onions, celery and bell peppers. Slowly add warm water to bring the mixture to the 4-cup mark. Stir and put the roux into a large heavy pot.

I had about two and one-half cups of *grimilles*, but you can substitute the same amount of cubed turkey, chicken, or whatever your heart desires. Then add six to eight cups of turkey or chicken broth – more if you want a thinner gumbo. Add salt, cayenne pepper and a pinch of thyme. Simmer for one to two hours.

Sprinkle with the minced parsley and green onions and serve over steamed rice.

Pour yourself a glass of hearty red wine and you will have a meal to warm the body and soul.

You would think I had learned my lesson about having the family for Thanksgiving, but I was determined to have a holiday meal that went smoothly and was enjoyable for everyone, so I tried again the following year.

I was amazed when everyone agreed to come. I was warned, however, that the teenagers seldom travel without friends these days, so I was to prepare for a few extras.

As for the Thanksgiving menu, I thought I was being real cute when I saw a menu for a Creole Thanksgiving dinner in a copy of a food magazine. I made a couple of changes. Instead of stuffing a turkey with jambalaya, I thought it would be fun to stuff Cornish hens instead. I would allow one little bird per person. Having the jambalaya would eliminate Mama having to make her rice dressing with oysters. I would make oyster tartlets, which would take the place of our usual giant oyster pie. We would have pumpkin-peanut butter pie and praline ice cream rather than our regular plain pecan pie.

I made copies of the food article and sent copies along with typed memos to those who had volunteered to bring dishes. The same day I mailed the memos, I purchased 25 Cornish hens. I was very pleased with myself. Everything was being well organized to make the day a pleasurable one.

Two days later I had a rash of phone calls. My sister-in-law informed me that her children do not eat carrots and brussel sprouts so would I mind if she made a sweet potato casserole instead. My brothers let me know very diplomatically that they weren't coming if Mama wasn't making her oyster dressing. My sister asked if it would be okay to have pecan pie *and* pumpkin-peanut butter pie.

Mama called and told me to buy a few more hens because the football player nephews would probably eat two instead of one each.

So much for trying to be cute and innovative. Since my family prefers traditional fare, I'll share with you the dishes we prepared.

Baked Cornish Hens

Makes 6 servings

3 Cornish game hens, about 1 pound each
Salt and black pepper, to taste
4 tablespoons of orange marmalade
3 tablespoons of soy sauce
6 bacon strips
3 tablespoons of olive oil
¾ cup of water or chicken broth
½ cup of dry sherry
3 tablespoons of minced parsley

Preheat the oven to 350 degrees.

Rinse the hens in cool water and pat dry. Season each hen generously with salt and black pepper. Set aside.

Mix the orange marmalade and soy sauce together. Rub the hens with this mixture and wrap each bird with two strips of bacon. Place the hens in a roasting pan and drizzle with olive oil.

Bake until the hens begin to brown. Then add the water or chicken broth to the pan. Loosely cover the pan with foil. Baste occasionally with the pan juices and cook until the wings pull away easily from the body, 30 to 40 minutes.

Remove the hens from the pan and set aside on a platter to keep warm. Remove any excess oil from the baking pan.

Place the roasting pan on top of the stove over medium heat. Add the dry sherry to the pan juices and allow to reduce by one-fourth.

To serve, cut the hens in half and spoon some of the pan gravy over each. Garnish with the parsley.

Oyster-Rice Dressing

Makes 6 to 8 servings

¼ cup of vegetable oil
¼ cup of of all-purpose flour
2 cups of chopped onions
1 cup of chopped green bell peppers
1 tablespoon of minced garlic
½ pound of chicken livers
4 chicken gizzards
2 pints of freshly shucked oysters
   with their liquor
3 cups of cooked long-grain white rice
Salt and cayenne pepper, to taste
¼ cup of finely chopped parsley

Combine the oil and flour in a large, heavy pot over medium heat. Stirring constantly, make a dark brown roux. Add the onions, peppers and garlic, and cook, stirring, until the vegetables are soft, about five minutes.

Grind the livers and gizzards in a food processor or meat grinder. Add the meat to the roux mixture and simmer for 20 minutes.

Add the oyster liquor and the cooked rice. Season with salt and cayenne pepper, being careful not to use too much salt if the oysters are salty.

Add the oysters and mix well. Add the minced parsley and cook until the edges of the oysters curl, about five minutes.

If mixture becomes too dry, add a little warm chicken broth.

Rum-Glazed Sweet Potatoes

Makes 8 to 10 servings

3 pounds of sweet potatoes, pricked
   several times with a fork
3 Golden Delicious apples, peeled and cut
   lengthwise
¼ cup of fresh lemon juice
1 cup of roasted pecan halves
8 tablespoons (1 stick) of butter
½ cup of firmly packed light brown sugar
½ cup of honey
2 tablespoons of dark rum
½ teaspoon of ground cinnamon
¼ teaspoon of ground ginger
¼ teaspoon of ground mace

Preheat the oven to 400 degrees.

Put the potatoes on a baking pan lined with foil. Bake until tender, about 45 minutes. Remove from the oven, cool and then peel.

Cut the potatoes into round slices. Toss the apples in the lemon juice. Arrange the sweet potatoes and the apples in a buttered baking dish and sprinkle with the pecans.

Combine the butter, brown sugar, honey, rum, cinnamon, ginger and mace in a saucepan over medium heat. Cook, stirring, until the sugar dissolves. Spoon the syrup over the potato-and-apple mixture and bake, basting occasionally with the pan juices, for 30 minutes.

Place under the broiler about four inches from the heat until the edges of the potatoes and apples are slightly brown. Remove from the oven and serve warm.

That holiday went quite smoothly except for a small child's mishap (he fell into a sewage ditch) – which brings me to the problem of children and holiday food.

Have you ever tried to serve a ten-year-old a plate of food from the Thanksgiving table?

"*Cher*, would you like turkey or roast?"

"Turkey, I guess."

"White or dark meat?"

"Maybe a drumstick?"

The turkey, as we all know, has only two drumsticks, so if you're late going through the line around the table, the kid is out of luck.

"How about some cauliflower *au gratin*?"

"Can you take off some of that white gook?"

"Ah, here's *grandmere's* specialty, oyster dressing. How about a little of that?"

"Can you take out the oysters?"

Sometimes you can pass off the cranberry sauce by telling the child it really is strawberry preserves. And if you're lucky, he might take a shot at the ambrosia if you pick out the grated coconut. French bread is usually a taker, but forget the giblet gravy.

Many times, I've seen a child's plate with nothing on it but a slice of turkey, bread and white rice with a lump of butter.

They'll sometimes take a slice of pumpkin pie, but they want to know why it's such a gross color. Any apple or cherry pie around? What would children really like to eat on Thanksgiving? I once gathered my 12 nieces and nephews and took a poll.

This is what is acceptable:

Chicken – baked or fried. Creamed potatoes or some kind of sweet potatoes. One five-year-old said pigs-in-a-blanket would be great. Vegetables are questionable. They just don't want gook on them. They want to be able to determine what they're eating. Hot apple pie with ice cream got the most votes for dessert.

So here goes for the children.

For the pigs-in-a-blanket, use canned flaky biscuits for the dough. Break each biscuit in half and roll each piece thinly on a lightly floured board. For adult tastes, put a dab of Creole mustard on the rolled dough; it's best to leave them plain for children. Wrap the dough around two-inch pieces of wieners or smoked mini-sausages. Pinch closed and bake at the temperature recommended on the biscuit can.

The fruit salad may be made with drained pineapple chunks, mandarin slices, apple slices, and whatever fresh berries that can be found at the market. Sprinkle the fruit with fresh mint leaves and stir in plain yogurt. If you want to sparkle some up for the adults, splash in some light rum.

Just about everyone can bake a chicken. I like to add a little oregano and paprika to softened butter and rub the bird well with this mixture. Add a cup of chicken broth to the roasting pan along with some chopped green onions or sliced yellow onions. Baste with pan juices. Kids love this gravy with plain old white rice.

And for the adults, a new twist for duck.

Baked Duck with Jalapeños

Makes 4 servings

2 wild ducks (Mallards preferably), dressed
2 teaspoons of salt
1 teaspoon of cayenne pepper
1 teaspoon of black pepper
2 tablespoons of olive oil
2 fresh jalapeños, seeded and cut into slivers (When handling fresh hot peppers, be sure to wear rubber gloves.)
4 bacon strips
2 tablespoons of all-purpose flour
3 tablespoons of vegetable oil
4 cups of chicken broth
¼ cup of dry sherry
2 cups of sliced fresh mushrooms
¼ cup of chopped parsley

Rub the dressed birds with salt, cayenne, black pepper and olive oil. With a sharp knife, make slits in the breasts and stuff with slivers of the jalapeños. Wrap each bird with two slices of bacon. Sprinkle the birds with flour and shake off any excess.

Brown them in hot vegetable oil (preferably in a black iron pot).

Turn the breast side of each duck up and add the chicken broth and dry sherry.

Cook slowly, covered, on the top of the stove or in a 350-degree oven until the birds are tender, one and a half to two hours.

Just before serving, add the sliced mushrooms and chopped parsley to the pot and cook for 10 minutes.

Remove from the pot and cool slightly before carving to serve.

This next dish is the star of Thanksgiving dinner, liked by both children and adults.

Sweet Potato Pone

Makes 6 to 8 servings

1 egg
1 cup of sugar
8 tablespoons (1 stick) of butter, at room temperature
2 cups of grated raw sweet potatoes
¼ teaspoon of salt
½ cup of milk
1 cup of chopped pecans

Preheat the oven to 325 degrees.

Beat the egg with the sugar and butter. Mix together with the grated sweet potatoes, salt and milk. Pour into a buttered casserole and bake for 30 minutes.

Sprinkle with the chopped pecans, return to the oven, and bake until the mixture sets, about 30 minutes.

While we're on the subject of sweet potatoes, I feel it is necessary to discuss Mama's addiction to them.

I ate so many sweet potatoes as a child, my nickname was *patate douce*. Mama was to blame. She was a fanatic about sweet potatoes any way they were prepared. Just about every day during the cold fall and winter months, she would put several potatoes in the oven to bake, and in the afternoon she and I would snack on them.

We would carefully pull off the skins and then douse the soft orange pulp with melted butter and cane syrup.

Sometimes we plopped them into a bowl of chicken and sausage gumbo. When pork was on the menu, sweet potatoes were the inevitable side dish – sliced, French fried, and sprinkled with sugar and cinnamon.

If a few somehow remained in Mama's sack under the sink and began to sprout, she would put them in jars filled with water and soon we would have a sweet potato vine framing the kitchen window.

She was an absolute diehard about the darn things. We knew we were in trouble especially around the holidays. She would pull out the recipe box and go through her collection of sweet potato recipes.

I once had a request for a sweet potato dish that was "different." My quest for yet another way to serve sweet potatoes led me to the source: I didn't have any new recipes, but I was sure Mama did.

So, I called Mama. After I hung up the phone, I knew she was already hot on the trail. Sure enough, a few days later, she called up with this unusual recipe.

Nutted Sweet Potatoes

Makes 6 to 8 servings

4 cups of canned yams, drained
1/2 teaspoon of salt
1/8 teaspoon of cayenne pepper
1/4 cup of miniature marshmallows
4 tablespoons of melted butter
1/3 cup of honey
1½ cups of chopped pecans

On the day before serving, mash the yams well and add the salt, pepper, marshmallows and one tablespoon of butter. Form into 12 balls, the size of small oranges. Place in a covered container and refrigerate for 24 hours.

The next day, preheat the oven to 350 degrees. Heat the honey and one tablespoon of the butter.

With two forks, roll each yam ball first in the honey, then in the chopped pecans. Place the yam balls in a baking dish.

Spoon the two remaining tablespoons of melted butter over the yams and bake uncovered for 15 minutes.

Serve warm.

I thanked Mama for her research and was about to hang up when I realized she had begun to dictate more sweet potato recipes. I dutifully copied down a few, and then made my excuses. I had to get off of the telephone. Mama was still talking when I hung up. She probably didn't even notice.

Sweet Treats

I love desserts just as much as the next person, but I'm terrible at preparing them. My cakes don't rise, cream won't whip, and soufflés simply flop. I made Floating Islands one time and the island sank. I tried a "can't-miss" lemon pie which turned out beautifully except that I forgot to add the lemon juice. One of my nieces called it "Nani Celle's Neuter Pie."

However, there are a few little Cajun desserts that I have mastered, probably because I literally learned them at my mother's knee – or rather, her stove. They are simple, but quite tasty. I wouldn't recommend them for one of your five-course, *haute cuisine*, candlelight, black tie affairs. Rather, serve them up at family dinners when the north wind blows and a pot of soup is simmering on the stove, or when dear old friends are coming for a weekend stay.

One of my favorites is *les oreilles de cochon*, which literally translated means the pigs' ears. But they are really deep-fried pastries dipped in cane syrup and sometimes sprinkled with chopped pecans. If you have a child who likes to play with a rolling pin, ask him to help. They're fun to do.

Les Oreilles de Cochon

Makes about 1 dozen pastries

1 cup of all-purpose flour
¼ teaspoon of salt
About ¼ cup of water
Vegetable oil for deep-frying
1 (12-ounce) can of cane syrup
1 cup of finely chopped pecans

Combine the flour and salt in a bowl. Stir in enough water to make a stiff dough.

Divide the dough into 12 equal parts and roll each into a ball about the size of a walnut.

Roll out the balls of dough very thin on a lightly floured surface.

Pour about two inches of oil into a heavy, deep pot and heat to 350 degrees.

Drop the pastry, one or two at a time, into the hot oil and, using a long-handled fork, stick the tines into the center of the pastry and twist quickly. Hold the fork in place until the dough sets. This will give it the appearance of a pig's ear.

Cook until golden brown and drain well on paper towels. Repeat the procedure with remaining pastry.

Bring the syrup to a boil in a heavy sauce pan and stir until it reaches the soft-ball stage (about 239 degrees).

Dip each pig's ear in the syrup, coating well. Sprinkle each with the chopped pecans and lay on buttered wax paper.

They're great warm or at room temperature.

This next little dessert can be used for breakfast as well and in the Cajun's version of tea cakes.

Croquignoles

Makes 1 dozen pastries

3 eggs
½ cup of sugar
1 tablespoon of butter, melted
2 tablespoons of water
About 3 cups of sifted flour, sufficient to make a stiff dough
1 teaspoon of baking powder
1 tablespoon of vanilla extract
Vegetable oil for deep-frying
Confectioners' sugar
Ground cinnamon

Beat the eggs in a large mixing bowl. Add the sugar and the melted butter, and then the water. Add the flour with baking powder sifted together. Add the vanilla.

Roll out the dough and cut into triangles about three inches long and two inches wide. Make a slash in the center of each using a sharp knife.

Heat the oil to 350 degrees in a heavy, deep pot. Add the dough, one or two pieces at a time, and fry until golden brown.

Drain on paper towels. Sprinkle with the confectioners' sugar and cinnamon.

A fresh batch of *croquignoles* can perk up a dreary November afternoon, especially if you have a nice pot of hot spiced tea to wash them down. Pull a chair up to the kitchen table and take a break from life's troubles.

Spiced Tea

Makes 4 servings

½ cup of sugar
4 cups of boiling water
6 tablespoons of fresh lemon juice
½ cup of fresh orange juice
¼ teaspoon of ground cinnamon
4 whole cloves
5 small tea bags (An orange pekoe blend will do just fine.)

Dissolve the sugar in one-half cup of the boiling water. Add the juices, the cinnamon and cloves.

Pour the remaining three and a half cups of boiling water over the tea bags and steep for five minutes.

Remove the tea bags and add the tea to the lemon- and orange-flavored syrup. Serve immediately.

Bread pudding is a staple dessert in south Louisiana, but rice pudding is seldom seen anymore. Mama used to make it for us with leftover rice, since nothing went to waste in her kitchen.

Baked Rice Pudding

Makes 6 servings

4 cups of milk
4 eggs, lightly beaten
¾ cup of sugar
2 teaspoons of vanilla extract
1½ cups of cooked white rice
1 cup of seedless raisins (optional)
1 teaspoon of grated nutmeg mixed with
1 teaspoon of ground cinnamon

Preheat the oven to 350 degrees. Grease a 2-quart casserole and set aside.

Scald the milk and gradually add the beaten eggs, stirring constantly. While stirring, add the sugar, vanilla, rice and raisins.

Pour the mixture into the prepared casserole and sprinkle with nutmeg and cinnamon mixture.

Set the casserole in a large baking pan which has about an inch of hot water in it. Bake uncovered for 15 minutes.

Stir the pudding with a fork. Bake until a knife inserted in the center of the pudding comes out clean, about 25 minutes longer.

When we returned home each afternoon after school, we always had a treat waiting for us. Sometimes it was a piece of French bread spread with homemade butter and topped with cane syrup and pecans. Sometimes it was condensed milk that had been cooked six hours in the can until it caramelized. Or maybe, just maybe, Mama would have a batch of silky-smooth egg custard waiting for us.

Burnt Cream

Makes 8 to 10 servings

8 egg yolks
½ cup of sugar
1 quart of heavy cream
1 tablespoon of vanilla extract

Preheat the oven to 350 degrees.

With a whisk or electric beater, beat the egg yolks and one-fourth cup of sugar together in a mixing bowl until the eggs are thick and pale yellow, three or four minutes.

Heat the cream in a heavy saucepan until small bubbles begin to form around the edges of the pan. Pour the cream in a slow stream into the egg yolks, beating constantly. Add the vanilla and strain the mixture through a fine sieve into a baking dish that is at least two inches deep.

Place the dish in another shallow pan and pour enough boiling water into the pan so that the water comes halfway up the sides of the custard dish. Bake until a knife inserted in the center comes out clean, about 45 minutes.

Remove the custard dish from the pan of water and cool to room temperature. Refrigerate for at least four hours.

About two hours before serving, preheat the oven broiler to its highest temperature. Sprinkle the top of the custard with the remaining one-fourth cup of sugar, coating the surface as evenly as possible. Slide the dish under the broiler about three inches from the heat; broil until the sugar forms a crust over the cream, four or five minutes. Watch carefully for any signs of burning.

Allow the cream to cool again and refrigerate before serving.

I often wish I could come home from work and a treat would be waiting for me. A friend told me what he sometimes does. He's a grown man, but still remembers his after-school treats and so shared this divine sweet with me. Make yourself a batch today, and tomorrow you too can have a sweet treat.

Crackers and Cream

Makes 8 to 10 servings

1 quart of milk
1 (12-ounce) can of evaporated milk
4 tablespoons of cornstarch, dissolved in 6 tablespoons of water
2 eggs, lightly beaten
1 cup of sugar
2 tablespoons of vanilla extract
Butter
2 packages of unsalted soda crackers (about 84 crackers)

Combine the milk and evaporated milk in a saucepan and bring to a gentle simmer. Add the cornstarch mixture and stir until the mixture begins to thicken. Add the eggs and sugar, and cook for two more minutes. Cool for about three minutes and add the vanilla.

Butter the crackers on one side and sandwich them together. Arrange the crackers in a large square glass baking dish. Pour the cream sauce over the crackers, cover and allow the crackers to absorb all the cream.

I have always loved October because it means Halloween, and that means carving jack-o-lanterns. Apparently this love is a family trait, because one year my nephew Nicholas, then age five, called me on the telephone.

"Nani Celle, let's go to the pumpkin stand. It's almost Halloween, and we don't want to be without a jack-o-lantern," he said.

Because I am a wonderful aunt, I agreed to take Nicholas into the country in search of the perfect *feu follet*.

We found that perfect pumpkin and were soon on my patio, spreading out newspapers to work on. I cut out the face; Nicholas scooped out the pulp with a spoon. We created one of the ugliest, scariest, most wonderful jack-o-lanterns ever made, and we had *lagniappe* from our efforts. We saved the pulp to make PUMPKIN CAKE WITH CREAM CHEESE ICING.

Pumpkin Cake

Makes 1 cake to serve 8 to 10

4 eggs
2 cups of sugar
1 cup of vegetable oil
2 cups of all-purpose flour
2 teaspoons of baking soda
2 teaspoons of ground cinnamon
1/2 teaspoon of salt
2 cups of cooked mashed pumpkin (Canned pumpkin purée can be substituted.)
Cream Cheese Icing (Recipe follows)

Preheat the oven to 350 degrees.

Cream the eggs and sugar together until light and well blended. Add the oil, continuing to beat.

Sift the flour, soda, cinnamon and salt together. Alternately add the dry ingredients and the pumpkin to the creamed mixture.

Pour into a greased and floured 9-inch tube pan. Bake until a straw or toothpick inserted into the center comes out clean, about 55 minutes. Let the cake stand in the pan for 10 minutes, then turn out onto a rack to cool.

Spread Cream Cheese Icing on the cooled cake.

CREAM CHEESE ICING

3 ounces of cream cheese, at room temperature
½ cup of butter, at room temperature
1 pound box of confectioners' sugar
1 teaspoon of vanilla extract
1 cup of chopped pecans

Cream together the cream cheese and butter. Add the sugar and vanilla, beating until very smooth. Stir in the chopped pecans.

Even back in 1952, my sister and my cousin and I liked to dress up for special occasions.
Sporting our Easter dresses are (left to right) me, sister Edna and cousin Laura Bienvenu.

When we were children, we all partici-pated in making the sweets for Halloween night. Nannan, Mama's aunt, joined us to make tac-tac, or popcorn balls. While we worked, Nannan told us scary stories. She would put a candle in the window over the sink and light several kerosene lanterns to get us in the mood. She had to set the stage, so to speak.

One of her favorite tales was about the burning scarecrow that haunted the old barn near her house. She liked to tell us, too, about the old bald lady who gathered Spanish moss from the trees to make her wigs. Oh, how we would laugh and be scared at the same time. And while we howled and she cackled, she would pop the popcorn and cook syrup for the popcorn balls. Then all was dumped into a huge wash tub on the back porch, and there we would sit and make our tac-tac.

Popcorn Balls

Makes about 3 dozen popcorn balls

1/2 cup of sugar
2/3 cup of pure cane syrup
1/3 cup of water
1 tablespoon of white distilled vinegar
1/3 teaspoon of salt
1 tablespoon of butter
1/8 teaspoon of baking soda
3 quarts of popped corn

Combine the sugar, syrup, water, vinegar and salt; stir until the sugar dissolves. Cook the mixture until it reaches a soft-crack stage, about 270 degrees.

Remove from heat and add the butter and baking soda, stir well.

Pour the mixture over the popcorn.

Now comes the fun part. Butter your hands to form the mixture into balls. Wrap the popcorn balls individually in wax paper.

Ping! Crash! Roll! Rat-tat-tat!

The noise on my roof early one morning woke me up out of a sound sleep. Clutching my robe around me, I slowly opened the patio door and looked up. I was promptly struck on the head with what felt like a big rock. What was going on? The sky was clear and no one was in sight. Then I spied several squirrels scampering around looking much like Mardi Gras revelers scooping up doubloons and beads. Ah, they were gathering pecans!

The brisk north wind that ushered in the cool front was shaking loose the fruit of the trees, and everywhere I looked were pecans – big, fat round ones and some that were long and narrow. In a second, I joined the squirrels. On my hands and knees, I gathered up a few handfuls within a matter of minutes. The pockets of my robe were soon filled and were akin to the puffed cheeks of my squirrel friends.

I pulled out a paper bag, retrieved my nut cracker from the back of the kitchen drawer, and was soon cracking and munching away.

I thought about the many times years ago that Papa, Mama and my old aunts would walk in a line through the yard scrambling for pecans. It was like finding gold nuggets. We had sacks, paper bags, cans, anything in which to put our nuts. Nannan fashioned herself a great tool so she wouldn't have to bend down because she had a bad back. On the end of a shortened broom stick, she had attached a small can with a nail. Her can acted like a scoop with which she could pick up several pecans at a time. Of course, along with her pecans she could not help but pick up a few leaves and twigs. Her sack was always a mess!

At the end of the day, Papa would take our sacks of pecans to Foti's Store, where they would be weighed and we would be paid. I was allowed to keep my money to do with as I pleased. Oh, what mad money it was! I could treat my friends to Grapettes at the drugstore, go to the movies, or to the football games. I was one of the last of the big spenders.

As the pecan season drew to a close, Papa would keep the last sack to crack and peel for our use. He sat for hours in the garage, cracking pecans and putting them in a large tray. On Saturday he positioned himself in front of the television and while watching football games he contentedly peeled pecans.

Mama's freezer looked like a squirrel's storehouse. She kept a ledger of sorts, designating so many bags for Christmas goodies, so many for roasting, and a few to give to relatives.

Here are a few tips for storing pecans that you gather yourself or receive as gifts.

As soon as they are thoroughly dry, pecans should be stored in airtight containers in a cool, dry, dark place. Pecans are rich in oil and will become stale or rancid quickly if not stored properly. Shelled or unshelled nuts will stay fresh for about a year stored in airtight containers in the refrigerator, or for several years in the freezer. Unbroken kernels stay fresh longer than broken pieces. Keep in mind that about two and a half pounds of pecans in the shell yield one pound of shelled nuts, or about four cups. Now you can use them in recipes.

Toasted (or Roasted) Pecans

4 tablespoons (½ stick) of margarine
3 cups of shelled pecan halves
Salt

Preheat the oven to 275 degrees.

Melt the margarine in a shallow baking pan. Put the pecans in the baking pan and stir to coat them evenly. Spread them out in one layer.

Roast, stirring about every 15 minutes, until they are evenly browned, 30 to 40 minutes, depending on the size of the pecans. Smaller pecans cook faster, and the amount of moisture in pecans affects the cooking time.

Remove the pan from the oven and sprinkle the pecans with salt while they are still warm.

When they are completely cool, store them in airtight containers.

Pecan pie is a fixture on holiday tables in Louisiana. I've tasted many versions of the delicacy, and this is absolutely the best. The secret is the dark corn syrup.

Enjoying coffee and dessert during a Christmas gathering circa 1949 are (left to right) "Pop-Pete" Broussard, Uncle George Broussard, Lazaire "Pop" Bienvenu, Tante Bell Judice, Aunt Eva Broussard and brother Henri Clay.

Pecan Pie

Makes 6 servings

3 eggs, lightly beaten
½ cup of sugar
1 rounded tablespoon of all-purpose flour
1½ cups of dark corn syrup
1 teaspoon of vanilla extract
1 cup of pecans
1 unbaked 9-inch pie shell

Preheat the oven to 350 degrees.

Put the eggs in a mixing bowl. In a separate bowl, mix the sugar and flour together and stir to blend. Add the sugar mixture to the eggs.

Add the corn syrup, vanilla and pecans. Fold into the mixture.

Pour mixture into the pie shell and bake until the filling sets, about 45 minutes.

Remove the pie from the oven and cool for a few minutes before slicing to serve.

Skillet Cookies

2 egg yolks
8 tablespoons (1 stick) of butter
  or margarine
½ cup of sugar
8 ounces of chopped dates
1 cup of chopped pecans
2 cups of Rice Krispies
Shredded coconut

Combine the egg yolks, butter and sugar in a large skillet over low heat. Cook, stirring, for five minutes. Add the dates and pecans, and cook, stirring, for five more minutes.

Remove from the heat, add the Rice Krispies and mix well.

Cool, then shape into small balls and roll in the coconut.

WINTER

Just as the last of the autumn leaves float to the ground, winter comes barreling through Louisiana fast on the heels of the first cold front that sweeps in from the west. Great storm clouds filled with torrents of rain burst open over the low-lying terrain.

With harvesting done, residents of south Louisiana gather around their stoves and kitchen tables to prepare for the upcoming holiday feasts. Papa Noel is on his way and *Le Petit Bonhomme Janvier* will be right behind. Then it's time for one of the favorites of all Louisiana celebrations – Carnival. Weeks of parades, balls and galas culminate with *Mardi Gras* (Fat Tuesday).

Following *Mardi Gras* are the 40 days of the Lenten season of penance, fasting and abstinence in preparation for the coming of Easter. As Easter approaches, the bleakness of winter begins to disappear and the warming days of March herald the coming of spring.

The birthday party for my grandfather, Lazaire "Pop" Bienvenu, was well attended, in January 1953. Among those at the party were 11 of his 12 children, plus a granddaughter, all shown here. Left to right are: Bobbie Lee Stewmon (granddaughter), Marcel M. "Blackie" Bienvenu (my father), Corinne Cecile "Coco" McCoy, Ralph Roch Bienvenu, Rita Rose Patout, Annabelle Valentine "Billy" Bienvenu, Marie Therese "Taye" Chataignier, Margaret Vida "Git" Laborde, "Pop" (the birthday boy), Msgr. Clay Anthony Bienvenu, Genevieve Gertrude "Jenny" Durand, and Louis Lawrence "Shorty" Bienvenu. Pop's other child, the one not in the photo, was Claudia Helen "Taudie" Brosius.

Cold Nights, Warm Food

I'm not particularly fond of winter in the South. The sun sets earlier and I can no longer have my quiet time watching the sun go down. If I want quiet time I have to get up earlier and watch the sun come up. My lush, semi-tropical plants must be moved indoors and my lawn furniture finds a new home in the shed, away from the elements.

But I like to think that I'm flexible, so I've learned to make the best of the shorter, colder days. When I'm up earlier I have time to linger over my cup of coal-black coffee and have a leisurely breakfast while catching up on my reading material. In the evenings I eat earlier and find that I want a sweet snack before I bury myself in the heavy quilts of my bed.

While my tiny kitchen is a bit warm in the summer, it's a cozy place to spend some time in the winter. Preparing a snack in my warm kitchen is a great way to end a winter day, and a snack that is close to my heart is FRIED SQUAW BREAD.

Fried Squaw Bread

Makes about 24 pastries

1½ cups of sifted all-purpose flour
½ teaspoon of salt
1½ teaspoons of baking powder
½ tablespoon of sugar
½ tablespoon of melted butter
¾ cup of water
Vegetable oil for deep-frying
Confectioners' sugar
Squaw Bread Syrup (Recipe follows)

Sift the dry ingredients together in a mixing bowl. Add the melted butter and water and stir to mix well.

Heat the oil to 350 degrees in a heavy pot. Drop the batter, by the tablespoon, into the hot oil. Cook, turning to brown evenly, for two to four minutes. Drain on paper towels, sprinkle with the confectioners' sugar and serve hot with the Syrup.

SQUAW BREAD SYRUP

1 cup of light brown sugar
2 cups of light corn syrup
2 tablespoons of vegetable oil
1 tablespoon of maple flavoring

Combine all the ingredients in a saucepan and heat to the boiling point, stirring constantly. Remove from the heat and serve warm.

This spiced coffee is a delightful accompaniment to the fried bread.

Spiced Coffee

For a four-cup coffee pot, put four rounded tablespoons of ground coffee in the drip cup. Sprinkle the ground coffee with one-half teaspoon of ground cinnamon, one-fourth teaspoon of grated nutmeg, and two pinches of ground cloves. Drip the coffee as usual. When serving, put a small dollop of whipped cream in the coffee.

Although winter days are short, they tend to seem long when they have to be spent indoors. To while away the hours, I find it therapeutic to put a pot of soup or gumbo on the stove to simmer while the wind and rain rattle the windows.

I remember waking one morning to the sounds of the north wind shaking the shutters and roaring through the lonely patio. In my centrally heated home I was as warm as toast, but I reflected on the countless mornings of my childhood when the mere thought of getting out from beneath the mound of quilts and blankets struck fear in my heart.

Suppose my slippers weren't right where I left them and I had to put my feet on the cold floor? Even the thought of moving my feet from their warm nest to the other side of the bed made me shudder.

But here in my present warm abode I didn't have to worry. If my slippers had been kicked under the bed, I knew the warm carpet awaited my feet. Once up, I peeped through the window. Yes, it was one of those cold, gray days, a perfect day for making a gumbo. I made a grocery list.

I braced myself against the wind and headed for my car. There wasn't a leaf left on the trees, and dark clouds were rolling in from the west. A real gumbo day indeed!

Chicken, Andouille & Oyster Gumbo

Makes 6 to 8 servings

1 roasting hen (3 to 4 pounds), cut into
    frying pieces
Salt and cayenne pepper, to taste
1 cup of vegetable oil
1 cup of all-purpose flour
2½ cups of chopped onions
1 cup of chopped green bell peppers
1 cup of chopped celery
10 cups of chicken broth
2 bay leaves
½ teaspoon of dried thyme leaves
1 pound of andoullie, cut crosswise into
    ¼-inch slices
1 pint of freshly shucked oysters
    with the liquor

Season the hen generously with salt and cayenne.

Combine the oil and flour in a large, heavy pot or Dutch oven over medium heat. Stirring slowly and constantly, make a roux the color of chocolate. (When I attempted to make my first roux years ago, I remember calling Papa and asking him how long it would take, and he told me "the time it takes to drink two beers." Not being a beer drinker, I had to come up with my own system. I now put on two record albums, and when they have played out my roux is usually just about right.)

Add the onions, bell peppers and celery, and cook, stirring, until they are soft, 10 to 12 minutes.

Add the chicken broth. (I usually warm it up in a pot just a bit before adding it to the roux mixture.) Stir to blend, and bring to a gentle boil.

Add the chicken. (There are those who will tell you to brown the chicken first, but I put it in raw.) Add the bay leaves and thyme, and cook at a gentle boil for one hour.

Add the andouille and cook, stirring occasionally, until the chicken is very tender, an hour to an hour and a half longer.

A few minutes before serving, add the oysters and simmer just until the oysters curl, about three minutes. Adjust seasoning to taste. (If the gumbo becomes too thick during cooking, simply add more chicken broth or water.)

Following a blustery storm we are sometimes blessed with a gorgeous bluebird day. The sky is deep blue, and, save for a few evergreens, it provides the only color in the landscape. A bluebird day is a great day for a trip to the country to see Mama.

With a couple of quarts of chicken, andouille and oyster gumbo packed in an ice chest in the trunk of my car, I forsook the interstate and opted to travel the back roads to St. Martinville.

At the time, I was living at Oak Alley Plantation, which is located upriver from New Orleans, below Baton Rouge. My usual route to St. Martinville, because it was the quickest, was Interstate 10, although it did mean that I had to cross the mighty Mississippi not once, but twice.

But that particular day I wasn't in a hurry, so I decided to drive along Highway 1 from Donaldsonville to Port Allen, thus eliminating any crossings over the Mississippi River. This route would allow me to drive through several small towns along the river, with a change of scenery for the first 50 or so miles of my trek.

The sugarcane harvest was just about at its end, and I watched the mills along Highway 1 belching white-gray smoke and emitting the sweet-sour odors of processed cane.

At Port Allen, just across the river from the State Capital of Baton Rouge, I turned west onto Interstate 10, a ribbon of concrete and steel that took me through the heart of the Atchafalaya Basin, which at this time of year was clothed in drab winter dress.

On this day the dancing rays of sunshine bounced over the quiet waterways, making the noble cypress trees look like soldiers guarding the sleeping land.

When I arrived at Mama's she had a pot of coffee brewing and a tray of her treasured demitasse cups set on the breakfast table. She had just poured our coffee when my brother-in-law Al came rushing in, looking for her big gumbo pot.

His wife, my sister Edna, has a cold weather ritual. She says that to keep warm and cozy all one has to do is keep a pot of gumbo simmering at the back of the stove all day while baking bread, muffins and biscuits. Like a squirrel, Edna hordes all the necessary ingredients for these items in the back of her freezer and pantry, and when cold weather strikes she is Boy Scout prepared.

As Al banged the screen door shut, he hollered to us to come join them for gumbo later. Mama and I wondered if it was going to be a seafood gumbo, or perhaps chicken and okra, or might it be a chicken and sausage gumbo?

We were on our second cup of coffee when the telephone rang. It was Maria, my sister-in-law, calling to invite us for a gumbo dinner the next day.

Mama's eyes rolled as she accepted the invitation. She said we were going to be gumboed to death. After hanging up the phone she admitted that earlier in the day she had given some serious thought to making a shrimp and okra gumbo. It was then that I confessed that my ice chest in the car was filled with a chicken, andouille and oyster gumbo. We howled. We agreed that we would eat them all.

We would lunch on mine, have supper with Al and Edna, and enjoy Sunday dinner with Maria and Henri Clay.

The day after my gumbo treat I thought about oysters, those salty, delectable bivalves that are a favorite treat among Creoles and Acadians alike.

During the cool months of fall and the cold ones of winter, oyster luggers can be seen following the jagged shoreline of the Gulf of Mexico and the neighboring bays, harvesting the oyster beds.

Many days find New Orleanians standing elbow to elbow at marble counters, behind which shuckers pry open oysters to fill the many orders during the noon hour.

"Joe, give me the biggest ones you have," says a hefty dock worker.

"Mister, I like the small ones, if you please," squeaks a fragile dowager.

Purists slurp the oysters straight out of the shell with no adornments. Others prefer them doused in a sauce that is custom-made by each consumer. In a small paper cup, ketchup, hot sauce, a splash of olive oil and a hefty dab of horseradish are stirred around and used for dipping the ice-cold oysters. Some people make a big to-do about squeezing lemon juice over

their oysters, and crackers, more often than a cocktail fork, are the means by which the oysters get from tray to mouth. Cold beer is the accepted liquid accompaniment.

While I didn't experience the oyster bar concept until I was well into my teens, many a late Friday night, upon returning from a high school football game, I found Papa, my uncles and their cronies sitting at the kitchen table slurping down raw oysters.

Earlier in the day Papa would have visited his old friend, Mr. Frank "Banane" Foti, who had a stand in St. Martinville where one could get roasted peanuts, fresh vegetables and freshly shucked oysters. Mr. Banane packed the oysters in little white cardboard boxes with wire handles (what we know now as "takee-outee" containers), which Papa would then store in the refrigerator for the Friday night feast.

I was allowed to put my stool next to Papa and watch the ritual of the men mixing up their cocktail sauce. On the table was a large bottle of ketchup, a jar of horseradish, several wedges of lemon, hot sauce and olive oil. Each man had his own cup, and with great vigor they would stir up their own concoctions according to individual tastes. A big basket of Saltine crackers was also on the table. The white containers of cold oysters were passed around and around as the men jabbed the oysters, dipped them in sauce, and threw them down their throats.

I watched in amazement. I was not quite ready to put the gray, slimy mollusks in my mouth. Papa sometimes gave me his cup of sauce into which he poured a little oyster juice; I would break up a couple of crackers in it and thought that was quite acceptable.

I ate my first oysters only after I was in college. A sophisticated upperclassman took me out to Poor Boy's Riverside Inn in Lafayette for dinner and asked if he could order for me. I, of course, thought that this was just the cat's meow. But, lo and behold, as a first course he ordered a dozen raw oysters on the half shell. I dared not refuse to eat them.

As I mixed up my sauce he told me he was a purist and didn't need all that razzmatazz. Somehow, with enough crackers, I was able to eat them all. And from that night on I was an avid raw oyster fan.

When oysters are at their peak, it's a perfect opportunity for an oyster feast.

If you have friends who will volunteer to shuck, get a sack of oysters in the shells. Or, if that seems like too much work, a couple of gallons of shucked oysters will do.

Allow for some to be eaten on the half shell. The rest may be used for a variety of delectable dishes that should satisfy the craving of even the most insatiable oyster lover.

Oyster & Artichoke Casserole

Makes 12 appetizer portions

6 whole fresh artichokes
8 tablespoons (1 stick) of butter
3 tablespoons of all-purpose flour
2/3 cup of finely chopped green onions
1 teaspoon of minced garlic
1 pint of oyster liquor
Pinch each of ground thyme, ground oregano, and marjoram
1/2 cup of finely chopped parsley
Salt and cayenne pepper, to taste
6 dozen oysters
Thinly sliced lemons sprinkled with paprika for garnish

Boil the artichokes in unsalted water until tender. Drain and cool. Scrape the tender pulp from the leaves. Clean the hearts and mash together with the pulp. Set aside.

Heat the butter in a large skillet over medium heat. Add the flour and stir constantly until the mixture is smooth and thick. Add the green onions and garlic, and cook, stirring, until they are soft, about one minute.

Add the oyster liquor, thyme, oregano, marjoram, parsley, salt and pepper, and stir.

Simmer for 15 minutes. Add the oysters and cook until the edges curl, about three minutes. Add the artichokes and blend into the mixture.

Spoon the mixture into individual casserole cups or shells, and garnish with the lemon slices.

This filling may also be put into small pastry shells, heated, and served as *hors d'oeuvre.*

There are some cooks who will tell you that OYSTERS CASINO is made with a tomato-based sauce, and indeed one version is. But this one was created by a chef friend who prepared it at my restaurant, Chez Marcelle, which I operated during the early 1980s near Broussard, Louisiana. It has not a bit of tomato in it, but it is a superb dish that can be served as an elegant appetizer or as a Sunday evening repast. It's perfect for a cold evening spent in front of a blazing fire with lots of hot French bread and a bottle of chilled white wine.

Oysters Casino

Makes 4 appetizer servings
or 2 main course servings

3 tablespoons of olive oil
1/3 pound of Italian sausage, removed from the casing and crumbled
1 cup of finely chopped green bell peppers
1 cup of finely chopped white onions
1/2 cup of chopped pimientos
1 teaspoon of minced garlic
1/2 cup of cream sherry
1 cup of half-and-half
1/2 cup of all-purpose flour
1 cup of melted butter
1 pound of grated sharp cheddar cheese
1 dozen freshly shucked oysters
Salt and cayenne pepper, to taste
2 slices of cooked bacon

Heat the olive oil in a large skillet over medium heat. Add the sausage, bell peppers, onions, pimientos and garlic, and cook, stirring, until the sausage is completely browned.

Add the sherry and the half-and-half, and cook, stirring, for 10 minutes.

Add the flour to the melted butter and stir to blend. Add this mixture to the pot and cook, stirring, until the mixture is thick. Add the cheese and season with salt and cayenne, and cook, stirring constantly, until the cheese is completely melted.

Remove from the heat and cool the mixture to room temperature. Cover and chill in the refrigerator until the mixture is firm, about an hour.

Preheat the oven to 350 degrees.

Place three oysters on each of four scallop shells or in small ramekins, and bake until the edges of the oysters curl, about three minutes. Remove from the oven and place two or three tablespoons of the chilled sausage mixture over the oysters, spreading it evenly. Place half a slice of bacon over each serving, return to the oven, and bake until the sauce bubbles, about 15 minutes. Serve warm.

Everyone has heard of Oysters Rockefeller, the famous dish created at Antoine's in New Orleans and named after one of the wealthiest men in the United States, John D. Rockefeller. Antoine's recipe has never been disclosed, but there are many versions served in and around New Orleans. Brian Richard, the same chef who created OYSTERS CASINO for my restaurant, came up with a rich soup which he dubbed OYSTERS ROCKEFELLER SOUP.

Oysters Rockefeller Soup

Makes 8 servings

1 cup of minced yellow onions
1 tablespoon of minced garlic
1/2 cup of minced celery
3 cups of chicken stock, divided
2 cups of cooked and drained spinach, puréed in a food processor
2 pints of oysters and their liquor
2 pints of half-and-half
3/4 cup of freshly grated Parmesan or Romano cheese
1/3 cup of cornstarch dissolved in 1/2 cup of Pernod
1 tablespoon of anise seeds
Salt and cayenne pepper, to taste
Lemon slices for garnish

Combine the onions, garlic and celery and one cup of the chicken stock in a large saucepan over medium heat. Cook, stirring, until the vegetables are very soft, eight to ten minutes.

Add the spinach purée and simmer, stirring, for five minutes. Add the remaining two cups of chicken stock and the liquor from the oysters, and stir to blend. Whisking constantly, gradually add the half-and-half and blend well. Cook, stirring constantly, for 10 minutes. Add the cheese and whisk to blend. Add the cornstarch and Pernod mixture, and stir to blend.

When the soup is thick and hot, remove from the heat and add the drained oysters, the anise seeds, and season with salt and cayenne.

Ladle the soup into soup bowls and garnish with lemon slices.

Mama dances with "Pop" Lazaire at a Christmas gathering in St. Martinville, as Tante May Haines looks on.

When they are at their peak, freshly shucked oysters invariably find their way into the pots of creative south Louisiana cooks. These innovative cooks give birth to a new oyster dish practically every day of the season. This was the case when I came home one late afternoon with a small carton of oysters swimming in their delicate liquor.

A golden moon was on the rise, glowing just above the horizon. There was a chill in the air, but it wasn't so cold that I couldn't grill outdoors. I had two nice, thick pork chops and some sweet potatoes. With a little ingenuity, I could have a delightful evening.

A small repast for two seemed to be in order. A neighbor accepted my invitation for dinner and came over with a bottle of good red wine.

While the charcoal was getting hot, I put lighted candles all around my deck, took out a couple of old hurricane lanterns and set them on the patio table. While my neighbor and I exchanged local gossip, I created an oyster dressing for the pork chops.

Pork Chops Stuffed with Oyster Dressing

Makes 2 servings

2 tablespoons of butter
1 pint of oysters, drained
3 tablespoons of finely chopped
　green onions
1 tablespoon of minced fresh parsley
1 tablespoon of finely chopped green
　bell peppers
1 egg, beaten
Seasoned bread crumbs
Salt, cayenne pepper, and garlic powder,
　to taste
2 center-cut pork chops, about
　1½ inches thick
Vegetable oil

Heat the butter in a large skillet over medium heat. Add the oysters and cook until the edges begin to curl, two to three minutes. Add the green onions, parsley and bell peppers, and cook, stirring for two to three minutes.

Remove from the heat and add the beaten egg and enough bread crumbs to bind the mixture. Season with salt, cayenne and garlic powder.

Cool the mixture to room temperature. While the dressing cools, prepare the pork chops.

Place the chops on a cutting board so that the bone is away from you. At the narrow tip end of the chop, insert the point of a stiff-bladed knife and push it in along the underside of the back fat, all the way up until you make contact with the bone. Be careful not to cut through the membrane that separates the back fat from the meat. That's what holds the dressing in.

When you have made contact with the bone, cut along the bone through the meaty part of the chop from right to left to form a pocket. (If you don't want to butterfly the pork chops yourself, your butcher can do it for you.)

Season the chops generously with salt, cayenne and garlic powder. Spoon the stuffing into the pocket, pressing it in firmly.

Rub the chops with a little vegetable oil. Grill until the juices run clear, about 30 minutes.

While the chops were on the grill, I spied some fresh mint growing near the deck. I chopped up a few leaves, added two tablespoons of vinegar and a teaspoon of sugar, and brought all to a boil in a small saucepan. I boiled the sauce briefly, then let it stand for a few minutes before pouring it over the grilled pork chops. The sweet potatoes had been baking slowly in the oven and were done when we sat down to supper.

It was quite an enchanting evening, and as we chatted I reminisced about an OYSTER SOUP Mama used to make on chilly winter nights.

Oyster Soup without Milk

Makes 6 servings

3 tablespoons of vegetable oil
3 tablespoons of all-purpose flour
1 ½ cups of chopped onions
3 tablespoons of chopped fresh parsley
4 dozen oysters and their liquor
1 quart of boiling water
2 tablespoons of butter
Salt and cayenne pepper, to taste

Heat the vegetable oil in a large, heavy pot over medium heat. Add the flour and cook, stirring constantly, to make a light brown roux. Add the onions and parsley, and cook, stirring, until the onions are wilted, three to five minutes.

Strain the oyster liquor from the oysters and add it to a quart of boiling water. Slowly pour the liquor-water mixture into the roux, stirring constantly. When the mixture comes to a boil, reduce to a simmer, add the oysters and the butter, and cook until the edges of the oysters begin to curl, about three minutes. Season with salt and cayenne.

If a thicker, heartier soup is desired, milk may be substituted for the water.

Serve with crackers or toast points.

On cold nights after football games Mama sometimes had hot oyster pies waiting for us. They were warm and spicy and took the chill off the bones.

Oyster Pie

Makes 6 servings

4 thick bacon slices
¼ cup of chopped onions
½ cup of chopped green onions
¼ cup of chopped parsley
½ teaspoon of cayenne pepper
1 quart of oysters, drained
Salt, to taste (The oysters may be salty enough.)
Two 9-inch pie crusts
Melted butter

Preheat the oven to 375 degrees.

Fry the bacon in a skillet until crisp. Drain on paper towels, cool, and then crumble. Set aside.

Add the onions to the bacon drippings in the skillet and cook until the onions are wilted, two to three minutes. Add the parsley and cayenne. Remove from the heat and scrape the mixture into a mixing bowl. Add the oysters and toss gently. Adjust seasonings.

Brush one pie crust with a little melted butter, then pour in the oyster mixture. Place the remaining pie crust over the mixture and prick with a fork.

Bake until the crust is golden brown, 30 to 40 minutes.

Remove from the oven and cool slightly before slicing to serve.

Joyeux Noel

The stoves and ovens of south Louisiana rarely get cold at any time of the year, but during the weeks between Thanksgiving and Christmas kitchens are frantic with preparations for the holidays.

Just about every day of the week found Mama and Aunt Lois whipping out batches of fudge, pralines and yummy Lizzies for gift-giving and for family consumption.

As a child I was sometimes put to work in what we all called "the candy factory." Pecans had to be chopped, pots had to be stirred and watched closely, and festive cans and jars had to be tied with ribbons and labeled before delivery was made to friends and relatives. I can't say I minded. After all, I got to lick the spoons and taste the crumblings, and I was always rewarded with a little stash of my very own.

My Aunt Grace, otherwise known as Cina by her many nieces and nephews, was the queen of pralines. Cina had a special black iron pot in which she made these delightful candies. There was really nothing special about the pot, other than its designation as "the praline pot."

Cina's Pralines

Makes about a dozen pralines

1 pound of light brown sugar (3 cups)
1/8 teaspoon of salt
3/4 cup of evaporated milk
1 tablespoon of butter
2 cups of pecan halves

Combine the sugar, salt, milk and butter in a heavy pot. Cook over low heat, stirring constantly, until the sugar dissolves.

Add the pecans and cook over medium heat to the soft-ball stage. Remove from the heat and cool for about five minutes. Stir rapidly until the mixture begins to thicken and evenly coats the pecans.

Drop by the tablespoonful onto aluminum foil or onto a lightly buttered baking sheet.

When the candy has cooled, gently lift it from the surface and store it in an airtight container.

Note: If candy becomes too stiff, add a few drops of hot water to the mixture.

I have another praline recipe from my time working and living at Oak Alley Plantation. Princess Margaret of Great Britain was visiting New Orleans and asked to be shown a plantation. Thus it came to pass that she came to Oak Alley for coffee, or tea, if you prefer. From our collection of old plantation recipes came this classic.

Althea's Pralines

Makes about a dozen pralines

1 cup of buttermilk
2 cups of sugar
1 teaspoon of baking soda
A large pinch of salt
2 teaspoons of vanilla extract
4 tablespoons of butter
2 cups of pecan halves

Combine the buttermilk, sugar, baking soda and salt in a deep, heavy pot over medium heat. Stir constantly until the mixture is mahogany in color.

Add the vanilla and butter, and beat until the mixture begins to thicken.

Add the pecans and drop by the tablespoonful onto a marble slab or waxed paper.

Cool and store in an airtight container.

We knew they were fit for a princess when she sent one of her ladies-in-waiting to the kitchen for the recipe and a box of the delicacies to take with her.

Mama is an absolute fanatic about fudge. At Christmas time she makes so much that we laugh at the number of tins she stashes. One year, several months after the holiday season, we came upon a couple of tins hidden in her armoire. We asked her if she hid those for her own snacking when no one was about! Her most special fudge is not chocolate and is called RUSSIAN TAFFY. When making pralines or candy, it's best to do so on a cool, dry day, or else the candy will not turn and you'll have a soggy mess on your hands.

Russian Taffy

Makes about 24 pieces

3 cups of sugar
1 cup of milk
1 (14-ounce) can of sweetened condensed milk
1½ cups of chopped pecans
4 tablespoons of butter
1 tablespoon of vanilla extract

Combine the sugar, milk and condensed milk in a heavy pot over medium heat. Cook, stirring, until the mixture forms a soft ball in a cup of cool water.

Remove from the heat and add the pecans, butter and vanilla. Beat until the mixture becomes thick.

Pour the mixture into a buttered 9x12-inch pan.

Cool completely before cutting into 1-inch squares.

This can become chocolate fudge by the addition of one-half cup of cocoa powder when mixing the sugar, milk and condensed milk.

My sister Edna and I always volunteered to make SANDIES, or COCOONS as they are sometimes called. For every one of these cookie-like confections that made it into the candy tin, we ate two.

Sandies (Cocoons)

Makes 4 dozen

1 cup of butter
1/3 cup of sugar
2 teaspoons of water
2 teaspoons of vanilla extract
2 cups of all-purpose flour
1 cup of chopped pecans
Confectioners' sugar

Cream the butter and sugar together in a mixing bowl. Add the water and vanilla, and mix well. Add the flour and pecans, and mix well.

Cover and chill the dough in the refrigerator for two to three hours.

Preheat the oven to 350 degrees.

Shape the dough into small balls, about the size of walnuts. Bake on an ungreased cookie sheet until slightly golden, about 20 minutes.

Cool slightly and then roll the cookies in confectioners' sugar.

We were some happy children on Christmas Day 1954. On the floor are my sister Edna Marie and cousin Billy Broussard. Standing, left to right, are cousin Curt Broussard Jr. and brother Henri Clay. That's me seated.

LIZZIES, which are little fruitcake cookies, were the specialty of Mama's good friend, Miss Do. She had no children, but many of us were like her adopted nieces and nephews. Each Christmas season she brought us each a box of the cookies, and we treasured them dearly.

Lizzies

Makes about 2 dozen

2 tablespoons of margarine
½ cup plus 2 tablespoons of brown sugar
1 egg
¾ cup of all-purpose flour, plus ¼ cup in which to dredge the fruit
¼ teaspoon of baking soda
¼ teaspoon of ground cinnamon
¼ teaspoon of ground cloves
1 tablespoon of buttermilk
¼ cup of bourbon
¼ pound of red candied cherries, chopped
¼ pound of green candied cherries, chopped
¼ pound of dark raisins
¼ pound of white raisins
2 cups of chopped pecans

Preheat the oven to 300 degrees.

Cream the margarine and sugar together in a mixing bowl. Add the egg and mix well. Add three-fourths cup of the flour, the baking soda, cinnamon, cloves, buttermilk and bourbon. Mix well.

Dredge the cherries, raisins and pecans in one-fourth cup of the flour. Add to the first mixture and mix well.

Form into tablespoon-size balls and bake on a greased cookie sheet for 15 minutes.

Cool completely before storing in an airtight container.

Unfortunately, I never knew either one of my grandmothers. One died before I was born and the other when I was a little baby. However, every time we have a Bienvenu family gathering, everyone talks about how good a cook "Mrs. Lazaire" was. Her name was Leoncia, but my grandfather's name was Lazaire, and back then people called them Mr. and Mrs. Lazaire.

Leoncia's family had a hotel and restaurant in St. Martinville, and that is where she learned her magic cooking secrets.

Most of Leoncia's eight daughters are pretty good cooks, and they all have their specialties. Aunt Taudie makes incredible pies, Aunt Taye is known for her divinity fudge, and Aunt Jenny makes *daube glace* or *daube froide*.

Aunt Jenny usually makes *daube* during the holidays, and I constantly nagged her for the recipe. She told me, "*Mais chere*, I don't have a recipe. I do it from memory, and you'll just have to come watch me do it."

So that is exactly what I did. Be forewarned: This is not a dish you can whip up in an hour. Reserve an afternoon for this one.

Aunt Jenny's
Daube Glace

3-pound round rump boneless roast
1 teaspoon of salt
½ teaspoon of cayenne pepper
3 tablespoons of vegetable oil
3 cups of chopped onions
3 garlic cloves, minced
2 cups of thinly sliced carrots
Equal parts of water and beef consomme
2 pig's feet, cut in half, lengthwise
2 bay leaves
½ teaspoon of dried thyme leaves
Water
½ cup of dry sherry
2 envelopes of gelatin
Pimiento strips
Fresh parsley leaves
6 green olives, thinly sliced
1 carrot, thinly sliced

Rub the roast with the salt and cayenne pepper. Heat the oil in a large, heavy pot or Dutch oven over medium heat. Add the roast and brown it evenly on all sides.

Add the onions, garlic, carrots and enough water and beef consomme to cover the beef. Cover and simmer until the meat is very tender, two to three hours. Add more liquid if necessary to keep the meat submerged in liquid.

In another pot, place the pig's feet (secured in a net bag), the bay leaves, thyme, enough water to cover, and the sherry. Boil for two hours, until the meat falls off the bones.

When the roast is tender, transfer it to a large platter and set aside.

Strain the cooking stock through a fine-mesh sieve, mashing the vegetables well to remove all the liquid. Set aside.

Remove the pig's feet and pick the meat off the bones. Strain the stock in which the pig's feet were cooked. Add the meat from pig's feet to the stock, stir in the gelatin and dissolve. Combine the roast stock with the pig's feet stock, skimming off the fat that rises to the top.

Place the roast in a 4-quart mold or bowl. (The roast can be cut in two, and two small molds can then be made.) On the bottom of the mold or bowl, place pimiento strips, several leaves of parsley, sliced olives, and sliced carrots and pour a little of the combined stock over the vegetables. Place in refrigerator and allow the stock to congeal. Sliced lemons and sliced hard-boiled eggs can also be used to garnish the bottom of the mold or bowl.

Remove from refrigerator. Place the roast on top of the garnishes in the bowl, then gently add the stock to cover the meat, and cool.

Return the mold or bowl to the refrigerator and chill for 10 to 12 hours.

Before unmolding, scrape off any fat that has floated to the top. Run a knife around the edges of the mold or bowl, then dip the bottom of the mold or bowl in hot water for a few seconds. Place an inverted plate or platter over the top of the bowl, and, grasping the plate and mold together firmly, turn them over. Rap bottom of mold or bowl sharply on a table or counter. The jellied beef should slide out easily.

Refrigerate until ready to serve. Cut into thin slices.

In the old days, the sliced daube was served for a meal along with boiled new potatoes or fresh green beans. If you wish to serve it for a cocktail party, slice the jellied meat into smaller pieces so guests can place it on toast points, crackers or toasted croutons.

The holidays are indeed a very special time in Acadiana. Not unlike the rest of the world, there's much visiting between friends and families. Gifts are bought or made, wrapped and delivered. Small children are urged to be very, very good because Papa Noel is watching to see who has been naughty or nice. There are tree-decorating parties and, yes, even yard-decorating *soirées*.

Because of the many bayous and streams that wind through south Louisiana, a great many homes are located on some body of water. In St. Martinville and Lafayette, for example, residents along Bayou Teche and the Vermilion River erect extravagant Christmas scenes that can be viewed from the water. These range from Papa Noel being pulled in his sleigh by festive alligators, to humble nativity scenes. Many a night before Christmas, boats loaded with children and adults, bundled warmly against the cold night air, putt-putt along the waterways observing the sights.

Children hum Christmas carols in between stops along the bayou to see friends and relatives. Cups of eggnog and trays of num-nums are passed around. It's a time of celebration and goodwill.

Celebration Eggnog

Makes 8 to 10 cups

6 eggs, separated
1 cup of sugar, divided
1 pint of bourbon
1 quart of heavy whipping cream
Grated nutmeg

Beat the egg yolks until they are pale yellow. Add two-thirds cup of the sugar and beat well. The yolks should be beaten until they are thick and lemon-colored, no matter how much your arm aches. Slowly add the bourbon, beating all the time.

When this much of your task is done, set aside the egg-and-bourbon mixture and turn your attention to the egg whites. Beat the egg whites until they are stiff but not too dry, adding the remaining one-third cup of sugar and beating as you would for meringue.

Then slowly pour the sugar-bourbon-egg yolk mixture into the egg whites, folding it in ever so gently.

Next, whip the cream and fold it into the other mixture. Even if you have been doing this by hand, you will not be too exhausted to stand back and admire the bowl of fluff you have produced.

Warm just a bit before serving. Serve in cups and sprinkle with ground nutmeg. This may also be served chilled.

The eggnog is especially good accompanied by fig cake. It's a perfect opportunity to use some of the fig preserves that were put up the previous summer.

Vicky's Fig Cake

2 cups of sugar
3 eggs
1 cup of vegetable oil
1 cup of milk
2 cups of all-purpose flour
2 teaspoons of ground cinnamon
1 teaspoon of salt
1 teaspoon of baking soda
2 cups of mashed fig preserves
1 cup of pecan pieces

Preheat the oven to 350 degrees.

Cream the sugar and eggs in a mixing bowl. Add the vegetable oil and mix to blend. Add the milk and mix well.

In a separate bowl, combine the flour, cinnamon, salt and soda. Add to the first mixture and then add the figs and pecans. Stir again to combine.

Pour into a 12-cup bundt pan and bake until golden brown, about an hour.

Remove the cake from the oven and cool slightly before slicing to serve.

A favorite num-num of mine is little sausages smothered in a sweet and sour sauce. These are easily stabbed with toothpicks for munching.

Sweet & Sour Sausages

2 pounds of smoked cocktail sausages
One 6-ounce jar of yellow mustard
One 10-ounce jar of tart jelly,
  such as currant

Slowly heat the mustard and jelly and stir until all is well mixed. Add the smoked sausages and cook until warmed through, 10 to 15 minutes.

Serve in a chafing dish and let guests pick them up with toothpicks.

From the time I was a toddler until I was eight or nine years old, my great-aunt Isabelle – fondly called Nannan by all of her family and friends – lived next door to us, and she always walked through the back yard to join us for libations early on Christmas Eve.

We would gather in the living room where the Christmas tree and the creche were the focal point. While Bing Crosby and Gene Autry sang Christmas songs on the radio, Mama would bring in a silver tray set with her best crystal. We all had a thimbleful of cherry bounce and got to open *one* present – just one, mind you.

More often that not, Mama made sure my sister and I opened the boxes that held our red Christmas nightgowns. They were always bedecked with lace ruffles and tiny silk ribbons, and I thought they were much too pretty to sleep in. It wasn't until I got older that I realized the gowns were hand-made by Nannan and her sister Tante May, and thus they became even more special to me. I still have a couple of them wrapped in tissue in my treasure trunk.

The boys, my two brothers, received warm plaid flannel pajamas, which I thought were rather plain but sensible.

Then we were all packed up to bed to dream about what Papa Noel was bringing to us. The boys were settled into their knotty pine-paneled room, which was decorated with plaid curtains and blankets (to match the pajamas). My sister and I were buried under piles of quilts in Mama's and Papa's room since we had to vacate ours to make room for Nannan, who always spent the night. She stayed with us while Mama and Papa went to midnight Mass.

Every Christmas morning I awoke to the smell of Mama's pork roast (which she had put in the oven when she returned from Mass), blended with the scents of brewing coffee and re-heated cinnamon rolls purchased the day before from Mr. Jack's Bakery on Main Street.

The doors to the living room remained closed until everyone had eaten breakfast and Tante May had been fetched to join us. Then with great ceremony, Papa opened the doors to wonderland.

Bikes, dolls, footballs, stuffed animals and baskets of gifts were everywhere!

The next few hours were complete pandemonium, with treks to church, the arrival of aunts and uncles, cousins and friends, and the exchanging of gifts. It usually wasn't until mid-afternoon that we calmed down enough to have Christmas dinner – a combination of dishes prepared by the numerous aunts and highlighted by Mama's pork roast, sometimes a turkey, or perhaps baked capons.

Mama's Stuffed Pork Roast

Makes 12 to 14 servings

10- to 12-pound fresh ham shank
1 large onion, finely chopped
1 large green bell pepper, seeded
   and finely chopped
10 garlic cloves, thinly sliced
3 teaspoons of salt
3 teaspoons of cayenne pepper
1 teaspoon of black pepper
Vegetable oil
2 cups of water

Preheat the oven to 450 degrees.

Set the roast on a large cutting board or platter. Combine the onion, bell pepper, garlic, salt, cayenne and black pepper in a small bowl and mix well.

With a sharp boning knife, make several deep slits in the roast spaced several inches apart. Using your index finger, stuff the seasoning mixture into the slits, packing it in firmly. Season the outside of the roast generously with more salt and cayenne. Rub the roast lightly with vegetable oil.

Place the roast in a heavy roasting pan and put it in the oven. When the bottom of the pan begins to sizzle, carefully add the water. Bake the roast until it browns evenly, 30 to 45 minutes.

More water can be added if the pan becomes too dry. This will mix with the roast drippings and make a dark gravy that can be used now for basting the roast, then later to pour over steamed rice.

When the roast is well browned, reduce the heat to 350 degrees, cover, and cook until the juices run clear and the roast is tender, three to four hours.

Remove from oven and cool slightly before carving.

Although most side dishes varied from year to year, Mama's roast, her rice dressing, and chicken and oyster patties bought from Aline Garrett (whose recipe was never given out) were always on the menu.

By the way, we never called rice dressing "dirty rice." I never heard that term until I was older.

The rice dressing is always made a day or two in advance to allow the flavors to marry.

Henri Clay on our Shetland pony, "Seabiscuit," and Daddy on his mount get ready to ride down Main Street St. Martinville in a parade, circa 1946.

Rice Dressing

Makes about 10 servings

¼ cup of vegetable oil
2 tablespoons of all-purpose flour
1 pound of lean ground pork
1 cup of chopped onions
½ cup of chopped green bell peppers
½ cup of chopped celery
1 pound of chicken gizzards, cleaned
Water
Salt and cayenne pepper, to taste
4 to 5 cups of cooked long-grain white rice
¼ cup of chopped parsley
½ cup of finely chopped green onions
1 pint of raw oysters and their liquor
  (optional)
1 cup of canned sliced mushrooms
  (optional)

Combine two tablespoons of the vegetable oil with the flour in a small, heavy sauce pan over medium heat. Stirring slowly and constantly, make a dark brown roux. Set aside.

Heat the remaining two tablespoons of vegetable oil in a large, heavy saucepan over medium heat. Add the pork and brown well. Add the onions, bell peppers and celery. Cook, stirring, until the vegetables are very soft, six to eight minutes.

In the meantime, place the gizzards in a pot with enough water (about three cups) to cover and boil until tender. Drain the gizzards and reserve the stock.

Grind the gizzards in a meat grinder or food processor. Add this to the pork mixture along with the roux. Add the reserved stock from the gizzards and season with salt and cayenne.

Reduce the heat to medium-low and simmer, stirring occasionally, for about an hour.

Immediately before serving, add the rice, parsley and green onions. Mix well and season with salt and cayenne.

If you like, add the oysters with their liquor and mushrooms and cook until warmed through.

There were many sweets at the Christmas table – remember the fudge, pralines and lizzies?

Aunt Eva could always be counted on to bring a cake of some sort. Her *pièce de résistance*, though, was coconut cake that always appeared to me to be too pretty to cut.

Coconut Cake

2¼ cups of all-purpose flour
1½ cups of sugar
3½ teaspoons of baking powder
1 teaspoon of salt
½ cup of softened shortening
1 cup of milk, divided
1 teaspoon of vanilla or almond extract
4 egg whites, unbeaten
Cream Filling (Recipe follows)
Fluffy Icing (Recipe follows)

Preheat the oven to 350 degrees.

Grease and flour two 8-inch layer pans or a 13 x 9½ x 2 oblong pan.

Combine the flour, sugar, baking powder and salt. Add the shortening, two-thirds cup of milk and the extract. Beat with a mixer for two minutes at medium speed. Scrape the sides and bottom of the bowl as needed.

Add the remaining milk and the egg whites. Beat for two more minutes, scraping the bowl frequently.

Pour the batter into the prepared pans. Bake the smaller cakes for 30 to 35 minutes or the oblong cake for 35 to 40 minutes. Cool on a wire rack.

If making a layer cake, spread the cooled Cream Filling between the two layers. Then top with Fluffy Icing and decorate with flaked coconut. Chopped pecans or almonds may also be sprinkled on top.

CREAM FILLING

¼ cup of sugar
1 tablespoon of cornstarch
¼ teaspoon of salt
1 cup of milk
1 egg yolk, lightly beaten
1 tablespoon of butter
1 teaspoon of vanilla extract

Combine the sugar, cornstarch and salt in a saucepan over medium heat. Gradually stir in the milk and bring to a boil, stirring constantly. Boil for one minute and then remove from heat.

Stir about half of the hot mixture into the egg yolk, then blend this mixture into the remaining mixture. Boil one minute more and then remove from heat.

Blend in butter and vanilla and cool, stirring occasionally.

FLUFFY ICING

½ cup of sugar
2 tablespoons of water
¼ cup of light corn syrup
2 egg whites
1 teaspoon of vanilla extract

Combine the sugar, water and corn syrup in a saucepan. Cover the pan and bring to a rolling boil. Remove the cover and cook until the mixture reaches 242 degrees on a candy thermometer.

Beat the egg whites until stiff enough to hold a point.

Pour the hot syrup very slowly in a thin stream into the beaten egg whites. Continue beating until the frosting holds peaks. Blend in the vanilla.

After the dinner table was cleared and the good silver and china had been washed and put away, it was time to bid everyone a long Creole good-bye. Some of us would be seeing each other again on New Year's Day, but there were always a few relatives who had come a long distance, so it might be another year before we would see them again. It was a sad-happy time for me, but I was always comforted by the fact that I could put on my red lacy gown and that my new doll for the year could sleep with me.

The week between Christmas and New Year's has always reminded me of a lull in a storm – a break between the Christmas feasting and the New Year's toasting. But it has also been a time to visit with friends who are in town for the holidays. I have made it a tradition to have an elegant dinner party at which we can all have an opportunity to dress up. What better time for the men to sport new ties or a cashmere jacket and the ladies to show off their baubles and beads?

And, too, it gives me a chance to use some of my treasured old china and silver pieces that have been handed down in my family from generation to generation. Among these heirlooms are several hand-painted oval fish plates, along with slender fish knives with curved points, designed to use to pick the bones out of a whole fish.

In genteel New Orleans homes of days past it was not uncommon to have fish for breakfast and again as a course for dinner.

More often than not, either small whole fish or fish steaks, with bone in, were served, rather than the fillets in vogue these days. The fish were served alone, with perhaps a sprig of parsley and a wedge of lemon, on colorful fish plates.

Also in my possession are several ornate bowls with six compartments, known as oyster plates – perfect for serving fresh-from-the-sea cold oysters. Instead of serving them on the half shell, the plates are ideal for a formal dinner party when the oysters can be plopped into the compartments, dabbed with cocktail sauce, and served with a wedge of lemon.

In my antique collection is an elegant set of pear-shaped glasses that were used for serving syllabub, a drink made with sweetened milk or cream mixed with wine or cider. I've been known to also use them for *parfaits* and frappés.

Probably my most treasured pieces are *café brulot* cups designed in the late nineteenth century by the proprietor of Antoine's Restaurant, Jules Alciatore. These fanciful cups feature a devil holding the bowl part of the cup.

Now on to dinner. I believe I'll serve the following dish on my beautiful fish plates.

This is me with my birthday cake in February 1953.

Broiled Spanish Mackerel

Makes 4 servings

4 tablespoons of butter
1 tablespoon of fresh lemon or lime juice
1/2 teaspoon of anchovy paste
1/8 teaspoon of cayenne pepper
1/2 teaspoon of salt
Four 6-ounce Spanish mackerel fillets
    (or any firm white fish), skinned
1 tablespoon of vegetable oil
Lemon or lime, cut lengthwise into
    4 or 8 wedges

Preheat the broiler to its highest setting.

Melt the butter in a small saucepan. Remove the pan from the heat and stir in the lemon or lime juice, anchovy paste, cayenne and salt. Set the sauce aside.

Pat the fillets completely dry with paper towels. Then, with a pastry brush, spread the vegetable oil evenly over the grid of the broiling pan. Arrange the fillets side-by-side on the grid, and brush them with two tablespoons of the butter sauce.

Broil four inches from the heat for four to five minutes, brushing the fillets once or twice with remaining butter sauce. The fish is done when the tops are golden brown and firm to the touch.

Transfer the fillets to fish plates and garnish with lemon or lime wedges.

Keep the meal light and serve with boiled new potatoes sprinkled with a bit of fresh dill and drizzled with melted butter.

For dessert, I'll make the SYLLABUB, which can also be served in wine goblets or *parfait* glasses.

Syllabub

Makes about 8 servings

2 cups of whipping cream
¼ cup of brandy
¼ cup of dry sherry
¼ cup of sugar
1 tablespoon of vanilla extract
2 lemons

Whip the cream until stiff and fluffy.

Add the brandy, sherry, sugar, vanilla and the juice and grated rind from two lemons. Mix well until blended.

Spoon into dessert glasses. Garnish with a pirouette cookie and a few chocolate sprinkles, or with grated lemon rind.

After dessert, and before my guests depart, I must serve coffee in my treasured *brûlot* cups.

Café Brûlot

Makes 4 to 6 servings (depending on the size of cups used)

If you don't have brûlot cups, demitasse cups may be used.

- Peel of 1 orange, cut into 1-by-1/8-inch strips
- Peel of 1 lemon, cut into 1-by-1/8-inch strips
- 3 sugar lumps
- 6 whole cloves
- 2-inch cinnamon stick
- 1 cup of cognac
- ½ cup of curaçao or other orange liqueur
- 2 cups of fresh strong black coffee

Light the burner under a *brûlot* bowl or chafing dish and adjust the flame to low. Drop the orange and lemon peel, sugar lumps, cloves and cinnamon stick into the bowl or pan, pour in the cognac and *curaçao*, and stir to dissolve the sugar.

When the mixture is warm, ignite it with a match. Stirring gently, pour the coffee into the bowl in a slow, thin stream. Continue to stir until the flames die out.

Strain the mixture, then ladle into *brûlot* cups or demitasse cups and serve at once.

Bonne Année et Le Petit Bonhomme Janvier

Christmas has come and gone. The presents have all been opened. All that is left of Christmas dinner is the turkey carcass. The Jolly Old Man has returned to the North Pole and Johnny Mathis has gone hoarse on the holiday music tape. The lights on the Christmas tree seem to have dimmed, and it seems that all we look forward to are endless football games on television.

But, if you believe in Acadian folklore, legend tells of *Le Petit Bonhomme Janvier*, the little man of January, who visits the homes of good little children (and adults) on New Year's Eve and brings small sacks of treats filled with such things as oranges, pecans, candy, coloring books and crayons.

I learned about this little man one New Year's Eve when we children were doled out to Nannan's so Mama and Papa could have a night on the town. We were all still young and we were allowed to bring one Christmas gift to Nannan's to play with. I had my Toni doll, Henri Clay had his electric football game, Edna had her blackboard and chalk, and Baby Brother Bruce had his white, fuzzy, stuffed lamb.

Nannan had laid down quilts over the cold, hard wooden floors and turned up the gas heaters that burned brightly in the living room, where the only other light came from the Christmas tree. No television then. Nannan had tuned to WWL radio, through which music was coming "live and direct" from the Roosevelt Hotel's Blue Room in New Orleans.

Since it was a special night, we were allowed to stay up later because Nannan had promised us a treat. Then we were going to be sent off to the big four-poster beds to sleep so that *Le Petit Bonhomme Janvier* could "make his pass" with his goodies.

I remember thinking, "Adults always think of a way to make us go to bed." But I trusted Nannan.

This was our first treat.

On a huge tray lined with her best linen napkins, Nannan brought out coffee cups

Enjoying a New Year's Eve party at the Buccaneer Club in St. Martinville are Mama (seated) and my Uncle Tilden Bonin (standing behind Mama), circa 1943. The other characters are unidentified.

filled with steaming hot chocolate thickened with lots of marshmallows and flavored with a bit of strong coffee, and plates of cheese toast.

Then it was off to bed to wait for that little man who comes only after children are asleep. I had full intentions of playing possum, but, alas, my body wasn't willing.

Early the next morning, hung on the posters of the beds, we found a colorful sack for each of us, filled with sussies of all kinds – apples, oranges, mandarins, candied pecans, little dolls made out of clothespins, and pralines wrapped in red cellophane paper tied up with gold ribbons.

I had a new hero! It is a tradition that is still practiced, and even now, as an adult, I can't wait to make and receive bags of goodies from the Little Man of January.

After I was grown, New Year's Eve remained a special night of parties and great celebration. Elegant evenings out on the

town became part of my holiday tradition, as they had been for my parents, so many years ago.

After they deposited us safely with Nannan, Mama and Papa would head out for a round of parties held in private homes and at popular supper clubs. One of their favorite nightspots was Toby's Oak Grove, the "in spot" and ultimate dinner club in Lafayette. Toby's holds a special place in my heart, for once, a long time ago, my parents took me there for an evening I'll never forget.

Mama was decked out in a sleek black silk crepe, over which she draped her fur wrap. Papa, with a smart bow tie and double-breasted suit, was quite dapper. The hair style for women then was the chignon, a bun caught at the nape of the neck. Mama's thick black hair was done just so, and she had ebony chop sticks with dangling rhinestones stuck in the bun that were absolutely divine. I thought I was pretty smart in a navy velveteen affair with a sterling silver barrette holding my pageboy hairdo to one side.

After we were seated, the waiter took our cocktail orders, and although I thought myself a bit old for a Shirley Temple, at least it was brought to me in a highball glass. Mama simply ordered a martini, dry, up. Daddy had his usual bourbon on the rocks with a splash.

When our drinks arrived, I watched as Mama sipped her martini from the frosted stem glass, her red fingernails gracefully wrapped round the stem. Then I noticed the red lipstick mark left on the glass, and I thought that most intriguing.

It was then that I decided that once I was old enough, I, too, wanted to always have red nails and red lipstick, and I would have a martini, dry, up.

Through the years I have been fascinated when people make or order a martini. It's a very personal matter, like your choice of a brand of toothpaste. If it's not just like you want it, it's not pleasurable.

At the Fairmont Hotel in New Orleans (still called the Roosevelt by many of us), I once observed a gray-haired, smartly dressed gentleman who came up to the bar, and who, with a nod to the bartender, was brought a small tray. On the tray was a silver shaker and strainer, a small glass ice bucket, a frosty stemmed glass, a sliver of lemon peel, a bottle of good gin, a bottle of dry vermouth, and a glass stirrer.

With great aplomb, the gentleman made his very own martini. His recipe was three jiggers of gin gently poured over a few cubes of ice in the silver shaker and a whisper of dry vermouth, which was then gently stirred, then strained into the stemmed glass. The lemon peel was passed around the top of the glass, then dropped in the cold liquid. With great relish, the gentleman sipped and smiled. He made another, and while sipping the second you could almost see the strain of the day slip away. Ah, what pleasure he had.

I had an aunt and uncle who had a nightly ritual. They had no children, lived in a gracious home, and were devoted to each other. Every evening, when my uncle got home from work, he and my aunt would sit in the parlor where the butler would set up a martini tray from which they would make their drinks. He would put a few chips of ice in a small glass martini pitcher, add several jiggers of iced vodka and a couple of drops of vermouth, give the liquid a swirl, and pour out the ice-cold martinis. Their preference was olives rather than lemon peel. The olives had to be the large Queen olives, which were speared on sterling silver monkeys that hung over the rim of the glass. How absolutely civilized.

When the New Year dawns in south Louisiana, pots are simmering on stoves, filled with the traditional black-eyed peas (for good luck) and cabbage (to ensure monetary success).

To get the juices flowing before embarking on a day-long feast (particularly if the New Year's Eve celebration included martinis!), an ice-cold MILK PUNCH or a tangy, spicy BLOODY MARY is in order.

Milk Punch

Makes 1 gallon

This drink is quite popular in old New Orleans restaurants and is a favorite during the winter holiday season. It is a soothing, pleasant drink after a night of partying.

1 (4/5-quart) bottle of bourbon
  (Brandy may also be used.)
3 quarts of half-and-half
4 tablespoons of vanilla extract
Simple syrup (Recipe follows)
Ground nutmeg

Combine the bourbon, half-and-half and vanilla in a 1-gallon container. Add Simple Syrup to attain desired sweetness. Chill thoroughly.

Serve in a chilled glass (not over ice) and sprinkle with ground nutmeg.

SIMPLE SYRUP

1 cup of water
1 cup of sugar

Combine sugar and water in a small saucepan. Boil until the sugar dissolves and the liquid becomes slightly thick. Cool completely before using.

Bloody Mary

Makes four 8-ounce cocktails

This is a real eye-opener when spiced up with Louisiana's own Tabasco®.

4 cups of good-quality, thick tomato juice
1 teaspoon of salt
1 teaspoon of black pepper
½ teaspoon of celery salt
1 tablespoon of Worcestershire sauce
8 dashes of Tabasco® brand pepper sauce
2 teaspoons of fresh lime juice
4 to 5 jiggers of vodka
Lime wedges

In a large pitcher, combine all ingredients and chill for at least an hour.

Stir again before serving. Pour into tall glasses over chipped ice and garnish with lime wedges.

To make the day last as long as possible, it is usually my choice to serve a brunch in late morning or early afternoon and keep the peas and cabbage for later in the day.

One of my all-time truly great breakfast dishes is *GRILLADES* (pronounced gree-yahds) and BAKED GRITS. Besides such traditional Acadian-Creole favorites as jambalaya, gumbo and red beans and rice, *grillades* is the epitome of what Southern cooks can do with simple ingredients to make a dish that will wake up your taste buds, warm your soul, and excite your heart! It is all in the way it is seasoned, cooked with patience, and served with great flair.

Baked Grits

Makes about 10 servings

2 cups of white or yellow grits (not the instant kind)
3 eggs, beaten
½ pound of grated cheddar cheese
1 cup of milk
8 tablespoons (1 stick) of butter

Preheat the oven to 350 degrees.

Cook the grits according to the package directions. Add the eggs, grated cheese, milk and butter. Stir until blended and the cheese melts completely.

Pour the mixture into a 2-quart baking dish and bake uncovered for one hour.

Serve hot.

Grillades

Makes about 10 servings

4 pounds of boneless beef round steak
1 tablespoon of salt
1 teaspoon of cayenne pepper
½ teaspoon of black pepper
½ teaspoon of garlic powder
½ cup of all-purpose flour
½ cup of vegetable oil
2½ cups of chopped onions
1½ cups of chopped green bell peppers
1 cup of chopped celery
4 cups of whole canned tomatoes, crushed, with their juice
2 cups of water or beef broth (or more as needed)
2 bay leaves
½ teaspoon of dried tarragon leaves
½ teaspoon of dried basil leaves
Hot sauce, to taste
1 cup of finely chopped green onions
½ cup of finely chopped parsley

Remove and discard excess fat from the meat and cut into 2-inch squares.

Make a seasoning mix by combining the salt, cayenne, black pepper and garlic powder in a small bowl. Have the flour at hand.

Lay several pieces of the beef on a cutting board and sprinkle with the seasoning mix and a little flour. Then with a meat mallet, pound each piece of meat until slightly flattened. Flip the pieces over and repeat the process.

Heat the vegetable oil in a large, heavy pot or Dutch oven over medium heat. Brown the meat, in batches, on both sides.

When all the meat has been browned, return it to the pot with the onions, bell peppers and celery. Cook, stirring, until the vegetables are soft and tender, six to eight minutes. Add the crushed tomatoes and their liquid, water or beef broth, the bay leaves, tarragon, basil and hot sauce.

Cook, stirring occasionally, until the meat is tender and the gravy is thick, one and a half to two hours. Season with salt and cayenne.

Add the green onions and parsley and serve over baked grits.

If you are an egg lover, you may want to opt for egg dishes at your brunch. I was introduced to the following potato omelet by my childhood friend Beau, who loves to cook almost as much as he loves to eat. He says this omelet was one of his mother's specialties.

French Fried Potato Omelet

Makes 1 serving

1 russet potato, skinned or unskinned,
   cut as for French fries
Vegetable oil
3 eggs
2 tablespoons of cold water
Salt and black pepper, to taste
Hot sauce (optional)

Fry the potatoes in enough hot oil to deep-fry. When the potatoes are golden brown, remove and drain on paper towels.

Lightly oil a medium-size skillet and heat over medium heat. Add the potatoes to the skillet. Beat the eggs with the water in a small bowl and then pour the mixture over the potatoes. Give it a couple of stirs and fold over.

Season with salt, pepper and hot sauce. Serve immediately.

Beau also parted with another egg dish, which is luscious.

Eggs Beauregard

Makes 2 to 4 servings

4 tablespoons of butter
½ cup of chopped celery
½ cup of chopped green bell peppers
1½ cups of heavy cream
4 eggs
½ cup of grated Swiss, cheddar
   or Colby cheese
Salt and black pepper, to taste

Heat the butter in an 8-inch skillet over medium heat. Add the celery and bell peppers, and cook, stirring, until they are slightly soft, about three minutes. Spread the vegetables evenly on the bottom of the skillet.

Pour in the cream, but do not stir. Allow the cream to set.

Drop the eggs, a couple of inches apart, into the cream and poach until desired doneness.

Sprinkle the cheese over the eggs and cook until the cheese melts. Season with salt and pepper.

To serve, cut into pie-shaped wedges with one egg in each slice.

A similar egg dish which is great when you have guests is something I call SKILLET EGGS. A friend of mine and I created this dish when we were testing a set of pots I had given myself as a birthday present. It is a dish that is as good as your creativity and imagination. Use whatever you have hanging around in the refrigerator. You can add boiled shrimp, leftover pieces of steak, chopped ham, or crumbled bacon. It's akin to creating your very own pizza.

Skillet Eggs

Serves 2, but it can be made for as many as 12 with ease. Adjust amounts accordingly.

1½ teaspoons of olive oil or vegetable oil
½ seeded and chopped green bell pepper
4 fresh mushrooms, wiped clean, stemmed
   and thinly sliced
½ cup of chopped cooked asparagus (or
   squash, green beans and tomatoes)
4 eggs
¼ cup of shredded cheese of your choice
Salt and black pepper
Fresh dill for garnish (optional)

Heat the oil in a medium-size skillet over medium heat. Add the bell pepper and cook, stirring, for about a minute. Add the mushrooms and whatever vegetables you've gathered and cook until warmed through. Spread the vegetables evenly over the bottom of the skillet.

Drop whole cracked eggs into the pan a couple of inches apart. Top with shredded cheese.

Cover and allow the eggs to poach to desired doneness.

Remove the skillet from the heat and cut the eggs into pie-shaped pieces. Season with salt and pepper and garnish with dill if you like.

Serve with hot French bread or biscuits.

Note: You can top the eggs with hollandaise, béarnaise, or even *marchand du vin* sauce.

If you have any leftover rice, let me introduce you to a very thrifty egg dish that Cina always served on Sunday nights. It is also perfectly fine for brunch, served along with LIGHT-AS-A-CLOUD BISCUITS, sweet butter and fig preserves.

Rice & Eggs

Makes 4 servings

2 tablespoons of vegetable oil or butter
2 eggs
2 cups of cooked long-grain white rice
1 tablespoon each of chopped green onions
  and parsley
½ cup of diced ham or crumbled cooked
  bacon
Salt and black pepper, to taste

Heat the oil or margarine in a heavy skillet over medium heat. Drop in the eggs and stir them until they begin to firm up, about a minute.

Add the cooked rice and blend with the eggs. Add the green onion, parsley and ham or bacon, and season with salt and pepper.

Serve hot.

Light-as-a-Cloud Biscuits

Makes 24 good-sized biscuits

4 cups of biscuit mix
1 heaping tablespoon of sugar
1 scant teaspoon of salt
½ teaspoon of cream of tartar
1 teaspoon of baking powder
1½ cups of vegetable shortening
1½ cups of milk

Preheat the oven to 400 degrees.

Sift all the dry ingredients together into a large mixing bowl. Drop the shortening into the middle of the dry ingredients and pour the milk over it. With your fingers, not with a spoon, pastry knife or anything else, mix everything together, working in the dry ingredients until the dough has formed a nice, slightly sticky ball.

If you want to roll the biscuits, generously flour a pastry board, roll out the dough to about 1/4-inch thickness, and cut with a biscuit cutter.

Otherwise, make drop biscuits by dropping the dough by the tablespoonful on an ungreased cookie sheet. Sometimes I dust my hands well with flour and pat out little rounds.

Bake until golden brown, 12 to 15 minutes.

Note: The uncooked dough can be frozen.

Now, you say, how can one possibly think about eating for the rest of the day? Never fear. Come six or seven o'clock, there are bound to be a few requests for something to eat. At least that's how it is down South. Besides, one could not think of letting New Year's Day go by without eating at least a small helping of BLACK-EYED PEAS, a dab of cabbage and, for *lagniappe*, a thick slice of baked ham, eaten alone or rolled inside a fistful of French bread. It wouldn't be proper.

I will admit, right here and now, I don't cook black-eyed peas from scratch. I can't find anything better than Trappey's Black-Eyed Peas with Jalapeño. I have been known to doctor them up a bit, but the Trappey company seems to have the secret to producing the peas cooked whole, yet swimming in a creamy sauce that's perfect for mixing with steamed rice.

Black-Eyed Peas

Makes 8 servings

2 tablespoons of vegetable oil
1 pound of smoked sausage, cut crosswise
  into ¼-inch slices
½ pound of diced ham
1 cup of chopped onions
½ cup of seeded and chopped green
  bell peppers
1 (15-ounce) can of black-eyed peas
  with jalapeño
Salt and black pepper, to taste
Hot sauce (optional)

Heat the oil in a large, heavy saucepan over medium heat. Add the sausage and ham and cook, stirring, for three to four minutes. Add the onions and bell peppers, and cook, stirring, until they are soft and lightly golden, about six minutes.

Add the black-eyed peas and simmer for 30 minutes. Season with salt and pepper, and simmer for 10 minutes longer.

Serve over rice. Or, better yet, make a jambalaya of sorts by mixing the black-eyed peas mixture with about four cups of cooked rice. If the mixture is too dry, add a little beef or chicken broth to moisten.

Smothered Cabbage

Makes 6 servings

2 tablespoons of vegetable oil
1 cup of chopped ham
1 cup of chopped onions
1 large head of green cabbage, cleaned
    and coarsely chopped
1 teaspoon of sugar
Salt and black pepper, to taste

Heat the oil in a large, heavy pot over medium heat. Add the ham and onions, and cook, stirring, for three to four minutes. Add the cabbage and sugar, and season with salt and pepper.

Cover and cook, stirring occasionally, until the cabbage is soft and tender, about 30 minutes. Serve hot.

I simply adore baked ham. I don't care that sometimes a baked ham can last for several days. Plus there's always the ham bone – a prize with which to make soups or bean dishes.

Glazed Ham

Makes about 12 servings

1 (8½-pound) ham shank
Whole cloves
1 cup of port wine
1 tablespoon of dry mustard
1½ tablespoons of dark brown sugar
½ cup of ginger ale

Most people prefer to remove any of the skin remaining on the ham, but I like to keep it on. Once the ham is cooked, the skin provides delightful tidbits to munch on.

Preheat the oven to 300 degrees.

Score the skin and/or fat by making long vertical and horizontal cuts. Bake the ham in a roasting pan for 30 minutes. Remove the ham from the oven and place a whole clove in the center of each scored square and return the ham to the oven for another 30 minutes, basting with one-half cup of port.

In the meantime, mix the dry mustard, brown sugar and the rest of the port together in a small bowl. Remove the ham once again from the oven and spread the sugar/mustard/port sauce over the whole fat side of the ham. Pour the ginger ale into the bottom of the pan.

Increase the oven temperature to 450 degrees and return the ham to the oven. Baste every 10 to 15 minutes with the pan juices. Continue to bake for an hour more. Loosely cover the ham with aluminum foil for this last hour of cooking. If you need more basting liquid, add some port and ginger ale.

Most folks are fairly tired of fancy eating after the Christmas and New Year holidays. If you have saved the ham bone from your holiday ham – and no self-respecting Louisiana cook would throw such a thing out – now is the time to stock up the freezer with humble but delicious bean dishes. Here are two of my favorites: WHITE BEAN SOUP and RED BEANS, MY WAY.

White Bean Soup

Makes 8 servings

1 pound of Great Northern beans
4 quarts of water or chicken broth
1 cup of chopped onions
1 cup of chopped green bell peppers
1 cup of chopped celery
1 (16-ounce) can of whole tomatoes,
    crushed with their juice
½ pound of salt pork or ham pieces
    (A leftover ham bone may be used.)

Soak the beans overnight in cool water.

Before cooking, drain and sort out any bad beans. Place the beans in a large soup pot or kettle along with the water or chicken broth, onions, bell peppers, celery, crushed tomatoes, and salt pork, ham pieces or ham bone. Bring slowly to a boil, then simmer until the beans are tender and can be mashed easily with a spoon against the side of the pot, about an hour and a half.

Adjust seasoning. Since the salt pork or ham may have made the beans taste salty enough, you may need to add only a little black pepper or cayenne.

Papa liked to eat his white bean soup with a couple of spoonsful of rice, a fistful of finely chopped green onions, and a generous dousing of hot sauce.

Just like gumbo, everyone in south Louisiana has his very own recipe for red beans. I've listened to people argue if they should add smoked sausage and ham, or either one or the other. Some like to use only ham hocks. Others like the red beans served along with a fried pork chop.

I'm not a purist when it comes to red beans. Do it any way you like. The following recipe happens to be a combination of Mama's way and my way.

Red Beans, My Way

Makes 8 servings

1 pound of red kidney beans
2 quarts of water
½ cup of beef broth
3 tablespoons of vegetable oil
2 cups of chopped onions
1 cup of chopped green bell peppers
1½ cups of chopped celery
1 teaspoon of minced garlic
1 pound of smoked pork sausage, cut crosswise into ½-inch slices
½ pound of ham pieces
3 bay leaves
2 pinches of dried thyme
Salt, black pepper, and cayenne pepper, to taste
Chopped green onions, for garnish

Soak the beans overnight in cool water.

Before cooking, drain and sort out any bad beans. Place the beans in a large soup pot or kettle along with the water and beef broth; bring to a gentle boil.

Heat the oil in a large skillet over medium heat. Add the onions, bell peppers, celery, garlic, sausage and ham. Cook, stirring, until the vegetables are soft and lightly golden, six to eight minutes.

When the beans have come to a boil, add the vegetable-and-meat mixture. Add the bay leaves, thyme, salt and peppers.

Reduce the heat to medium-low and cook, stirring occasionally, until the beans are very tender, about two hours.

I like my red beans a little creamy, so I remove about two cups and cream them in a food processor or blender, and return them to the pot.

Serve the red beans over rice topped with a sprinkling of minced green onions.

Mardi Gras Beads

While the rest of the country is taking a much-needed break from festivities once the holiday season comes to a close, the people of south Louisiana are moving quickly into one of their favorite seasons – Carnival.

The Carnival season officially begins on Twelfth Night, and from New Orleans to Lake Charles there will be countless balls, parades, and *soirées*. The round of parties will continue until *Mardi Gras* Day, which is also known as Shrove Tuesday or Fat Tuesday. The Carnival season ends at midnight on Shrove Tuesday, ushering in the somber Ash Wednesday morning and the Lenten season of penance and abstinence.

But until midnight on Fat Tuesday, the prevailing attitude is, *Laissez les bon temps rouler*!

Mardi Gras is celebrated in a variety of ways all across south Louisiana. Sure, most people in the United States have heard about the New Orleans *Mardi Gras* – a big-city party with big-city traditions. Most people aren't aware of the country-style *Mardi Gras* I grew up with in St. Martinville.

We didn't have king cakes, elaborate parades or krewes. Our Carnival traditions were a little less formal, but fun nonetheless.

On the Sunday before *Mardi Gras*, the St. Martinville Lion's Club always sponsors the Children's Carnival. For weeks mamas piece together crepe paper, bits and pieces of net and ribbon, cardboard – anything at hand – and create a bit of mythical wonder for the children of the town.

The night before *Mardi Gras* is reserved for adults when the Rotary Club presents a magnificent tableaux and dance. I've often said that the costumes outshine those I've seen at most balls in the city. Since my father was a charter member of the St. Martinville club, my brothers, sister and I have run the whole gamut from being pages, entertainers, maids, dukes, captains and queens.

For weeks before the affair the women – and, yes, many times the men – can be found bending over tables and work benches, beading, spray painting, sewing

Ruling over the St. Martinville Rotary Club Mardi Gras Ball in 1954 are my father, King Blackie Bienvenu, and Queen Virginia Fournet.

and building sets in preparation for the big event.

I'll never forget the year I was queen. In the week before *Mardi Gras*, everyone ran around like chickens with their heads cut off. There were teas, receptions and last minute dashes to Lafayette for more beads and long white gloves. I can still smell the scents of velvet, starched net and glue.

On the magical day, those without hangovers would march down Main Street attired in makeshift costumes, banging on tin cans shouting, "*Mardi Gras* chick-a-la-pye, run away and tra-la-la." Sometimes, if Mama and Papa could handle it, we would drive to Lafayette to see a parade. There were no doubloons, beads or ladders back then. The float riders threw candy, bubble gum and whistles. The big hurrah was the costumed horses and riders from neighboring towns. Even the hooves of the horses were painted and glittered.

If time warranted, we drove to Church Point and Mamou to see the *Courir du Mardi Gras* (the running of the *Mardi Gras*). The men of the rural communities, dressed in colorful costumes, gather on horseback. The maskers visit farm houses along a planned, or sometimes unplanned, route. At each stop, *Le Capitaine* asks for a donation. Sometimes the donation is a bag of rice, a small fat hen, or other ingredients for a big gumbo. Sometimes the maskers thank the farmers and their families by performing dances and singing Cajun songs. At the end of the day, they ride back to town, shouting invitations along the way, telling everyone to come to the town hall where the cooks prepare a big gumbo and a *fais do do* is held.

Here is a recipe for a traditional gumbo much like the one which might be prepared in Mamou or Church Point on *Mardi Gras* Day.

Carmen Bulliard Montegut's Chicken & Oyster Gumbo

Makes 8 servings

¾ cup of vegetable oil
¾ cup of all-purpose flour
1 large onion, finely chopped
8 garlic cloves, minced
1 large hen, cut up as for frying
Salt, cayenne pepper, and black pepper, to taste
3 quarts of water (or more as needed)
1 pint of oysters with their liquor
Filé powder
Chopped parsley
Chopped green onions

Make a roux by heating the oil, adding the flour, and blending until smooth. Cook over low heat until the roux is golden brown.

Add the onions and garlic.

Season the chicken with salt, cayenne and black pepper. Add the chicken to the roux and cook until the oil comes out around the edges, about an hour.

Add warm water and cook slowly until the chicken is tender, about two hours.

Add the oysters and their liquor five minutes before serving.

Serve with rice. To each serving of gumbo add a small amount of filé powder, to taste. Garnish each bowl with chopped parsley and chopped green onion tops.

Once I moved to New Orleans as a young adult, I was introduced to a whole other kind of Carnival celebration. There were before-parade parties, during-parade parties and after-parade parties. There were weekly king cake parties and parties before balls and parties after balls.

I quickly got the hang of it, and during the several years I lived in the French Quarter my apartment became the meeting place for all of the above.

Not to be outdone by my new group of friends, I broadened my cooking repertoire to include not only gumbos, jambalayas and *etouffées*, but also simple but good *hors d'oeuvres* that could be put out for the hungry hordes that stopped at my door.

Sausage-Cheese Biscuits

Makes about 6 dozen

1 pound of extra-sharp cheddar cheese, shredded
1 pound of spicy bulk pork breakfast sausage, crumbled
3 cups of buttermilk biscuit mix

Preheat the oven to 450 degrees.

Melt the cheese in the top of a double boiler. Add the sausage and cook, stirring, until the sausage is evenly browned, about 20 minutes.

Transfer the mixture to a large mixing bowl and cool just a bit. Add the biscuit mix and mix well.

Shape the dough into 1-inch balls. (The dough may be frozen at this point.)

Place the balls on ungreased cookie sheets and bake until golden brown, 15 to 20 minutes. Serve warm.

If *Mardi Gras* season is late and crawfish are beginning to show up at the market, MINI CRAWFISH PIES are also good finger food.

Mini Crawfish Pies

Makes 4 dozen bite-sized pies

8 tablespoons (1 stick) of butter
1 cup of finely chopped onions
1 cup of chopped green bell peppers
1 teaspoon of salt
½ teaspoon of cayenne pepper
½ teaspoon of white pepper
¼ teaspoon of black pepper
2 tablespoons of tomato paste
1 teaspoon of paprika
2 tablespoons of cornstarch dissolved in 1 cup of water
1 pound of peeled crawfish tails
1 bunch of green onions, finely chopped
2 tablespoons of minced parsley
4 dozen bite-sized, pre-baked patty shells

Preheat the oven to 350 degrees.

Heat the butter in a large, heavy pot over medium heat. Add the onions and bell peppers, and cook, stirring until they are soft, about six minutes. Add the salt and peppers, and reduce the heat to medium-low.

Add the tomato paste and paprika and let the mixture bubble for a few minutes. Add the cornstarch dissolved in water, and cook until a fine glaze appears on the mixture.

Add the crawfish, green onions and parsley. Cook, stirring occasionally, for about ten minutes. Adjust the seasonings to taste.

Spoon the mixture into pre-baked patty shells and bake until golden brown, five to eight minutes. Serve warm.

I am also a firm believer in finger sandwiches that are filling and easy to make. For *Mardi Gras*, I usually opt for a great HAM SALAD spread on hearty rye bread.

Ham Salad

Makes 20 finger sandwiches

3 cups of diced ham
¼ cup of minced green onions
¼ cup of minced celery
¼ cup of minced black olives
2 tablespoons of minced pimientos
Mayonnaise
Creole mustard
Hot sauce
Worcestershire sauce
10 slices of rye bread

Chop the ham very fine in a food processor.

Combine the ham with the green onions, celery, black olives and pimientos. Blend with mayonnaise, Creole mustard, hot sauce, and Worcestershire, to taste.

Spread the mixture on the bread and cut each sandwich into quarters.

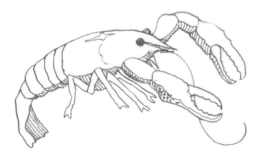

The final hurrah of Carnival (which translates from the Latin as "farewell to the flesh") is *Mardi Gras* Day. Even before dawn on Fat Tuesday, inhabitants of south Louisiana are crawling out of warm beds to pull themselves together for the last wallop of festivities. Even with hangover headaches pounding at their temples, revelers are bristling with excitement.

Parade riders, armed with costumes, beads and doubloons, are winding through the streets heading for krewe dens and other designated meeting places, where they will board their assigned floats. Members of marching bands have one more practice session as they line up in the streets. Horseback riders give their mounts one more brushing. Maskers add the final touches to costumes before taking to the streets. Families load up station wagons and vans with ladders, picnic baskets and folding chairs.

It's going to be a long day and everyone will need sustenance for the action-packed festivities. Knowing that the day after *Mardi Gras* is Ash Wednesday, which opens the Lenten season of 40 days of penance and abstinence prior to Easter, everyone is prepared to fill their tummies with all the good things they love.

In rural communities, pots of gumbo, both seafood and sausage, *sauce piquantes*, and possibly *fricassées* are bubbling on stoves long before the sun comes up. After all, there will be aunts, uncles, many cousins and friends who will be dropping by in the late afternoon after much dancing in the streets to play *bourrée* (a popular card game) and enjoy a hearty meal.

For those who will ensconce themselves along parade routes, picnic hampers and small ice chests are the order of the day.

A couple I know always goes to parades in style with a few bottles of good champagne, caviar and all the fixings, a stash of STEAK TARTARE, and an assortment of good breads. A bowl of strawberries rolled in sour cream and sprinkled with brown sugar will be for later in the day, along with a thermos of coffee and brandy. A tin of PECAN LACE COOKIES are brought along for good measure.

An Uptown New Orleans family who

lives right off St. Charles Avenue gathers each *Mardi Gras* Day, and in between parades they warm themselves with hot, thick SPLIT PEA SOUP. Food tables are laden with finger food and decorated with piles of doubloons, beads and tiny handmade flambeaux figures. A huge king cake is the traditional dessert. Children fill up on hot dogs and hamburgers. At the house next door, guests enjoy chicken galantine, pistolettes, MARDI GRAS PASTA SALAD and MINIATURE CREAM PUFFS. The choice of food that can be served on *Mardi Gras* Day is endless and limited only by one's tastes and imagination.

Whatever you should choose to serve, use the colors of *Mardi Gras* – green, gold and purple, symbolizing faith, power and justice. It is traditional to decorate homes with yards and yards of bunting. Carnival flags fly from balconies, and vases and baskets are filled with purple and yellow tulips. Bouquets of balloons are sometimes tied to parked cars and serve as markers for family members who may stray from the group. Green, purple and gold frostings are used on cakes and cookies. And those who may not choose to mask should at least wear *Mardi Gras* colors.

It's a time for frivolity. That's what it's all about. We say eat, drink and be merry, because for the next six weeks of Lent we must pay for our sins.

Steak Tartare

Makes 2 to 4 servings

1 pound of beef tenderloin or sirloin, freshly ground
2 teaspoons of capers, mashed
6 anchovy fillets, mashed
½ cup of minced onions
¼ teaspoon of black pepper
2 to 3 dashes of hot sauce
¾ teaspoon of salt (or to taste)
2 to 3 dashes of Worcestershire sauce
4 tablespoons of dry red wine (optional)
½ teaspoon of Dijon or Creole mustard
1 teaspoon of brandy
2 eggs, separated

Combine all the ingredients, except the eggs, together in a chilled bowl. Blend well. Just before serving, break the egg yolks into the mixture and blend with a fork. It's best served chilled. Serve on assorted thinly sliced breads.

Pecan Lace Cookies

Makes about 2½ dozen cookies

6 tablespoons of softened butter
4 tablespoons plus ½ cup of unsifted all-purpose flour
1 teaspoon of double-acting baking powder
Pinch of salt
2 cups of sugar
2 eggs, well beaten
1 teaspoon of vanilla extract
2 cups of coarsely chopped pecans

Preheat the oven to 400 degrees.

With a pastry brush, spread two tablespoons of the softened butter over two large baking sheets. Sprinkle each sheet with one tablespoon of flour, distributing evenly. Shake the sheets to remove any excess flour.

Combine one-half cup of flour, the baking powder and salt, and sift them together in a bowl. Set aside.

In a deep mixing bowl, cream the remaining two tablespoons of softened butter until light and fluffy. Add the sugar, beat in the eggs and vanilla, and stir the flour mixture into the dough. Add the pecans.

Drop the batter by the heaping teaspoonful onto the baking sheets, spacing the cookie dough about three inches apart.

Bake until the cookies have spread into lace-like 4-inch rounds and have turned golden brown, about five minutes.

Allow the cookies to cool for a minute or so and then transfer them to wire racks to cool completely.

Repeat the process until all the dough has been used. Store in airtight containers.

An old New Orleans drink, popular during Carnival, is an OJEN (pronounced oh-hen) COCKTAIL. Ojen is short for Bobadillojean, a Spanish liqueur that is difficult to find. However, anisette or any other anise-flavored liqueur may be substituted.

Ojen Cocktail

Makes 1 serving

1½ tablespoons of anisette
3 dashes of Peychaud bitters
2 to 4 ice cubes

Combine the liqueur, bitters and ice in a mixing glass and place a bar shaker on top. Shake vigorously. Remove from shaker and strain into a chilled cocktail glass.

Miniature Cream Puffs

Makes 24 pastries

1 cup of water
½ cup of butter
¼ teaspoon of salt
1 cup of all-purpose flour
4 eggs
Cream Filling (Recipe follows)
Frosting (Recipe follows)

Preheat the oven to 425 degrees.

Combine the water and butter in a medium saucepan and bring to a boil. Add the salt and flour, and stir vigorously over low heat until the mixture leaves the sides of the pan and forms a smooth ball.

Remove and cool slightly. Add the eggs, one at a time, beating well after each addition. Beat the batter until smooth.

Drop the batter by the rounded teaspoonful, three inches apart, onto a greased baking sheet.

Bake until puffed and golden brown, about 15 minutes. Transfer to wire racks and cool.

Cut the tops off of the puff pastries, pull out the soft inside dough and discard. Fill the bottom halves with Cream Filling, replace the tops, and spread with Frosting.

Serve slightly chilled.

CREAM FILLING

3 1/2 tablespoons of all-purpose flour
1 1/3 cups of sugar
Pinch of salt
3 egg yolks, beaten
3 cups of milk
1 teaspoon of vanilla extract

Combine the flour, sugar and salt in a heavy saucepan.

In a separate bowl, combine the egg yolks and milk, mixing well. Add this mixture with the vanilla to the dry ingredients and cook over medium heat, stirring constantly, until smooth and thickened.

Chill thoroughly before filling the puffs.

FROSTING

½ cup of softened butter
2 tablespoons plus 2 teaspoons of milk
4 cups of sifted confectioners' sugar
Green, purple, and orange paste food coloring

Cream the butter in a mixing bowl, then add the milk, mixing well. Gradually add the sugar, beating well.

Divide the Frosting into thirds. Add the food coloring to each portion until you have attained the desired color.

Spread the Frosting over the cream puffs after they have been filled and topped.

Split Pea Soup

Makes 8 to 10 servings

1 pound of dried split peas
1 ham bone, 2 ham hocks, or 2 cups of diced ham
3 quarts of beef broth (If using canned broth, dilute it; use half broth and half water to make 3 quarts.)
1 cup of chopped celery
1 cup of chopped onions
1 cup of coarsely chopped carrots
1 teaspoon of dried ground thyme
1 bay leaf
Salt and black pepper, to taste
1 cup of dry sherry

Combine all the ingredients, except the sherry, in a large soup pot over medium-high heat. When the mixture comes to a boil, reduce the heat to medium-low and simmer, stirring occasionally, until the peas are soft and tender, about an hour.

Add the sherry and cook for another 20 minutes. Adjust seasonings to taste.

Mardi Gras Pasta Salad

Makes 8 servings

1 pound of pasta, such as capellini, vermicelli, or fusilli
2 tablespoons of butter
1 cup of whole-kernel corn, frozen or freshly cut from the cob
1 cup of shredded purple cabbage
1 bunch of green onions, finely chopped
1 cup of mayonnaise (more or less to taste)
1 teaspoon of Dijon mustard
½ teaspoon of dried basil
Salt and black pepper, to taste

Cook the pasta in boiling salted water according to package directions. Drain well and place in a large mixing bowl.

Heat the butter in a skillet over medium heat. Add the corn and cook, stirring, for two minutes. Add the corn, purple cabbage, and green onions to the pasta and toss with mayonnaise to lightly coat the ingredients. Add the mustard, basil, salt and pepper, and toss gently.

Serve at room temperature or slightly chilled.

Lenten Fare

The Catholic religion is deeply rooted in the hearts and souls of Acadians. The French immigrants who made *Acadie* (now Nova Scotia) in Canada their New World paradise were expelled from their new homeland in 1755 when they refused to pledge allegiance to the British.

During the *grand derangement* families were separated, and many wandered along the Eastern Seaboard of what is now the United States before finding their way to New Orleans, where they could speak their own language and practice their religion among fellow Frenchmen. The city was not for hunters and trappers, however, and they soon spread out into the countryside, settling along the bayous, in the swamps and on the fertile prairies.

Religious faith was very important to the Acadians who came to Louisiana from *Acadie*, and it remains an integral part of the lives of modern Acadians. Feast days of the Church are honored with tradition all across south Louisiana.

So it is that on Ash Wednesday, the Catholic Creoles and Acadians descend upon the many Catholic churches to receive ashes, a reminder of their mortality (and immortality). Ash Wednesday is a solemn day, and the foreheads of the faithful are marked with dark ashes in the form of a cross.

One Ash Wednesday morning, I slowly opened my eyes and thought, "I've made it through the siege."

I now had some idea of what it must have been like on Sherman's march through Georgia. I had begun my trek during the Christmas holidays, then went on to New Year's and the Sugar Bowl, plowed through Super Bowl week, and stood my ground during *Mardi Gras*.

Why, in the last four days I had joined the throngs along parade routes, attended two balls, climbed on reviewing stands, and watched the Krewe of Gabriel parade in Lafayette. I then sped down the back roads to Mamou to watch the running of the *Mardi Gras* – eating all the while.

Ah, but that was all behind me now. It was the first day of Lent, and I looked forward to getting my ashes at church. Just as it was a time to cleanse my soul, it was also a time to cleanse my body.

Some people choose to give up something they especially like – sweets, soft drinks, whatever. Others pledge to attend daily Mass and Way-of-the-Cross services, or to spend more time in meditation. The nuns always impressed upon us to "offer it up" to the Lord whenever we had a sacrifice to make, such as being quiet or giving our candy money to the poor box in church.

Mama's Lenten tradition was to eat light and clean. No heavy, festive meals, save for perhaps on Sunday, and, of course, there was no snacking between meals. If nothing else, we were healthy for at least 40 days of the year.

Because of certain Lenten rules, there was less eating of meat so consumption of seafood was up. Shrimp, crabs, crawfish and fish were on just about every table, which didn't seem like penance to me. Sometimes we had dishes made with canned salmon or tuna. With a deft hand, Mama was able to stretch the salmon or tuna into absolute delights.

Salmon Croquettes

Makes 4 servings

If formed into tiny balls, these may be used as hors d'oeuvres (makes about 2½ dozen).

1 egg, beaten
1 cup of mashed potatoes
1 (6½-ounce) can of salmon (or same amount of tuna), drained and flaked
1 tablespoon of chopped pimientoes
1 tablespoon of minced onions
¼ teaspoon of salt
Pinch of black pepper
Pinch of cayenne pepper
¼ to ½ cup of dry unseasoned bread crumbs
1 egg, lightly beaten
½ cup of seasoned bread crumbs
Vegetable oil for deep-frying

Mix the first nine ingredients in a bowl, adding enough bread crumbs to bind the mixture. Pat the mixture into hamburger-sized patties or, if you prefer, into balls the size of walnuts.

Put the lightly beaten egg into a shallow dish and the seasoned bread crumbs into another shallow dish. Dip the patties (or balls) into the beaten egg and then roll them in seasoned bread crumbs, coating evenly. Place them on a platter lined with waxed paper and chill for one hour.

Fry the patties (or balls) in deep, hot oil until golden brown, three to four minutes. Drain on paper towels.

The croquettes may be served with tartar sauce or a mayonnaise-mustard sauce.

Mayonnaise-Mustard Sauce

2/3 cup of mayonnaise
2 tablespoons of prepared yellow mustard
2 tablespoons of capers
1 teaspoon of fresh lemon juice

Combine all the ingredients in a bowl and blend well.

This next dish is also a good Carême (Lenten) dish. Although it is not a seafood dish, it is one Mama often served to us during Lent because it was a meal in itself and could be made with chicken or turkey leftovers.

Chicken (Or Turkey) Tetrazzini

Makes 6 servings

5 tablespoons of vegetable oil
3 tablespoons of all-purpose flour
¼ teaspoon of salt
1½ cups of chicken broth
1 (4-ounce) can of sliced mushrooms, with the liquid
2 cups of cooked chicken or turkey, chopped
4 ounces of spaghetti, cooked and drained
1 cup of grated cheddar or American cheese
¼ cup of unseasoned bread crumbs

Preheat the oven to 275 degrees.

Blend three tablespoons of the vegetable oil with the flour in a large saucepan over medium heat, stirring until smooth. Add the salt and broth, and continue stirring until the sauce begins to thicken. Add the mushrooms and their liquid.

Lightly oil a 2-quart casserole dish with one tablespoon of vegetable oil. Alternate layers of turkey, spaghetti, cheese and sauce. Top with bread crumbs sprinkled with the remaining tablespoon of oil.

Bake uncovered until the sauce begins to bubble, 25 to 30 minutes.

With either of these dishes, Mama served a salad that we children thought rather odd, but we never turned it down.

Perfection Salad

Makes 6 servings

2 envelopes of unflavored gelatin
½ cup of sugar
1 teaspoon of salt
1½ cups of boiling water
1½ cups of cold water
½ cup of distilled white vinegar
2 tablespoons of fresh lemon juice
2 cups of finely shredded cabbage
1 cup of chopped celery
½ cup of chopped green bell peppers
¼ cup of chopped pimientoes

Mix together the gelatin, sugar and salt in a mixing bowl. Add the boiling water and stir until all is dissolved.

Add the cold water, vinegar and lemon juice, and stir to blend. Add the cabbage, celery, bell peppers and pimientoes, and mix gently. Chill until set, then serve.

During my years in New Orleans, Lenten Fridays found me in line at the seafood market checking to see what was fresh off the boats. Sometimes it was redfish or trout. If I had a few extra dollars, I purchased fish *and* a pound or so of shrimp. If I had to abstain from meat, no one said I couldn't enjoy my seafood meal.

Trout with Shrimp *Provençal*

Makes 4 servings

1 cup of milk
1 teaspoon of salt
1 teaspoon of cayenne pepper
½ cup of all-purpose flour
4 trout fillets, about 6 ounces each
8 tablespoons of butter

Combine the milk, salt and cayenne in a shallow bowl. Put the flour in another shallow bowl. Dip the trout first in the milk mixture, then dredge in the flour, coating evenly.

Heat the butter in a 10-inch skillet over medium heat and cook the fillets about five minutes on each side. Remove from skillet and drain on paper towels. Keep warm.

Place the fillets on a serving plate and top with sauce.

SAUCE

4 tablespoons of butter
2 tablespoons of olive oil
¼ cup of finely chopped green onions
¼ cup of finely chopped green bell peppers
1 garlic clove, minced
2 cups of peeled and deveined shrimp
2 tablespoons of brandy
1 cup of peeled and chopped fresh tomatoes
Salt and cayenne pepper, to taste

Heat the butter and oil together in a large skillet over medium heat. Add the onions, bell peppers and garlic, and cook, stirring, until slightly soft, two to three minutes. Add the shrimp and stir until they turn pink, three to four minutes.

Pour in the brandy and shake the pan. Add the tomatoes and seasoning and shake the pan again.

I'm not usually real crazy about casseroles, but this SPINACH BAKE is perfect with seafood.

Spinach Bake

Makes 6 servings

2 (10-ounce) packages of frozen chopped spinach
4 tablespoons of butter
1 cup of chopped onions
1 cup of chopped celery
Salt, cayenne pepper and garlic powder, to taste
8 ounces of cream cheese, softened
1 pint of sour cream
1 cup of canned sliced mushrooms, drained
Grated cheddar or Mozzarella cheese
Paprika

Preheat the oven to 350 degrees.

Cook the spinach according to package directions and drain well. Set aside.

Melt the butter in a large skillet, add the onions and celery, and cook, stirring, until wilted. Season with salt, cayenne and garlic powder.

Add the cream cheese and sour cream, and, with a fork, cream together with the vegetables. Add the mushrooms and spinach and stir to blend.

Spoon the mixture into a buttered casserole dish and sprinkle with grated cheese and paprika.

Bake uncovered until the cheese is melted and bubbly, 15 to 20 minutes.

St. Patrick's Day and the feast of St. Joseph usually fall right smack dab in the middle of Lent. These religious feast days are grandly celebrated in New Orleans with parades (Whenever New Orleanians can parade, they do.), feasting (Never mind Lent for a couple of days.) and, of course, some praying.

Every year around this time, I wish I had some Irish blood running through my veins, because I sure like their style. They're flamboyant, like to sing, love good food, and even mourn well. Definitely my kind of people. Red hair is also associated with the Irish, and I have a particular fantasy about red hair.

Since I was a child, I have prayed that my hair would one day turn bright red, or at least strawberry blond. Coming from south Louisiana, where there aren't too many redheads, I thought having titian hair would make me magic. Papa added fuel to the fire. When I was little, he allowed me to visit with him while he was shaving in preparation for an evening out. It was my job to stir up the soap in his mug; then after he shaved, I got to splash with Old Spice along with him.

I always knew when he and Mama were going out because his best suit and bow tie were laid out on the bed along with a starched white shirt. We would then play a little game.

"Where y'all going, Papa?"

"Well, I don't know about your Mama, but I have a date with a redhead."

I knew he was teasing, but I often wondered why he always talked about a redhead.

Even Mama would play along.

"And, Blackie, just where are you going to find you a redhead?"

And Papa would wink at me and grin.

Yes, I definitely wanted to be a redhead and have emeralds dripping from my neck and ears. I've finally given up. I've come to terms with the fact that I will go through life as a brunette. And anyway, emeralds are not so bad on brunettes.

But back to St. Patrick's Day.

While living in New Orleans and working for the Brennan family at Commander's Palace, I quickly learned how to be Irish for at least one day out of the year. I now make CABBAGE ROLLS and toast my Brennan friends with one of their very own St. Paddy's Day desserts, AVOCADO CREAM.

Cabbage Rolls

Makes about 24 rolls

1 large head of green cabbage
1 cup of uncooked short-grain white rice
2 pounds of lean ground beef
2 garlic cloves, minced
2 medium onions, finely chopped
1 green bell pepper, seeded and chopped
Salt and cayenne pepper, to taste
1 (6-ounce) can of tomato paste
4 (15-ounce) cans of tomato sauce
2 cans of water, measured in tomato
   sauce cans

Boil the head of cabbage until tender. Drain well and cool.

Combine the rice, ground beef, garlic,

onions, bell pepper, salt and cayenne in a large mixing bowl. Add the tomato paste and mix well.

Carefully separate the cabbage leaves. Spoon two to three tablespoons of the meat mixture into the cabbage leaves and roll up. Be sure to tuck in the ends so that the filling won't fall out.

Make a layer of the rolls in a large roasting pan or pot. Pour some of the tomato sauce evenly over the rolls. Then add another layer of the rolls, then more sauce, seasoning with salt and cayenne as you make the layers.

After all the layers are made, pour in just enough water to cover the rolls. Cover the pot and cook over low heat until the rice is tender, about an hour.

Avocado Cream

Makes 4 servings

1 ripe medium-sized avocado
1½ tablespoons of fresh lime juice
6 tablespoons of sugar
½ cup of heavy cream
1½ teaspoons of vanilla extract
4 cups of French vanilla ice cream

Peel and slice the avocado. Purée the avocado with the lime juice, sugar, cream and vanilla in an electric blender or food processor.

Transfer the mixture to a large mixing bowl and blend in the softened ice cream.

Spoon the mixture into parfait glasses, cover and freeze until serving time.

Garnish with a slice of lime.

I've wanted to be Italian just as often as I've wanted to be Irish. I can eat pasta any time of the day and tomato sauce on anything.

On the feast of St. Joseph, an altar is laden with dishes that the Italian community spends weeks preparing. This happens not only in New Orleans but in towns and cities all over Louisiana. When I have the opportunity to visit such an altar I always make sure to taste the stuffed artichokes and grab a few lucky fava beans.

Artichokes were not part of my childhood. It wasn't until I was a working woman straight out of college, living in New Orleans, that I was introduced to a fresh artichoke. I was acquainting myself with a large supermarket when I spied these fabulous light green globe-like objects in the produce section. Just about everyone who passed them grabbed a few and chunked them into their baskets. I followed suit.

The only artichokes I had ever tasted were those in jars, packed in oil. All I could figure out was that the tiny artichokes must grow up and become these wondrous things.

I quickly got over my timidity and asked my neighbor, an old-time New Orleanian, what to do with these artichokes I brought home. She was amused.

"And I thought you Acadians knew everything about cooking!"

Stuffed Artichokes

Makes 4 appetizer servings

1 cup of seasoned bread crumbs
1/2 cup of grated Romano or Parmesan cheese, or a combination of both
3 green onions, finely chopped
1/3 cup of finely chopped ham or shrimp
1 garlic clove, minced
3 teaspoons of olive oil
2 large artichokes, trimmed, washed, and drained
1 teaspoon of salt
1 teaspoon of black pepper
Pinch of dried oregano leaves
2 tablespoons of fresh lemon juice

Combine the bread crumbs, cheese, green onions, ham or shrimp, and garlic in a bowl. Add one to two teaspoons of olive oil to moisten the mixture.

Pull gently on the artichoke leaves and stuff each with about one teaspoon or so of the bread crumb mixture.

Place the artichokes in a deep Dutch oven or heavy pot with about two inches of water. Season the water with salt, black pepper, the rest of the olive oil, oregano and lemon juice. Cover and bring to a boil.

Reduce the heat to medium-low, cover the pot, and simmer until the leaves easily pull away, about an hour. If the water evaporates, add a little more water to the pot.

Serve warm or at room temperature.

Following the short break in Lent for the celebration of the feast days, solemn Holy Week services are observed in anticipation of Easter Sunday.

Church altars are stripped bare and ceremonies commemorating the last days of Jesus Christ on earth are held in the grandest cathedrals and the most humble chapels. Many hours are spent in meditation and prayer by the faithful. Perhaps the most solemn day of Holy Week is Good Friday, when customs regarding food, drink and behavior are strictly observed by many.

As I have noted before, there are many types of gumbo in south Louisiana. It can be made with everything from chicken, turkey, seafood and, yes, even sometimes rabbit or squirrel. But there is one gumbo that is truly the king of them all – *gumbo aux herbes* or *gumbo z'herbes*.

This unique gumbo is said to have been originated by the superstitious Creoles especially for Good Friday, when, it was believed, you would have good luck for the coming year if you ate seven greens and met seven people during the day. Some folklore has it that for every green that was put into the gumbo a new friend would be made during the coming year. Since it was to be eaten on Good Friday, no meat was added. Oysters were sometimes used.

In Acadiana, it was not the traditional Good Friday meal, since there *gumbo z'herbes* is usually prepared with salt meat or ham. However, it is a hearty gumbo often prepared by Cina when the hordes of aunts, uncles and cousins flock to her house on weekends.

In addition to the controversy regarding the inclusion of meat in *GUMBO Z'HERBES* is the debate about whether it should be made with a roux. Here are two versions, one made with a roux and one without. If you can find fresh greens, I highly recommend using them, but if not, frozen will suffice.

Gumbo Z'herbes
(Without a Roux)

Makes about 10 servings

1 pound of collard or mustard greens
1 pound of spinach
1 pound of turnip greens
1 pound of green cabbage leaves
1 large bunch of fresh watercress (optional)
1 large bunch of fresh parsley (optional)
Tops of 6 carrots (optional)
Tops of a large bunch of radishes (optional)
½ teaspoon of cayenne pepper
½ teaspoon of black pepper
2 bay leaves
½ teaspoon of ground thyme
¼ teaspoon of allspice (optional)
3 tablespoons of vegetable shortening
1 pound of salt meat or ham,
   cut into small cubes
1 bunch of green onions, finely chopped
1 cup of chopped yellow onions
1 garlic clove, minced

If using fresh greens, trim and wash well. Put the greens in a large, deep pot and add enough water to cover. Add the cayenne, black pepper, bay leaves, thyme and allspice. Boil until the greens are tender. Drain and reserve the cooking liquid. (You should have three to four quarts of liquid.)

Once the greens are well drained, chop them fine, either by hand or with a food processor. If you are using frozen greens, cook according to package directions with spices, drain, and reserve the cooking liquid.

Melt the shortening in a large skillet and brown the salt meat or ham, green onions, yellow onions, and garlic. Return the greens to the reserved liquid and add the cooked salt meat, onions and garlic. Simmer for about two hours.

Some people add a couple of teaspoons of white vinegar during this cooking time. Adjust the seasonings to taste.

When it is prepared in this manner, you can choose to eat the gumbo with or without rice. If it is to be a Lenten dish, substitute two pints of oysters and their liquor for the salt meat or ham.

Gumbo Z'herbes
(With a Roux)

Makes about 10 servings

Use the same ingredients listed at left, with this addition:
½ cup of vegetable oil
3 tablespoons of all-purpose flour

Make a roux with the oil and flour. When the roux is a warm brown color, add the yellow onions and garlic, and cook until the onions are soft, about four minutes.

Add the salt meat or ham and cook for a few more minutes.

Combine the roux mixture with the cooking liquid from the greens in a large, heavy soup pot over medium heat. Add the green onions and cook for 30 minutes.

Then add all of the greens. Continue to simmer for two hours.

The only step omitted from the first recipe is the browning of the onions and salt meat in the shortening.

Papa liked to douse his bowl of gumbo and rice with vinegar in which tabasco peppers had been steeped.

On Holy Saturday preceding Easter Sunday, while eggs were being dyed and the final touches were given to our Easter bonnets, there was one final meatless supper. It was a simple but delicious repast.

Shrimp Creole

Makes 6 servings

4 tablespoons of butter
2 tablespoons of all-purpose flour
1 cup of chopped onions
1 cup of chopped green bell peppers
1 cup of chopped celery
3 garlic cloves, minced
1-pound can of whole tomatoes, crushed
    with their juice
2 bay leaves
2 cups of shrimp stock or water
¾ teaspoon of salt
½ teaspoon of cayenne pepper
2 pounds of medium shrimp,
    peeled and deveined
Chopped parsley

Melt the butter in a large, heavy pot over medium heat. When the butter begins to foam, add the flour and whisk quickly to make a light brown roux. Be careful not to burn the roux.

Add the onions, bell peppers, celery and garlic. Cook, stirring, until the vegetables are soft, about five minutes. Add the tomatoes and their juice, the bay leaves and shrimp stock or water, blending well.

Add the salt and cayenne and gently simmer for 30 minutes, stirring occasionally.

Add the shrimp and cook for about 10 minutes. Just before serving add the parsley.

Serve over steamed or boiled rice.

Baked Macaroni

Makes 6 servings

12 ounces of elbow macaroni
4 tablespoons of butter
1 (12-ounce) can of evaporated milk
3 eggs, beaten
8 ounces of American cheese, cubed
Salt and cayenne pepper, to taste

Preheat the oven to 350 degrees.

Cook the macaroni in boiling water just until tender. Drain and rinse in warm water.

Place the macaroni in 9 x 13-inch baking dish and add the butter; stir until it melts completely.

Add the milk and beaten eggs, and mix well. Add the cheese and mix again until cheese is slightly melted. Season with salt and cayenne.

Bake for 45 minutes. Serve hot.

Fried catfish, crisp and well seasoned, is the perfect complement to baked macaroni. The secret to this catfish recipe is the marinade.

Roger's Catfish

Makes 4 servings

1 pound of catfish fillets, cut into
    1 x 3-inch strips
½ teaspoon of salt
½ teaspoon of black pepper
1 cup of milk
2 tablespoons of yellow mustard
2 tablespoons of fresh lemon juice
Hot sauce, to taste
2 cups of corn flour
1 tablespoon of cornstarch
Vegetable shortening for deep-frying

Season the fish with salt and pepper. Place the strips in a bowl with the milk, mustard, lemon juice and hot sauce. Cover and refrigerate for up to two hours.

Put the corn flour and cornstarch into a brown paper bag.

Remove the catfish from the marinade a few pieces at a time, allowing the marinade to drain off a bit. Put the strips in the bag and shake well to coat each piece.

Heat the shortening to 350 degrees and drop a few pieces of fish at a time into the hot oil. When the fish pieces pop to the surface, remove and drain on a brown paper bag.

Index of Recipes
– Alphabetical –

Index of Recipes
– By Food Category –

About the Author

MARCELLE BIENVENU is a cookbook author and food writer who has been preparing Cajun and Creole dishes since the 1960s.

— Photography by Steve Comeaux, St. Martinville, Louisiana

A native of St. Martinville, Louisiana, in the heart of the Cajun country, she has written a weekly food column, "Creole Cooking," for *The Times Picayune* of New Orleans since 1984. She's worked as a researcher and consultant for Time-Life Books, contributing to a series of books titled *Foods of the World*. She's been featured in *Food & Wine, Southern Living, Redbook, The New York Times, Louisiana Life* and *Acadiana Profile*.

She is the author of three books: *Who's Your Mama, Are You Catholic and Can You Make a Roux?, Who's Your Mama... (The Sequel)*, and *Cajun Cooking for Beginners*.

She co-authored several cookbooks with renowned chef Emeril Lagasse, including *Louisiana: Real & Rustic, Emeril's Creole Christmas, Emeril's TV Dinners* and *Every Day's A Party*. She also co-authored *Eula Mae's Cajun Kitchen* with Eula Mae Doré, a longtime cook for the McIlhenny family on Avery Island, and *Stir the Pot: The History of Cajun Cuisine*, with Carl A. Brasseaux and Ryan A. Brasseaux.

Ms. Bienvenu edited the 1987 edition of *The Times Picayune's Creole Cookbook*, originally published in 1901 and re-issued to celebrate the newspaper's 150th anniversary.

She owned and operated a restaurant, Chez Marcelle, near Lafayette, La., in the early 1980s, and has worked for several restaurants, including Commander's Palace and K-Paul's Louisiana Kitchen in New Orleans.

A graduate of the University of Southwestern Louisiana, she lives on Bayou Teche in St. Martinville, La., with her husband, Rock Lasserre.

Cookbooks by
Acadian House Publishing
The Nation's leading publisher of authentic Cajun and Creole recipes

Who's Your Mama, Are You Catholic, and Can You Make A Roux?

A 160-page hardcover book containing more than 200 Cajun and Creole recipes, plus old photos and interesting stories about the author's growing up in the Cajun country of south Louisiana. Recipes include Pain Perdu, Couche Couche, Chicken Fricassée, Stuffed Mirliton, Shrimp Stew, Grillades, Red Beans & Rice, Shrimp Creole, Bouillabaisse, Pralines. (Author : Marcelle Bienvenu. ISBN 0-925417-55-6. Price: $22.95)

Cajun Cooking For Beginners

A 48-page saddle-stitched soft cover book that teaches the basics of authentic Cajun cooking. It contains about 50 simple, easy-to-follow recipes; cooking tips and hints; a glossary of Cajun food terms, such as roux, gumbo, jambalaya and etouffee; and definitions of basic cooking terms, such as beat, blend, broil, sauté and simmer. (Author: Marcelle Bienvenu. ISBN: 0-925417-23-8. Price: $7.95)

The Top 100 NEW ORLEANS Recipes Of All Time

A 192-page hardcover book containing 100 of the recipes that have helped to make New Orleans food world-famous. For example, Shrimp Creole, Red Beans & Rice, Blackened Redfish, Oyster Loaf, Muffaletta, Beignets, Café au Lait and King Cake. (ISBN: 0-925417-51-3. Price: $14.95)

The Top 100 CAJUN Recipes Of All Time

A 160-page hardcover book containing 100 recipes selected by the editors of *Acadiana Profile*, "The Magazine of the Cajun Country." For example, Boudin, Couche Couche, Maque Choux, Mirliton, Crawfish Etouffee, Chicken Fricassee, Pralines–the classics of South Louisiana cuisine. (Hardcover ISBN: 0-925417-52-1, Price $14.95; Softcover, 7x10 size with 48 pages, ISBN: 0-925417-20-3, Price: $7.95)

Cajun Cooking, Part 1...

...contains about 400 of the best Cajun recipes, like Jambalaya, Crawfish Pie, Filé Gumbo, Cochon de Lait, Chicken & Okra Gumbo, Sauce Piquante. Special features include a section on homemade baby foods and drawings of classic south Louisiana scenery. (ISBN: 0-925417-03-3. Price: $17.95)

Cajun Cooking, Part 2...

...picks up where Part 1 left off. It contains such delicious dishes as Shrimp & Crab Bisque, Fresh Vegetable Soup, Seafood-Stuffed Bellpepper, Broiled Seafood Platter, Yam-Pecan Cake. The recipes appear in the same easy-to-follow format as in Part 1, except they're in real large print for an arm's-length reading. (ISBN: 0-925417-05-X. Price: $15.95)

The Louisiana GUMBO Cookbook

A 192-page hardcover book with more than 100 recipes for the Cajun and Creole gumbo dishes that have made south Louisiana food world-famous. Special sections on the history of gumbo and filé, plus instructions for making rice and gumbo stocks. (Authors: Bea & Floyd Weber. ISBN: 0-925417-13-0. Price: $17.95)

TO ORDER, list the books you wish to purchase along with the corresponding cost of each. Add shipping & handling cost of $3 for the first book and 75¢ per book thereafter. Louisiana residents add 8% tax to the cost of the books. Mail your order and check or credit card authorization (VISA/MC/AmEx) to: Acadian House Publishing, Dept. WYM, P.O. Box 52247, Lafayette, LA 70505. Or call (800) 850-8851.